AF504003

Fig. 1   Class J92 B Works shunting at the locomotive works at Stratford, June 1939.

LOCOMOTIVES OF THE L.N.E.R.

Part 10A

DEPARTMENTAL STOCK, LOCOMOTIVE SHEDS, BOILER AND TENDER NUMBERING

Published by
THE RAILWAY CORRESPONDENCE AND TRAVEL SOCIETY

ISBN 0 901115 65 7
First Impression 1988
Second Impression 1991

Printed by Icon Impressions Ltd., Yorkshire Street Mill, Bacup, Lancs. OL13 9AF

Published by:
R.C.T.S.
21 Winthorpe Road
Lincoln
LN6 3PG
England

CONTENTS

INTRODUCTION

The final Part in this series is devoted to miscellaneous locomotives, additional information, railcars and statistics. The amount of material has once again demanded that two volumes will be required.

In this book, the L.N.E.R.'s limited use of internal combustion driven locomotives is described — only eight, all for shunting duties. However, the Company also possessed several narrow gauge machines used for special purposes.

The L.N.E.R. had a number of steam locomotives which were used only for departmental work, i.e. non revenue earning. Many were of types represented in Running Stock and these have already been noticed in earlier Parts. There were others which were unique to Service Stock, such as three locomotives inherited from the G.N.R., a 0-4-4 crane locomotive, a small saddletank of interesting origin and a peculiar four-wheeled machine constructed from parts salvaged from a steam-driven traverser. The G.E.R. provided the three well-known 0-6-0 crane tanks dating from 1868 which lasted at Stratford Works until the early fifties. Then there was the little Fox, Walker 0-6-0ST taken over from the M. & G.N. in 1936. As well as full descriptions of these engines, the opportunity is taken to give the complete story of the Service Stock fleet at their location of use, with additions during the B.R. period. There were also three 4-wheel petrol inspection cars of N.E.R. origin which survived until 1939 in Service Stock.

There are chapters dealing with locomotives on loan both to and from the L.N.E.R. during its 25-year existence and on preserved locomotives, the Company having established the York Railway Museum.

Part 1, The Preliminary Survey, formed the general introduction to this entire series. In it were chronicled details of the locomotive building programme, classification, numbering systems, liveries and so on. It is thought that certain other matters require extended mention and accordingly chapters are included herein on projected designs and standardisation proposals, locomotive sheds, and boiler and tender numberings — all fascinating subjects in their own right.

Throughout this series mention has been made under individual locomotive class headings of the Engine Order numbers issued by Doncaster Works and it is felt that readers will welcome a complete list of these. Similarly, a full list is included of the engines that carried the short-lived "E" prefix letter to their L.N.E.R. running numbers in early B.R. days.

Finally, there is a statistical analysis of locomotives and a numerical index to assist readers to locate the appropriate class article by reference to the engine number.

The second volume (Part 10B) will contain chapters covering the L.N.E.R.'s railcars — petrol, diesel and steam driven — together with its electric stock, both locomotive and multiple unit.

Certain information in the present work will be found to differ from previously published material, and in such cases every effort has been made to ensure the accuracy of the data now given. Generally speaking official records have been accepted unless clear proof to the contrary has been established. Where any doubt exists this will be indicated in the text.

The individual class articles in this series have been arranged on a uniform basis, each class being divided under sub-headings. This method was preferred by the authors to a chronological history as it facilitates reference, but some unavoidable repetition does occur. The following notes on these sub-headings are offered to assist the reader:—

ENGINES AT GROUPING (or at subsequent date of absorption).— For convenience the locomotive numbers quoted are wherever possible on an L.N.E.R. basis. In some instances, however, locomotives were withdrawn without actually receiving new L.N.E.R. numbers.

STANDARD L.N.E.R. DIMENSIONS. — These are standardised for each class and have generally been taken from the first engine diagram issued by the L.N.E.R. for the class concerned, unless otherwise stated. The pitch of the boiler is its centre line height above rail level. Boiler diagram numbers refer to those brought into use from 1928 onwards by the L.N.E.R. These numbers have also been used for locomotive classes which became extinct before that date where the particular boiler type survived in use on some other class at 1928 and thus received a diagram number.

REBUILDING. — Generally this section is confined to major rebuilding, or reboilering with a different type of boiler. All other variations appear under other headings, e.g. "Details" and "Brakes".

ENGINE DIAGRAMS. — The diagrams issued by the L.N.E.R. are listed under this heading. Generally the diagrams were prepared at the end of the year quoted and issued early in the following year. In certain classes an indication is given of major variations not recognised by the issue of a diagram.

SUMMARY. — (i) Engine Numbers: Numbers in brackets indicate that the number in question was never actually borne. Dates of renumbering are given, except in the case of many of the 1924 L.N.E.R. numbers where the relevant information is not uniformly available. (ii) Rebuilding and other alterations: As this work is primarily a history from Grouping to the present day, the summary normally lists only alterations that occurred after 1923. Alterations made in pre-Grouping days are therefore generally confined to the body of the class article, except that, where a particular alteration to a class was initiated before Grouping and continued by the L.N.E.R. complete details will be given in the Summary.

Dates of building, rebuilding and detail alterations are on the basis customarily employed by the various companies before Grouping. For the L.N.E.R. and B.R. periods they are "to traffic", i.e. when the locomotive took up revenue earning work. Differences may thus occur between these and previously published information where, for instance, "ex-works" or "official" rebuilding dates may have been quoted. "Ex-works" frequently meant the date an engine emerged from the erecting shop: a further period then elapsed during which time it ran one or more trial trips and was painted and varnished. Rebuilding dates were often recorded when a new boiler was allotted to or installed on an engine then under repair and could precede the date the engine returned to traffic by several months. From about 1929, ex-works dates ceased to be quoted in L.N.E.R. records, dates to traffic being solely used thereafter.

INTERNAL COMBUSTION LOCOMOTIVES

At Grouping, the L.N.E.R. inherited two standard gauge petrol-engined 0-4-0 shunting locomotives, one from the N.B.R. and the other from the G.E.R. These machines could develop 40 b.h.p. and were of generally similar design, the product of Motor Rail & Tram Co., Bedford. A third locomotive of this type was purchased by the L.N.E.R. in 1925 for use by the Civil Engineer of the North Eastern Area. It was never entered in the Running or Departmental stock lists during the L.N.E.R.'s existence and it was not until 1949, when a replacement was requested, that this was done. The classification Z6 was used for a few years by the L.N.E.R. for these machines, but this lapsed and class Y11 was finally adopted for them in 1943. The class became extinct in 1956, although it should be noted that other locomotives of this type previously owned by the G.W.R. lasted until 1960 under B.R. ownership. The L.N.E.R. also owned several narrow gauge petrol locomotives for special purposes and these are noted on page 9. In addition there were petrol driven gangers' trolleys but these are outside the scope of this publication.

Early in 1934 an order was placed with Karrier Motors Ltd. of Huddersfield for a 2-ton lorry to be used by the permanent way maintenance people on the West Highland line. As it could be used equally on public roads as on rails, it was known as a Ro-railer (fig. 149). The road wheels were raised and lowered by crank action and transference from rail to road was effected by lowering them fully and running the vehicle on to a rail-level ramp, so lifting the flanged wheels clear of the metals. To reverse the process, the vehicle was driven slowly along the ramps until the flanged wheels dropped into position on the rails. The sphere of operations of the vehicle was from Crianlarich northwards, using the road from that point to Bridge of Orchy, thence the railway to Tulloch and back to the road again from that place to Fort William. It was also run as a rail vehicle only on the Mallaig extension and its use relieved rail traffic congestion by the elimination of ballast engine workings. Its stock number was KE 6001 and its road registration number was AYH 947. When not in use it was kept at Fort William shed in the rail version, and with the road wheels out of contact.

As far as diesel shunting locomotives were concerned, the first step taken by the L.N.E.R. involved the trial in 1924 of a small diesel-hydraulic 0-4-0 built in Austria (the "Railway Magazine" could bring itself only to describe it as "of foreign manufacture"!). This machine was tested on the G.E. Section (see also page 40). Then, in 1932 a lengthy trial was conducted in the Newcastle area of a diesel-electric 0-6-0 constructed by Armstrong Whitworth & Co. (see page 41). This was at a time of severe industrial depression in the country and nothing came of it. The L.N.E.R. had a more than adequate stock of steam shunting locomotives at that time and was short of finance for new ventures. However, the L.M.S. developed the diesel-electric shunting locomotive and was able to demonstrate clear advantages in economy of operation and the ability of such units to operate twenty-four hours a day without refuelling or attention. So at last, when war came the L.N.E.R. placed an order in July 1941 for four 350 h.p. six-coupled locomotives of this type, the frames and bodywork being built at Doncaster with the propulsion unit and traction motors supplied by the English Electric Co. They entered service during 1944-45 and were at first classified J45 but became type DES1 in September 1945. A fifth diesel-electric shunter was also ordered by the L.N.E.R. of similar type but powered by a Petter engine in conjunction with G.E.C. electrical gear. This locomotive was rated at 360 h.p. and did not enter service until B.R. days, in 1949. It was classified DES2 and lasted until 1962, the earlier four being withdrawn in 1967. In October 1947 the L.N.E.R. announced that it was to put into traffic 176 further 350 h.p. diesel-electric shunting locomotives to replace 217 steam engines, but nationalisation of the railways prevented the placing of orders for these, although B.R. did in fact build large numbers of such machines.

Although not strictly within the period covered by the L.N.E.R., it may be mentioned that the Company expected for trial during 1947 a 0-6-0 diesel-mechanical shunter of 204 h.p. This did not arrive until February 1948 and was recorded by B.R. (Eastern Region) as 2217, its works number. It was based at Gorton shed and was tried at Openshaw, before later going to Ipswich, Cambridge and Stratford depots. This locomotive had been built on behalf of the Drewry Car Co. by Vulcan Foundry and was painted in L.N.E.R. green complete with black and white lining. It was transferred to Southern Region in October 1948 and found a home at Hither Green Engineers Yard where it was known as DS1173. It was the forerunner of a large number of similar machines used on B.R. and was ultimately withdrawn as D2341 from Ashford in December 1968.

In the field of main line diesel locomotive traction, on 28th July 1928 Gresley obtained permission from the Locomotive Committee to purchase a diesel motor from Beardmores and a generator and control gear from English Electric in order to convert one of the ten ex-N.E.R. Bo-Bo electric locomotives to diesel power. These locomotives (to be described in Part 10B) were used to work the Shildon to Newport (Middlesbrough) coal traffic, which at that time was in a state of decline leading to the complete abandonment of electric working on the route in 1935. The idea behind converting one of these locomotives was to gain experience on the economics of diesel traction on the heavy coal trains operating between Peterborough and Hornsey on the G.N. main line. In the event the contractors became worried about the feasibility of the conversion and the scheme lapsed, noted in the Locomotive Committee minutes of 28th November 1929 "no further action to be taken".

In addition to the experimental diesel shunting locomotive, Armstrong Whitworth produced an 880 h.p. diesel-electric 2-6-2 (or 1-Co-1 in modern parlance) intended for main line work. This was tested in 1933-34 by the L.N.E.R, mostly on empty coaching stock and goods trains from Newcastle, both on the Carlisle road and on the East Coast main line, but again nothing came of it, although similar locomotives were sold for use overseas (see also page 41).

Throughout this period another 2-6-2, the experimental steam/diesel locomotive built by Kitsons was under trial by the L.N.E.R. A description of this remarkable machine, known as the Kitson-Still, will be found on page 41.

Consideration was given by Gresley in 1934 to the introduction of a diesel multiple unit based on the German "Der Fliegende Hamburger" for a high-speed service between London and Newcastle. Trials with class A1 and A3 Pacifics demonstrated that faster times and heavier loads could be operated by using steam engines, and the A4 Pacific and "Silver Jubilee" train introduced in 1935 had a lasting effect on L.N.E.R. locomotive policy. Gresley did not seriously consider main line diesel traction again and Thompson also showed no interest in it — his locomotive standardisation programme of 1945 contained no proposals to use diesel power.

After the end of the 1939-45 War the L.N.E.R. Board reviewed the Company's locomotive policy and some of its officials visited the U.S.A. to study diesel traction in that country, but nothing was done until the British coal industry reached a point of crisis in the winter of 1946-47. The Government then instructed the main line companies to convert a number of steam locomotives to burn oil. This scheme never came to full fruition but it did trigger the need to re-examine the question of diesel propulsion, a more economic way of burning oil and saving coal. The impetus came from the Chief General Manager's Office who, in July 1947, persuaded the Board to sanction the purchase of twenty-five 1600 h.p. diesel-electric A1A-A1A locomotives at an estimated cost of £1,127,500 to replace thirty-two Pacifics. The diesels were to be used in pairs to work eight weekday services each way between King's Cross and Edinburgh, together with three shorter round trips (King's Cross-Doncaster, King's Cross-Grantham and Edinburgh-Aberdeen) to provide for the full employment of the machines in traffic. A lesser number of duties were to be worked on Sundays. Maintenance depots were to be constructed in London (at either Finsbury Park Goods Yard or Holloway Carriage Sidings) and Edinburgh (at Leith Central Station) at a further cost of £260,000.

The memorandum, dated 24th July 1947, containing full details of these proposals was addressed to the Joint Locomotive & Traffic Committee, marked Approved by the Board, and a public announcement was made. Tenders from manufacturers were invited for the design and construction of the locomotives — no design work was done at Doncaster. Six tenders were submitted to the L.N.E.R. and were opened on 12th November in the presence of Sir Ronald Matthews. Nationalisation was then only seven weeks away and the Government had imposed restrictions on capital expenditure by the railway companies, so nothing further could be done by the L.N.E.R. and the complete scheme was dropped by the new administration.

CLASS Z6 (LATER Y11)
SIMPLEX 3ft. 1in. FOUR-WHEEL PETROL ENGINES

ENGINES AT GROUPING (2):

RUNNING STOCK (ex-N.B.R., built 1921): "Petrol Engine No. 1", numbered 8431 in 1930.

MISCELLANEOUS STOCK (ex-G.E.R., built 1919): Unnumbered. Transferred to Running Stock in 1925 and numbered 8430 in 1930.

ENGINE PURCHASED AFTER GROUPING (1):

MISCELLANEOUS STOCK (Obtained 1925): L4. (Transferred to Departmental Stock by B.R. in 1949).

Shortly after the end of the 1914-18 War a number of railways purchased small four-wheeled petrol shunting locomotives of the "Simplex" pattern constructed by the Motor Rail and Tram Company, Simplex Works, Bedford. Though limited in power these locomotives were ideal for use in small yards, in particular where the shunting had been performed by horses. The L.N.E.R. inherited two such standard gauge locomotives at Grouping and purchased a third in 1925.

The N.B.R. had obtained their petrol locomotive in 1921 (Works No. 2037) and this was known as Petrol Engine No.1. It was in Running Stock and was classified Z6 in the miscellaneous series by the L.N.E.R. In 1919 the G.E.R. had purchased a similar locomotive (Works No. 1931) for use on departmental duties. It bore no number and at Grouping was in Miscellaneous Stock (not even in Departmental Stock, hence not included in the official totals of locomotives). However, a reference to it as "LNER 2" has been found in M.R.T. records. In 1925 it was transferred to Running Stock and received the number 8430 in 1930, while Petrol Engine No.1 became 8431, also in 1930, the two locomotives settling down on their respective duties at Brentwood and Ware until withdrawal in 1956. The classification Z6 appears to have fallen into disuse and the engines were known simply as petrol shunters until December 1943 when they were officially classified Y11, at the end of the 0-4-0T series. Their final B.R. numbers were 15098/9.

The third petrol shunter under review was purchased second-hand by the L.N.E.R. in August 1925. It had been built in 1922 as Works No. 2126 and was supplied to Preston Water Works in Lancashire. Motor Rail bought it back in 1925 and, after overhauling the engine, resold it to the L.N.E.R. under Works No. 3783. The machine appears to have spent the rest of its career at Greenland Creosote Works, West Hartlepool in almost total obscurity. Until May 1949 the locomotive was neither in Running nor Departmental Stock and its existence was scarcely recognised at all. An un-numbered engine was noted as being in the N.E. Area at 31st December 1926 and the "Railway Magazine" in August 1929 referred to a "N.E. petrol, Z6 8434". Reference to the engine was omitted from the "Locomotives of the L.N.E.R., 1923-37" (R.C.T.S. 1941) on the grounds of insufficient evidence and it was not until late 1947 that it was firmly tracked down at West Hartlepool, by then identified as L4 in the N.E. Area Engineer's Stock List. Even so the C.M.E.'s Department did not officially rediscover it until a replacement was requested by the Civil Engineer, when at last it was taken into Departmental Stock in May 1949 under British Railways and numbered 15097. Soon afterwards it was replaced at the sleeper creosote works (by 0-4-0 diesel-mechanical shunting engine No. 11104) and withdrawn in June 1950.

L.N.E.R. Dimensions, 1943

	No. 8430 (ex-G.E.R.)	No. 8431 (ex-N.B.R.)
Cylinders (4)	120 x 160mm.	120 x 140mm.
Horse power	40	Not given
Drive (chain)	10:51	Two speed
Wheels	3' 1"	3' 1"
Wheelbase	5' 6"	5' 7"
Length over buffers	13' 4"	13' 5"
Weight (full)	About 8 tons	
Petrol capacity	About 26 gallons	

No engine diagram was issued by the L.N.E.R. until 1943.

L.N.E.R. and B.R. Renumbering

When the former G.E.R. petrol shunter was added to Running Stock and sent to Brentwood in September 1925 it was, either then or soon afterwards, allotted the number 8430. However, it is reasonably certain that this number was not actually applied until July 1930. (This corrects the statement given in Part 1, page 35.) In the meantime the machine was referred to in official records as *Peggy*, said to be the name of the horse it replaced at Brentwood. This name was probably painted on, although no photograh has been discovered showing it. A contemporary observer has confirmed that the name was carried, either in chalk or painted. The name had disappeared by December 1933 and was not subsequently displayed.

The N.B.R. machine, Petrol Engine No. 1, continued to carry this description, even after it reached the G.E. Section. When in July 1930 it was permanently transferred from the Scottish Area it was renumbered 8431. No trace has been found of any proposed allocations for 8432/3 but 8434 was apparently allotted (but not applied, as far as is known) to the petrol shunter L4 in Miscellaneous Stock at West Hartlepool.

Nos. 8430/1 were allocated 7591/2 in the 1942 partial renumbering scheme, which was designed to clear numbers for the future construction of class B1 4-6-0's. These numbers were never carried and in 1946 Nos. 8430/1 became 8188/9 under the 1943 renumbering scheme.

Nos. 8188/9 entered British Railways stock but only the latter received its first B.R. number 68189 before it was decided to number the internal combustion locomotives in a new series. In May 1949 the petrol shunter at West Hartlepool was transferred from Miscellaneous to Departmental Stock, and was renumbered 15097. Nos. 8188, 68189 became 15098/9 respectively at the same time.

Details

N.B. Petrol Engine No. 1 was a standard four-wheeled Simplex shunting locomotive (fig. 8). It weighed 8 tons and had a 4-cylinder Dorman petrol (or paraffin) engine developing 40 brake horse-power at 1,000 r.p.m., with chain drive on to both axles through a two-speed gearbox. The low gear provided a tractive effort of 3,400 lb. at a speed of 3 m.p.h., whilst the corresponding figures for high gear were 1,250 lb. at 9 m.p.h. The wheels were of split spoke pattern.

The sides were completely open, with the typical Simplex simple flat roof higher in the middle than at the ends. The overall height to the top of the exhaust silencer on the roof was only 9ft. 7in. Ordinary buffers and three-link couplings were fitted. Standard N.B. shunter's foot boards were also provided at each side at an early date. In August 1927 during the course of a shopping at Cowlairs Works a fully enclosed tall cab was fitted (fig. 9). This was made from steel plate and had an arched roof. The cab was clearly based on N.B.R. locomotive practice with its typical Cowlairs style window on each side, though set rather low in order to correspond with the seated driver's line of vision. Doors were constructed of wood and the handrails were of the type employed by the N.B.R. on goods brake vans. No. 1 returned to its duties at Kelso in December 1927. Some previously published

accounts have stated that the new cab was fitted following fire damage whilst at Ware in August 1929 but this was not so.

At some time shutters were added to fill in the space above the half-height doors, and rear view mirrors were provided (fig. 10). Until B.R. days there was only one lamp iron at each end, set in the middle above the maker's plate. At some time after April 1949, but before August 1951, additional lamp irons were added, one over each buffer (fig. 11).

The L.N.E.R. did not issue an engine diagram for this machine (by then No. 8431) until 1943, for which purpose it was necessary to take actual measurements on site at Ware. Some of these are at slight variance with those shown on the N.B.R. diagram, including: wheelbase (5ft. 6in.), length over buffers (13ft. 4in.) and petrol capacity (20 gallons). The diagram also showed the overall height to the top of the exhaust silencer on the roof of the tall cab as 11ft. 8½in. The width over eaves was 7ft. 4½in.

This locomotive was re-engined at Holloway Road Motor Depot in January 1954, with what was described as a Crossley 180 b.h.p. petrol engine from a former World War II tank.

Little is known about the former G.E. petrol locomotive (later to become No. 8430) prior to its transfer to Running Stock in 1925, by which time it too had acquired a tall cab though to a different design from the N.B.R. locomotive. Much of it was made of wood, one side being almost fully enclosed except for a low aperture at one end. On the other side there was a tall entrance, centrally placed, with a curved top rail (figs. 2&3). A removable wood door was provided. The curved roof was set sideways on (the driver sat facing across the engine) and measured 12ft. 2¾in. to the top of the silencer mounted on it. The width over eaves was only 6ft. 0½in. In addition to steps on the frames there was a bracket step each side adjacent to the left-hand axlebox. Unlike the N.B.R. machine, the single lamp iron at each end was mounted on top of the "bonnet" on the left-hand side (facing). According to the engine diagram which was prepared at Stratford, the 40 b.h.p. Dorman engine had 160|mm. stroke cylinders instead of 140mm. and the chain drive had a ratio of 10:51. The petrol capacity was shown as being about 26 gallons.

No technical information is available concerning L4, the petrol locomotive at West Hartlepool, other than the painted tare weight on the solebar: 8 tons 18 cwt. The manufacturer's records gave the engine as 40 h.p. It retained to the end its spartan cab roof though at some stage it acquired some form of protection for the driver in the form of glass windows and tarpaulin sheeting on one side only. Also at some time dumb buffers had been fitted, placed closer together than the original buffers, and projecting well out at both front and rear (fig. 13).

Maintenance

Whilst in the Scottish Area, N.B. Petrol Engine No. 1 made at least one appearance at Cowlairs Works. This was in August 1927 when the tall cab was fitted. The petrol locomotives in the Southern Area were the responsibility of Stratford Works, though they also visited the road motor depot at Holloway, which was situated in the vicinity of Ashburton Grove. The shunter at West Hartlepool is known to have visited Darlington Works in September 1938 and York in 1947 for repair.

Liveries

The N.B.R. locomotive displayed "N.B. PETROL ENGINE No. 1" on its solebars in 6in. letters for PETROL ENGINE and 9in. for N.B. and No. 1. No evidence has been found to suggest that any change was made after Grouping and the letters N.B. may even have been retained after its visit in August 1929 to Stratford to repair the fire damage, as at that time it was still officially on loan from the N.B. Section, though this is pure conjecture and, on balance, unlikely. From July 1930 it displayed "L N E R 8431" (afterwards 8189) high up on the cab side alongside the windows (figs. 9 & 10). After nationalisation the words "BRITISH RAILWAYS" were painted on the cabside below the windows with the running number 68189 (afterwards 15099) on the bufferbeams (see fig. 37, Part 1). The lion and wheel emblem replaced "BRITISH RAILWAYS" in January 1954 (figs. 11 & 12). It is believed that throughout its existence this locomotive was painted black, though there is a possibility that red lining was applied in early L.N.E.R. days. The same situation obtained with the former G.E.R. machine.

After its transfer to Running Stock the last-mentioned locomotive displayed "L N E R 8430" on its solebars (probably from July 1930), the company initials eventually giving way to "NE" during wartime, probably at its November 1943 repair (figs. 3 & 4). It was renumbered 8188 in July 1946 and at an unrecorded date between June 1948 and April 1949 these letters were painted out (fig. 5). From May 1949 it carried its final number 15098 on both solebars and "No. 15098" at the ends above the bufferbeam (fig. 6). By July 1954 the shaded numerals had been replaced by plain unshaded, with "No." omitted at the ends (fig. 7). At no time during its B.R. career did it carry evidence of its new ownership.

The locomotive at West Hartlepool was observed in September 1938 numbered L4 whilst towards the end of 1947 it was carrying a plate which bore "L.N.E.R. N.E. Area L4 Engineer's Dept." From May 1949 it carried "No. 15097" at both ends above the maker's plate and "N E" on the solebars (fig. 13).

Allocation and Work

Prior to 1921 the yard shunting at Kelso was performed by horse haulage. Three horses and three horse drivers were required for six months of the year, and two horses and two drivers for the remaining six months, at a total cost of £1,100 per annum. Horses were employed because access to the pair of sidings alongside the premises of Messrs. A. Dunn & Sons had originally been by means of a wagon turntable, though by 1921 the sidings had been connected up with the head shunt and the turntable removed.

On 23rd February of that year No. 1 was delivered at Kelso and cost £1,200. It was capable of hauling up to five loaded wagons or nine empty wagons and was in traffic for 8 to 8½ hours per day, single-manned by one of the former horse drivers. One result of the shunting work being dealt with more expeditiously than before was that the shunter was able to spend half his time on platform duties and a porter was dispensed with. When not available No. 1 was replaced by a class Y9 0-4-0ST from St. Margaret's shed, with a driver and fireman from Hawick; for instance No. 9546 was at Kelso in August 1927 when No. 1 was away in shops.

A memorandum dated 1st May 1923 prepared by the General Manager's Office, Scotland compared the annual costs for working and maintenance, £483, of the petrol shunter with those for a light type of steam locomotive, £998. The implications were obvious and resulted in some trials being made in England. The first recorded trial was at Brentwood, from which No. 1 returned to Kelso on 26th October 1923. Shortly afterwards arrangements were made for the St. Margaret's steam crane to go to Kelso to load it on to a low wagon on 20th November preparatory to a week's trial at Selby, though its actual appearance there has not been confirmed. It may be wondered why trouble and expense was taken to transport No. 1 all the way from Scotland to Brentwood when an almost identical machine was working in the Civil Engineer's yard at Lowestoft. The probable answer is that the Locomotive Running departments and the Scottish Area General Manager were at that time totally unaware of the latter's existence. An illustration of No. 1 shunting at Brentwood appeared in the November 1923 edition of the "North Eastern Magazine" (the all-line magazine did not emerge until January 1927) and it is possible that this prompted a reminder from someone in the G.E. permanent way department.

No. 1 left Kelso in June 1928 when it was transferred to Connah's Quay, near Chester, being replaced on its former duty by a newly-built Sentinel locomotive, class Y1 No. 9529. The petrol shunter was then transferred to Ware in August 1928, where it replaced a Hertford East class J15 engine and a local horse named *Dobbin*. The petrol shunter caught fire at Ware on 12th May 1929 though it may not have been so extensively damaged as some reports have suggested. During this time it was still officially in Scottish Area stock but it was permanently transferred to the Southern Area in July 1930, when it became No. 8431. The locomotive continued to shunt at Ware until its withdrawal in November 1956, though it was noted at Brentwood towards the end of 1943 at a time when No. 8430 was in Stratford Works. Earlier that year, on 24th March, No. 8431 was observed passing New Barnet in an up goods train hauled by class J39 No. 1927. It was bound for repair at Holloway and would have been routed via the connection from Hertford East to North where it would have been conveyed by one of several daily goods trains via Cole Green to Hatfield sidings for inclusion in a train travelling up the main line. On occasions when No. 8431 was absent from Ware, a G.E.R. 0-6-0T was shedded at Hertford East to replace it.

The G.E.R. petrol shunter started work in the Engineer's Yard at Lowestoft Harbour in December 1919. In September 1925 it was transferred to Brentwood and later numbered 8430. The late F.E. Wilson could recall only one occasion when No. 8430 left the confines of the goods yard during its working day. This was to detach a van with a hot axlebox from the rear of a down passenger train. No. 8430 continued to work at Brentwood until its withdrawal in September 1956. When not in use, both the above engines stood in the open in their respective goods yards.

Engine Diagrams

Not issued, 1923. Z6. Petrol Engine No. 1.

Not issued, 1925. Petrol Shunting, No. 8430. (Diagram prepared by Stratford not generally issued).

Section E, 1943. Y11. Composite diagram for Nos. 8430/1 with separate drawings for each.

Classification: Route availability 1; no B.R. power class.

Summary of Petrol Shunting Locomotives

2nd B.R. No.	1st B.R. No.	1946 No.	1942 No.	1st L.N.E.R. No.	Orig. identity
15097 5/49	—	—	—	(8434)	L4 (a)
15098 5/49	(68188)	8188 7/46	(7591)	8430 7/30 (d)	—
15099 5/49	68189 12/48	8189 6/46	(7592)	8431 7/30	(f)

Purchased by	Maker	Works No.	Built	To Dept. Stock	Withdrawn
L.N.E.R.	M.R.T.Co.	3783	8/1925 (b)	5/49 (c)	6/50
G.E.R.	M.R.T.Co.	1931	12/1919 (e)	—	9/56
N.B.R.	M.R.T.Co.	2037	2/1921	—	11/56

(a) N.E. Area Engineer's Dept. series.

(b) Originally built as Works No. 2126 in 1922 and supplied to Preston Water Works. Returned to makers in 1925 and refurbished before purchase by the L.N.E.R. under Works No. 3783.

(c) In Miscellaneous Stock until added to Departmental Stock, May 1949.

(d) Named *Peggy* for a time upon transfer to Brentwood in September 1925.

(e) In Miscellaneous Stock on G.E.R., then L.N.E.R. until added to Running Stock, September 1925.

(f) N.B. Petrol Engine No. 1.

NARROW GAUGE LOCOMOTIVES

In addition to the standard gauge 4-wheel petrol driven shunting locomotives, the L.N.E.R. inherited four similar narrow gauge machines, one each from the G.N.R. and G.E.R. and two from the N.E.R. Four more were purchased after Grouping. The G.N.R. locomotive was built by Baguley/McEwan Pratt, whilst all the others were the product of Motor Rail & Tram. During the Second World War the L.N.E.R. purchased two narrow gauge diesel locomotives from Ruston & Hornsby, again of the 4-wheel type.

None of these ten narrow gauge locomotives figured in the Company's annual stock returns but are here mentioned for the sake of completeness. Two of them may possibly account for the missing running numbers 8432/3 referred to on page 6. All these locomotives were for use either at works and depots or on civil engineering contracts.

Maker	Works No.	Date	Gauge		Location	Notes
B.M.P.	747	4/1918	2′	3″	Boston P.W. Depot	(a)
M.R.T.	1905	5/1920	2′	11¾″	Lowestoft Sleeper Depot	(b)
,,	2077	4/1923	2′	0″	Whessoe Lane P.W. Shops, Darlington	(c)
,,	2103	4/1921		,,	Croft Jct. P.W. Store Yard, Darlington	(d)
,,	2104	4/1921		,,	Gateshead P.W. Shops	(e)
,,	4514	3/1928		,,	Cuffley	(f)
,,	5337	7/1931		,,	Queen's Dock, Hull	(g)
,,	5338	7/1931		,,	Queen's Dock, Hull	(g)
R.H.	202005	7/1940	2′	2¾″	Boston P.W. Depot	(h)
,,	224337	–/1944	3′	0″	Lowestoft Sleeper Depot	(i)

Notes:—

(a) Ordered by War Department Light Railways 14th February 1917. Despatched to Calais (Running No. LR284) 29th April 1918. 10 h.p., 60 cm. gauge. Regauged to 2ft. 3in. by Baguley in 1921 and purchased by G.N.R. for use at Boston (fig. 14).

(b) "For passing through tanks" (presumably the 6ft. diameter tanks used for pressure creosoting the sleepers). Said to be numbered "LNER 1" and named *Billy* latterly. ("LNER 2" was the standard gauge petrol shunter that became No. 8430.) Dorman 2-cylinder engine developing 20 b.h.p., 17¾″ wheels, weight 4 tons. Still at Lowestoft in 1958.

(c) Dorman 2-cylinder engine, 20 b.h.p., 17¾″ wheels, weight 2½ tons. Ordered by Stores Superintendent's Office L.N.E.R. (N.E. Area), Gateshead on 11th April 1923.

(d) Ordered by MacLachen & Co., Haughton Bridge Wagon Works, Darlington, on 31st March 1921 for delivery to N.E.R. Same dimensions as (c) above. Later owned by Shanks & McEwan, Corby.

(e) Ordered by MacLachen 2nd April 1921 for N.E.R. Dimensions as (c).

(f) Ordered by L.N.E.R., Secretary's office, Marylebone Station, 6th March 1928, for conveying spoil tubs at a major earth slip at Cuffley because the existing tractor was not powerful enough to enable the job to be completed quickly. Gresley authorised the purchase of the Simplex machine on 5th March 1928 — Motor Rail could deliver ex-stock. The engine developed 20 b.h.p., 17¾″ wheels, 2½ tons weight, length 8′11″, width 4′10″, height 4′4½″, wheelbase 3′6½″. There was another serious earth slip at Mill Hill where work could be found after Cuffley. The machine was to be retained in stock for similar use as required.

(g) Ordered by L.N.E.R. Secretary's office, Marylebone, 25th July 1931. Used during the work of filling in Queen's Dock (the first Hull dock of 1776). The filling largely consisted of household rubbish which was dumped at one end and then distributed along each side of the dock by trucks on the 1′11½″ gauge line. The job was completed in 1932 and the disposal of the two locomotives is unknown. Dorman 4-cylinder engine of 35 b.h.p., 17¾″ wheels, weight 2½ tons, wheelbase 3′4⅛″.

(h) The Ruston & Hornsby machine was of the maker's standard design and was ordered by the Secretary of the L.N.E.R., York, 17th February 1940. It was powered by a diesel engine (all the M.R.T. locomotives used petrol) which developed 20 h.p. at 1200 r.p.m. Wheel diameter 16 ⁵⁄₁₆″.

(i) Carried "LNER 3" and the name *Monty* (fig. 15). Engine developed 48 h.p. Still at Lowestoft in 1958.

CLASS J45 (LATER DES1)
DONCASTER 4ft. 0in. 0-6-0 DIESEL-ELECTRIC ENGINES

ENGINES BUILT AFTER GROUPING (1944-45): 8000-3. TOTAL 4.

Shortly before Gresley's death, an Emergency Board meeting on 19th February 1941 authorised the construction in the Company's Doncaster Works of four 350 h.p. diesel-electric 0-6-0 shunting locomotives, the equipment to be supplied by English Electric. The L.N.E.R. was the last of the four main line companies to embark on this venture, and strangely at a time when oil imports were curbed during the War. The main contractor was English Electric and quite naturally the equipment was standard in almost all respects with that which was fitted to the latest L.M.S. diesel-electric shunting locomotives Nos. 7120-5. The mechanical parts also closely followed the L.M.S. in outline, whilst incorporating where possible standard L.N.E.R. details. One novel feature was the provision for acting as mobile generators during power failures, resulting for example from enemy action during wartime.

The four locomotives appeared in 1944-45 and their construction is summarised in the accompanying table. At first they were classified J45 in the steam locomotive series but became DES1 (Diesel Electric Shunting) in September 1945. A further reclassification, used internally in the Eastern and North Eastern Regions of B.R., took place in October 1954 when they became DEJ1. A fifth locomotive was ordered in 1945 with Brush the main contractor, and this is described separately under DES2. On the eve of nationalisation at a Joint Locomotive and Traffic Committee meeting on 30th October 1947, the purchase was recommended of 176 diesel-electric shunting engines to displace 217 steam locomotives. These form part of the history of British Railways and are not described in this work. Nos. 8000-3 (latterly 15000-3) survived until 1967, having spent most of their working life at Whitemoor yard (March).

Engine Nos.	Doncaster E.O. No.	Date ordered	Works Nos.	Built	No. Built	Date
8000-3	370	July 1941	1960/3/73/8	Doncaster	4	1944-45

Standard L.N.E.R. Dimensions

Diesel engine	English Electric type 6KT
Cylinders (6)	10″ x 12″
Max. cont. rating	350 h.p. at 680 r.p.m.
Main generator	English Electric type 809
Rating	200 kW
Traction motors (2)	English Electric type 506
Hourly rating (x2)	135 h.p.
Cont. rating (x2)	115 h.p.
Tractive effort (starting)	32,000 lb.
Wheels	4′ 0″
Length over buffers	29′ 1″
Wheelbase	5′ 9″ + 6′ 0″ = 11′ 9″
Weight (full):	
Engine	51T 0C
Max. axle load	17T 16C
Fuel capacity	580 gallons

L.N.E.R. Numbering

The engines were allocated Nos. 8000-3 in Thompson's 1943 comprehensive renumbering scheme, which had still to be implemented when Nos. 8000/1 appeared in August 1944. To avoid duplication of these and further contemplated diesels, class N7 Nos. 8000-11 were hurriedly renumbered 7978-89 as a temporary expedient in July and August 1944 (see Part 9A of this series).

Details

The design followed closely that of the contemporary diesel-electric shunting locomotives on the L.M.S. Externally they appeared similar, though the L.N.E.R. engines had a 3in. longer wheelbase. The six-cylinder four-stroke diesel engine was rated to give 350 b.h.p. at 680 r.p.m., and was directly coupled to a generator in addition to driving by belts the various auxiliaries such as compressor and radiator fan. The generator supplied two nose-suspended traction motors with a voltage varying up to a maximum of about 600 volts. Each motor drove one axle through double-reduction spur gearing (ratio 27:7:1), which ensured a reasonable speed of rotation of the motors when the locomotive was hump shunting at very low speeds. The motors could be easily and quickly uncoupled from the axles to allow the locomotive to be hauled at speeds above the normal maximum of 20 m.p.h., this feature being useful if it became necessary to despatch the locomotive in a hurry to act as an emergency power plant at a remote site. Whilst hump shunting, speeds as low as ½ m.p.h. could be smoothly operated.

There were small detail differences between the engines (figs. 17, 18 & 19). The rain strip above the cab entrance on No. 8000 was straight. On No. 8001 extra pieces were added at the ends, whilst Nos. 8002/3 had curved strips instead. The sandboxes on No. 8000 at the cab end had no external fillers, whereas these were provided for the remaining engines when new. Nos. 8002/3 were more readily distinguishable from the first two engines as their battery boxes on the running plate were shallower with slanting tops, and the hand grips for the side panels had recesses behind them to prevent grazed knuckles. On Nos. 8002/3 the lower part of the air inlets to the fan compartment at the front end were plated over (fig. 19). These distinguishing features were retained except that No. 8000 was soon brought into line with No. 8001 in regard to its rain strips and sandbox fillers. By July 1955 No. 15000 (ex-8000) was running with L.N.E.R. Group Standard buffers and seems to have been the only one of the four so altered (fig. 20).

Latterly all four carried radio equipment (evidenced by an aerial on the cab roof) for use at Whitemoor Yard (fig. 20).

Apparently with the intended role as a mobile power plant, a 4,000 gallon tank was constructed from the oil gas tank taken from service vehicle No. 962033 and fitted to the adapted frames and running gear from tender No. 9879 (from class C11). The converted fuel tank, service No. 961880, retained its tender hand brake but had a through brake pipe also. The profile of the vehicle was designed to clear the Poplar loading gauge. The subsequent fate of this fuel tank has not been discovered.

Brakes

Westinghouse direct acting brakes were provided for the locomotive, with vacuum for train braking.

Maintenance

The engines were maintained by Stratford and March but after nationalisation (from February 1950) maintenance was transferred to Derby Works, until January 1960 when it reverted to Eastern Region at Stratford.

Liveries

The engines appeared in plain black with shaded numerals on their sides below the letters "N E", though No. 8000 had acquired "L N E R" in full by nationalisation (fig. 16). In B.R. days after renumbering had taken place, variations included the number either in its original position or on the cab side, and one or other variety of B.R. emblem either high up on the sides or low down on the battery box (figs. 20 & 21). No. 15000 was noted at Derby Works painted green in October 1958.

British Railways

The engines were duly renumbered 15000-3 although it took from June 1950 to June 1952 to effect the change.

Allocation and Work

The engines were first allocated to Stratford for working at Temple Mills and, later, Goodmayes yards, but were transferred to March during 1945: on 20th June No. 8002 hauled 8000/3 to March together with one oil tank wagon, two wagons containing spares and a goods brake van. No. 8001 was laid up at that time at Stratford with a burnt out main generator and it was not sent to March until the following November. Here they settled down to regular work at Whitemoor Yard, apart from occasional trials elsewhere, such as No. 8000 loaned to Eastfield in November 1946 for a short spell at Cadder and Sighthill yards, No. 15003 at Feltham on Southern Region in February 1952 and No. 15001 at Immingham in January 1956.

At Feltham No. 15003 was used on hump shunting trials following the unsuccessful trial use of L.M.S.-type DE 0-6-0 No. 12066 which seriously overheated due to the continuous low speed running needed on this type of work.

The engines were intended to work continuously for two weeks followed by a few hours off for inspection and maintenance, in order to obtain the most economical use out of them, and the reason for their concentration at one depot was that special maintenance facilities were required.

In January 1966 all four were transferred to the London Midland Region, where they were allocated to Crewe South shed. They were withdrawn from L.M.R. stock during 1967.

Engine Diagrams

Section L.N.E., 1945	Not issued. Type Diesel-Electric Shunting. Reproduced April 1945 from original scheme drawing dated July 1942.
1945.	Small scale. Type J45. Reclassified DES1 in September 1945.
1947.	Replacement diagram. Reclassified DEJ1 in October 1954.
DE/353/1, ?1964	Reissue (by Swindon).

Summary of J45 Class

B.R. No.	Orig. No.	Maker	Works No.	Built	Withdrawn
15000 6/52	8000	Doncaster/	1960	8/1944	8/67
15001 5/52	8001	English Electric	1963	8/1944	4/67
15002 6/50	8002	,,	1973	12/1944	8/67
15003 11/51	8003	,,	1978	3/1945	5/67

CLASS DES2
BRUSH 4ft. 0in. 0-6-0 DIESEL-ELECTRIC ENGINE

ENGINE BUILT AFTER NATIONALISATION (1949): 15004. TOTAL 1.

Shortly after the completion of the four diesel-electric shunting locomotives described under class J45, an Emergency Board Meeting on 26th April 1945 authorised the construction of one more 0-6-0 locomotive, with however Brush as the main contractor instead of English Electric. At that time Sir Ronald Matthews was Chairman of both the L.N.E.R. and Brush and an arrangement was made that the Railway would make the structure of the locomotive, leaving Brush to install the equipment. Doncaster Engine Order 384 covered the construction of the underframe, upperstructure body and certain mechanical parts, and the locomotive was noted standing in the works yard at Doncaster on 13th December 1946 awaiting despatch to Brush at their Falcon Works at Loughborough for the installation of the motor and electrical equipment. No works number was allocated by Doncaster to this locomotive. It was completed in November 1947 and shortly afterwards began working trials at Temple Mills yard, Stratford. However, it was not taken into B.R. stock until 25th April 1949 as No. 15004. Until then it carried no running number, although allotted 8004 by the L.N.E.R.

No. 15004 had a chequered career of thirteen years, never seeming to settle down for long at any one shed, and was withdrawn in October 1962. At first classified DES2, it became DEJ2 in October 1954 under a reclassification scheme used internally in the E. and N.E. Regions of B.R.

Standard Dimensions

Diesel engine	Petter type SS4
Cylinders (4)	8½″ x 13″
Max. cont. rating	360 h.p. at 600 r.p.m.
Main generator	Brush
Rating	190 kW
Traction motors (2)	Brush
Hourly rating (x2)	135 h.p.
Cont. rating (x2)	115 h.p.
Tractive effort (starting)	32,000 lb.
Wheels	4′ 0′
Length over buffers	29′ 1″
Wheelbase	5′ 9″ + 6′ 0″ = 11′ 9″
Weight (full):	
Engine	51T 8C
Max. axle load	*
Fuel capacity	800 gallons

* Not quoted on engine diagram issued by Doncaster.

Engine No.	Doncaster E.O. No.	Date ordered	Maker	No. Built	Date
15004	384	February 1946	Doncaster/ Brush	1	1949

Details

The principal difference between No. 15004 and the earlier L.N.E.R. diesel-electric shunting locomotives lay in the four-cylinder two-stroke engine, with a slightly higher brake horse-power, in place of the six-cylinder four-stroke engine.

No. 15004 was readily distinguishable from Nos. 8000-3 by the absence on the running plate of the battery boxes, as compressed air was used for starting the diesel engine.

Brakes

Westinghouse direct acting brakes were provided for the locomotive, with vacuum for train braking.

Maintenance

The engine was maintained at Derby Works, but from January 1960 was transferred to Eastern Region maintenance : its visit to Doncaster in October 1962 for scrapping was probably its first and last after being built there. It was still lying in the yard at Doncaster as late as 7th July 1963.

Liveries

When new it appeared in grey livery with no markings or number. It was taken into B.R. stock in April 1949, painted plain black and numbered 15004 on 12th May (fig.22).

Allocation and Work

Following trial in the L.M.S. yard at Loughborough, it went to Stratford where it was noted in January 1948. Extended trials took place in Temple Mills Yard and later at Whitemoor Yard, March. The locomotive was officially allocated to March shed in April 1949, where it joined Nos. 8000-3 on similar duties at Whitemoor.

On 9th December 1951 it was transferred to Hornsey where it immediately commenced running a fortnight's trials against class J50 No. 68949 on a South London goods transfer trip to Herne Hill via the Widened Lines. Departure from Ferme Park Yard was about 9-30 a.m., returning through Platform 16 at King's Cross about 3-0 p.m. It was turned at the end of each journey. On 24th December it arrived at Cricklewood for similar trials which began three days later and lasted until 11th January. Brent sidings were left at 10-22 a.m., with arrival at Hither Green at 12-26 p.m. The return working was at 2-15 p.m., arriving Brent 3-43 p.m. Loads were varied, about 20 - 30 wagons each trip and accomplished without banking assistance up the Snow Hill incline.

No. 15004 returned to March in January 1952. Its next move was to Woodford in December 1956 and then in January 1957 it was involved in a final transfer to New England. In addition to use in the yards there, it was also seen at work at Peterborough East and Fletton.

Engine Diagram

1949	Reclassified DEJ2 in October 1954.
DE/358/1, ?1964	Reissue (by Swindon).

Summary of DES2 Class

B.R. No.	L.N.E.R. No.	Maker	Built	Withdrawn
15004 5/49	(8004)	Doncaster/Brush	11/1947*	10/62

* Taken into stock in April 1949 although completed in November 1947.

DEPARTMENTAL STOCK

Some railway companies maintained a number of non-revenue earning locomotives whose purpose was to carry out shunting and movement of materials at the workshops or depots to which they were allocated. A few of the locomotives had cranes mounted on them in order to carry out lifting operations. Other locomotives in Departmental (or Service) Stock undertook the haulage of officer's saloons on tours of inspection. The L.N.E.R. never used departmental locomotives to work ballast trains, but this was the practice on at least one large pre-group railway (the L.N.W.R.).

The G.N.R., G.E.R. and N.E.R. companies all contributed a separate stock of departmental locomotives to the L.N.E.R., but the G.C.R., N.B.R. and G.N.S.R. did not, contenting themselves with the use of locomotives from Running Stock to shunt at their workshops. Throughout the life of the L.N.E.R. the same position largely obtained. At Grouping, there were 17 locomotives in Departmental Stock, as follows (using their L.N.E.R. numbers):—

ex-G.N.R. (2) :   0-4-4T "Doncaster Works"; 0-6-0T 3470A.

ex-G.E.R. (7) :   J66 7281; Z4 (later J92) B, C, D; Y4 7210; Y5 7230, 07228.

ex-N.E.R. (8) :   J71 263; J78 590, 995; J79 1662; X1 66; X3 190; Y7 129, 898.

As can be seen, where appropriate they were included in the same classification as other members of the class which were in Running Stock, viz. J66, J71, J78, J79, X3 and Y7. In addition X1 was allotted to No. 66 *Aerolite*, the solitary member of its class, afterwards transferred to Running Stock in 1926. All these engines have been described in detail under their respective class headings in Parts 8A, 8B and 9B of this series of books. The remaining three classes, comprising the two unclassified G.N.R. engines and the G.E.R. crane locomotives of class Z4 (later J92), were never represented in Running Stock and are dealt with herein at pages 28-35. The L.N.E.R. also possessed a number of self-propelled vehicles which figured neither in Running nor Departmental Stock returns. In the account which follows, reference will be made to some of these which were of unusual interest, such as the G.N.R. tram engine at Peterborough, the 0-4-4T kept for test purposes at Doncaster Carriage Works, the two Sentinel cranes bought by the L.N.E.R. for use at engine sheds in Scotland, and two Simplex petrol-engined shunting tractors — one from the G.E.R. and the other purchased after Grouping. Both the petrol shunters eventually found their way into the locomotive stock returns.

Over the years there were a number of deletions and additions to the official total of locomotives in Departmental Stock and these have been summarised in the table on page 23. The first changes occurred in 1925 when three petrol-driven inspection cars which had not previously figured in the returns were added to Departmental Stock in the North Eastern Area. During 1925-26 all eight N.E. Area steam locomotives in Departmental Stock were transferred to Running Stock. In the period 1925-33 nine new class Y1 Sentinel shunting locomotives were added to Departmental Stock, either as replacements for existing service engines or to take up new duties. Engines displaced were the ex-G.N.R. 0-6-0T and the 0-4-4 crane engine, the latter being replaced by a class J54 saddle tank taken from Running Stock. One of the Y5's was also withdrawn in 1927.

In 1934 a class B13 4-6-0 was taken into Departmental Stock for use during the road testing of other locomotives. A class J52 0-6-0T became an official additional works shunter at Doncaster in 1936 following the use in previous years of several condemned locomotives which had acted briefly in that capacity. The takeover of the M. & G.N. locomotive stock by the L.N.E.R. resulted in the addition in 1937 of the Melton Constable Works shunter to Departmental Stock, but it was withdrawn before the end of that year. The three petrol cars already referred to were condemned in 1939. In 1940 a class Y3 Sentinel locomotive was transferred to Departmental Stock, followed by two more during 1942, and these moves completed the changes during L.N.E.R. days, a summary of which appears on pages 24 and 25.

In view of the continued independent course with regard to Departmental Stock followed by each of the L.N.E.R. Areas throughout the Company's existence it will be convenient to describe events under those headings.

SOUTHERN AREA

G.N. SECTION. — There has been some confusion regarding the status of ex-G.N.R. departmental engines and it is regretted that a diligent search of available records still does not enable the authors to present a satisfactory solution. At Grouping, G.N.R. returns recorded the total as two, one of which was almost certainly the 0-4-4 crane tank engine which served the locomotive workshops at Doncaster. It had been built as No. 533 in 1876 as one of a class of 46 back tanks for use on the London suburban services. After withdrawal in 1905, No. 533 was rebuilt in March 1906 with a crane for handling material in Doncaster Works as well as use there on shunting duties. It then carried no number and was merely lettered "Doncaster Works" (fig. 23). However, as explained in the full account of this engine on page 28, it was known in official records as No. 3. This had repercussions after it was condemned (still un-numbered) on 23rd November 1928 and replaced by class J54 No. 3920 (see later).

The other departmental engine on the G.N.R. was an 0-6-0 saddle tank, No. 470, which Stirling had completely rebuilt in 1872 from an engine built only nine years earlier by Manning Wardle for the West Yorkshire Railway. In 1919 it was transferred to the Duplicate list as No. 470A and then, on 19th December 1921, it was put into Service Stock for use at Hall Hills Sleeper Depot at Boston, where it spent the rest of its life. At this period it was running as an 0-4-2 with the rear section of its coupling rods removed. Following a general repair at Doncaster, which took from 23rd October 1924 until 10th January 1925, it emerged painted black with red lining and lettered and numbered "LNER 3470A" (fig. 24), but it was never given any L.N.E.R. classification and was condemned on 19th April 1927 after its duties were taken over by a new Sentinel shunting locomotive.

The two locomotives just described were all that Doncaster recognised in official stock totals, but there was another one in regular use from 1908 until the end of 1926 in the Civil Engineer's Yard at Peterborough. This was a curious 0-4-0 tank engine which had a vertical boiler and a two-cylinder vertical engine geared to one of its axles, the whole almost fully enclosed in a metal box-like structure (fig. 26). The engine portion was built in 1892 at Doncaster and was used to power a traverser at the Carriage Works until supplanted by electric power.

Further details of this machine, and No. 3470A are to be found on pages 29-30.

The discovery of this extra G.N.R. departmental locomotive could well have significance when considering the classifications adopted by the L.N.E.R. On page 24 of Part 1, the probability is put forward that Z1 and Z2 were intended for No. 3470A and the 0-4-4 crane tank. If Z3 was in mind for this third ex-G.N.R. departmental, then the original choice of Z4 for the ex-G.E.R. crane tanks (and which was used by them until they were reclassified J92 in April 1927) has credibility. On the other hand, it should be mentioned that the third classification number was deliberately omitted initially by the L.N.E.R. in other wheel arrangement groups i.e. C (4-4-2), N (0-6-2T), O (2-8-0) and Y (0-4-0T), in the expectation that development of G.N.R.

designs might require their future use. So Z3 could have been a deliberate omission. To cloud further the question of the status of ex-G.N.R. service locomotives there was a puzzling drop of two in the overall official total of Departmental Locomotive Stock on the L.N.E.R. at the end of 1923, and restoration in the following year. It is possible that the crane locomotive and the Peterborough machine were those concerned even though the latter had not previously figured in the official totals. The fact that 470A retained its number, and received the L.N.E.R. 3000 addition, could have significance because it was the only one of the three so treated, but it is now unlikely that what really happened will become known.

In L.N.E.R. days three class Y1 Sentinel four-wheel shunting engines were ordered (see also page 17) from the makers and delivered in November 1926 to G.N. Section departmental establishments (fig. 31, Part 1), one each going to Boston, Peterborough and Doncaster, but it was not until April 1930 that they were given numbers (see Part 9B of this series for a full description of these engines).

The Boston engine replaced 0-6-0T No. 3470A and became No. 4801. In September 1937 this was changed to 4991 so that class V2 locomotives then being constructed could carry consecutive numbers. On 9th February 1940 No. 4991 was replaced at Hall Hills Sleeper Depot by class Y3 No. 49, which was transferred to Service Stock on 9th April 1940. No. 4991 then went to Doncaster Works as spare shunter and for much of its subsequent L.N.E.R. days it was stored and only used on rare occasions, its usual habitat being a corner of the Paint Shop. However, early in B.R. days, and by then renumbered 8132, it was found further employment at Ranskill Wagon Works (see page 20).

The Peterborough engine (No. 4802 later) superseded the vertical boilered 0-4-0 tank as the shunter for the Civil Engineer's Yard. It became No. 4992 in March 1937 and remained on the same job until withdrawn as Departmental No. 6 in November 1955, having previously carried numbers 8133 (1946) and 68133 (1948).

The Doncaster engine went to Carr Wagon Shops, which had hitherto not been allocated a permanent shunter. Like the other two G.N. Section service stock Y1's, the Carr Wagon Works shunter was initially lettered only with its allocation. However, it became No. 4803 in April 1930, being changed to No. 4993 on 17th April 1937 (figs. 27 & 28) and it only just managed to outlive the L.N.E.R., being withdrawn as No. 8134 (under the 1946 scheme) in February 1948. As it was normally used at the wagon shops it was rarely visible to outside observation.

The 0-4-4 crane tank continued in use as yard shunter at the Plant until it was condemned on 23rd November 1928, its duties then being taken over by class J54 No. 3920 hitherto stationed at

Colwick shed, which lost its running number to become "Service Stock No. 3" (fig. 25).

It will be noted that this title perpetuated the book entries for the crane tank. If the original reason for the numbering of the crane tank in 1906 was suggested on page 28, then this would quite likely have been forgotten by 1928 when it was a straightforward matter of finding a suitable replacement for a worn-out locomotive, as the crane itself had not been used for many years. However, as with the Sentinels mentioned above, No. 3 was given a proper number in April 1930 when it became 4800. In September 1933 it was rebuilt to class J55 and in August 1937 it was renumbered 4990. Under the 1946 scheme it became 8319 and survived into B.R. days, being withdrawn in June 1950 as No. 68319 (fig. 39, Part 8A). Throughout this time its sphere of operation continued to be the locomotive works yard at Doncaster. Its history is fully described under classes J54 and J55 on pages 35 to 50 of Part 8A.

From time to time a withdrawn tank engine was employed as an additional works shunter at the Plant for a further short period before being broken up. Class J54 No. 3676 was used as such from January to August 1929, as was J55 class No. 3802 from July 1934 to November 1935, when class J53 No. 3928 took its place until June 1936 and was then superseded by class J52 No. 3924. The latter was scrapped in November 1936, but this continuity from July 1934 had established the permanent need for an extra Service Stock engine at the locomotive works, and this was met by taking class J52 No. 3980 from traffic in November 1936 (fig. 29) and it remained on this duty until condemned as No. 68782 on 23rd June 1950. At the time it entered Service Stock, No. 3980 had not had a heavy repair since September 1933 but it continued in use until September 1939. On 7th October it went into Plant for a general repair, which took until 2nd December, and over this period its job was covered by class J52 No. 3964 which had been taken out of Running Stock for withdrawal on 15th August 1939. Apart from No. 3980, none of the other five was included in official returns for Service Stock totals, and they were quickly scrapped after they ceased to be works shunters.

During the years 1924 to 1932 Doncaster Works also had another engine available for service duties, but as it was not mobile it was never regarded as a Departmental locomotive. G.N.R. No. 824, a 0-4-4 tank of class G1, was taken out of traffic in June 1924, and in the following month it was fitted with a modern vacuum ejector and (additionally) Westinghouse brake pump with connections at each end, together with steam heat connection at the front end. It was stationed in the Carriage Works sidings and used for testing carriage braking and heating apparatus until August 1929. It then stood derelict until its boiler was condemned on

12th January 1933 — during which period the Westinghouse pump was removed for use elsewhere — but it was September 1933 before it was actually cut up. From July 1924 it carried neither number nor lettering, and from a 1932 photograph (fig. 152 in Part 7) it is impossible to judge the colour of its weather-worn paint after standing outside for so many years. As its last repair was in August 1919, it would then be turned out in grey and without lining, but whether it was painted black in July 1924 does not appear to have been recorded. The history of class G1 will be found in Part 7, pages 84-7.

G.E. SECTION. — The G.E.R. listed seven locomotives as being in Departmental Stock. All but one of these were continuously employed in and around the company's extensive workshops at Stratford. The engines concerned were No. 7281 (class J66) and the 0-6-0 crane tanks known as B, C and D, together with 0-4-0T's Nos. 7210 (class Y4) and 7230 (Y5). The remaining engine, class Y5 No. 07228, was also attached to Stratford Works at the time of Grouping. In December 1924 it was sent to the Norwich District, but returned to Stratford in the following March. It again went to Norwich in May 1926 and was noted during the following August at the Engineer's Yard at Lowestoft. In January 1927 it once more returned to Stratford and ended its days providing hot water for carriage foot warmers. It was withdrawn on 30th June 1927. Further details of these engines, and their duties will be found in Parts 8A (class J66), and 9B (Y4 and Y5), whilst the crane tanks are described on pages 31-35 of this work.

The G.E.R. also owned a small 40 h.p. petrol tractor, which was used at Lowestoft, but this did not figure in Departmental Stock lists and was regarded as miscellaneous equipment. As recorded below, it was replaced by a Sentinel locomotive in September 1925, then transferred to Brentwood to replace the horses used previously for moving wagons in the yard there. It was added to Running Stock in 1925, numbered 8430 in 1930 and later classified Y11. Further details are given on pages 5-8.

It was on the G.E. Section that the capabilities and economics of Sentinel shunting engines were first assessed. Traffic Committee Minute 488 of 30th April 1925 authorised the purchase of a "Super-Sentinel" for use in the Engineer's Yard at Lowestoft. It began work there as class Y1 No. 8400 on 27th September (fig. 59, Part 9B) and the costings of its work for the first six months showed an estimated saving of £316 per annum compared with the previous method of working. This was by the 40 h.p. petrol tractor mentioned above which was insufficiently powerful, so that a considerable amount of supplementary shunting had to be done by an ordinary steam locomotive. Except when it was undergoing its quarterly overhaul, the Sentinel's use obviated any supplementary shunting in the depot. On 26th

Fig. 2   Petrol shunting locomotive (later class Y11) No. 8430 at Brentwood, October 1932.

Fig. 3   Class Y11 No. 8430 at Brentwood, c.1946.
Wartime lettering "N E". Showing entrance to cab.

Fig. 4   Class Y11 No. 8188 at Brentwood, April 1948.

Fig. 6   Class Y11 No. 15098 at Brentwood, August 1951.

B.R. number on sides and ends in shaded numerals, but without indication of ownership.

Fig. 5   Class Y11 No. 8188 at Brentwood, April 1949.

Repainted, but without indication of ownership.

Fig. 7   Class Y11 No. 15098 at Brentwood, July 1954.

Unshaded numerals.

Fig. 8   Petrol shunting locomotive N.B. Petrol Engine No. 1 at Kelso, September 1923.

Fig. 9   Petrol shunting locomotive No. 8431 at Ware, c. 1935.
As rebuilt with tall cab and fitted with footboards for shunting staff.

Fig 10   Class Y11 No. 8189 at Ware, May 1948.

Wooden shutter fitted above half-height door, rear view mirror.

Fig. 11   Class Y11 No. 15099 at Ware, June 1951.

"British Railways" lettering, additional lamp irons added over buffers.

Fig. 12   Class Y11 No. 15099 at Stratford, September 1956.

Lion and wheel emblem.

Fig. 13   Class Y11 No. 15097 at Greenland Creosote Works, West Hartlepool, September 1949.

With B.R. number but still lettered "N E". Showing dumb buffers additionally fitted.

Fig. 14   Baguley/McEwan Pratt 2ft. 3in. gauge petrol locomotive conveying
sleeper lengths at Hall Hills Sleeper Depot, Boston.

Fig. 15   Ruston & Hornsby 3-foot gauge diesel locomotive "L N E R 3 *Monty*" at
Lowestoft Sleeper Depot.

Fig. 16   Class DES1 diesel-electric Nos. 8000/1/2 at March, June 1948.
No. 8000 lettered ''L N E R'', others ''N E''.

Fig. 17   Class J45 (later DES1) No. 8000 at Doncaster Works, June 1944.
Straight rain strips on cab roof, no external filler to rear sandbox.

July 1926, the Locomotive & Traffic Committee was asked to sanction purchase of three more of these Sentinels in a memorandum from the Divisional General Manager, Alex. Wilson, in which he also mentioned that the C.M.E. was recommending the purchase of another one for use in Doncaster Wagon Shops. If four were ordered, Sentinel would reduce the price of each from £1,400 to £1,362.10.0. On 29th July 1926 Minute 543 authorised purchase of these four for use at Hall Hills Sleeper Depot Boston, Peterborough Engineer's Shops and Doncaster Wagon Shops on the Western Section, the fourth to go to the Eastern Section for use at Lowestoft North Beach. There an ordinary steam locomotive still had to be used for procuring sand and shingle from the beach required for concrete (see class Y5, page 89 in Part 9B). These four Sentinels all went into Departmental Stock, those on the Western Section on 5th November 1926, and the Lowestoft engine on 31st December 1926. In due course, the former were numbered 4801/2/3 (see page 15), but the fourth engine became No. 8401 immediately.

The one at Doncaster Wagon Shops had been expected to show a saving of £480 and, after its first six months, Gresley was able to report that experience had justified this claim. On 25th May 1927 he recommended purchase of two more, one for use at the wagon shops at Temple Mills (near Stratford) and the other at Faverdale in the N.E. Area. This purchase was duly authorised and the two engines were delivered on 27th August 1927, numbered 8402 and 44 respectively. The encouraging results obtained from the class Y1 locomotives in Departmental Stock led to the purchase in 1927 of further examples for Running Stock use, together with a two-speed gearbox variety which was classified Y3. The complete story of these locomotives will be found in Part 9B.

The demand on Nos. 8400/1 was eased when class Y3 Nos. 96 and 98 were sent to Lowestoft running shed in 1936 and 1937, and particularly when these two were transferred to Departmental Stock on 4th September 1942 for use at Lowestoft Civil Engineer's Depot. It may be mentioned that it was common practice at most locations to borrow a Sentinel locomotive from the Running Department whenever the local departmental Sentinel was stopped for repair or away undergoing general overhaul. The further history of the above four engines is continued under "Lowestoft" on page 21.

No. 8402 remained attached to Temple Mills Wagon Works until the early part of the 1939-45 War. It is recorded as receiving a new ash pan in March 1940 and it is believed to have ceased work at Temple Mills at this time because its record card was then marked "to go to Parkeston". However, it was never recorded as being there. It is known (see page 79, Part 9B) that serious concern was expressed about the glare at night from the Sentinel boilers contravening the wartime blackout regulations, and it is suggested that this was the reason why No. 8402 ceased work as Stratford was a key area and particularly susceptible to German air raids. No. 8402 received no further repairs and spent the rest of its existence stored in the paint shop at Stratford Works — the last entry on its record card (2nd July 1948, by which time it had been renumbered 8135) was cryptic and significant, simply reading "Has been standing in Paint Shop for years — not much of it left". It was condemned on the following 9th August.

G.C. SECTION. — The G.C.R. did not allocate any engines to a separate Departmental Stock list, preferring instead to utilise an elderly locomotive still retained in Running Stock. At Grouping, Gorton's nominated engine was G.C.R. No. 309B, already fifty years old and the last surviving 0-6-0 tender engine of 68 built by Sacré in 1869-73. It took over this job in December 1920 and bore the word "LOCO" on the cab side sheets above its number (fig. 62, Part 5). This it retained until withdrawal in October 1924, and full details of this engine are given on pages 46/47 of Part 5. It was replaced by No. 6442 of class J12 which dated from January 1882, but this engine did not have the word "LOCO" applied and after its demise in November 1927, Gorton did not nominate any engine to the job of works shunter.

M. & G.N. SECTION. — When the M. & G.N. system was absorbed by the L.N.E.R. on 1st October 1936, Melton Constable had a works shunter numbered 16A. This was an outside cylinder 0-6-0 saddle tank, built by Fox Walker & Co. in 1877 and is separately described on page 35. The L.N.E.R. added it to their Departmental Stock as from 1st January 1937, but it did not survive the year end, being condemned on 25th October and cut up at Stratford Works.

NORTH EASTERN AREA

The eight N.E.R. locomotives shown in returns as being in departmental use at Grouping were divided between the works at Darlington (J71 No. 263, Y7 Nos. 129, 898) and Gateshead (J78 No. 995, J79 No. 1662), with J78 No. 590 at Percy Main where its crane was used in connection with the breaking up of condemned locomotives. The two single drivers, X1 No. 66 and X3 No. 190, were stationed at Darlington and Heaton respectively for hauling officer's saloons on their tours of inspection.

In January 1924 No. 590 was sent from Percy Main to the former Hull & Barnsley works at Springhead in Hull. This railway had not previously had a departmental locomotive attached to the works, any handy engine from the adjacent running shed hitherto performing this function. The purpose of No. 590's transfer was to assist in the melancholy task of dismantling the works after they ceased operation in August 1924, and during the run-down period earlier in that year. During the following October No. 590 departed to York, where it became the resident shunter at the locomotive running shed.

In September 1925 No. 1662 was transferred to Capital Stock, then in August 1926 the other seven also became Running Department responsibility. All eight engines have been dealt with fully under their respective classes in Parts 8B and 9B.

Three petrol-engined 4-wheeled inspection saloons were put into Departmental Stock during 1925. They were not new, having been built at York Carriage Works in 1908, 1912 and 1923, but they had not previously been included in Stock Returns. All three remained in Departmental Stock until withdrawn on 4th February 1939, after a decision that it was more economical to use a steam engine to haul an inspection saloon. Running costs were some 30% less for the cars, but a steam engine could also be used on other work whereas the cars simply stood idle when not on inspection duty. A full description of these cars will be found on pages 37-39.

Under L.N.E.R. auspices there were four more additions to N.E. Area Service Stock. The success and lower running costs of the single-manned Sentinel shunters enabled them to be used as a firm allocation at depots which did not hitherto have their own engine. In August 1927 class Y1 No. 44 began work at Faverdale Wagon Works, Darlington, followed in September 1930 by No. 45 at the York Civil Engineer's Yard (fig. 63, Part 9B), and in December 1933 by No. 59 at the Geneva Permanent Way Depot at Darlington. All three remained on these same duties until withdrawn in 1956, 1959 and 1961 respectively.

From March 1934 until withdrawn for scrapping in the following September, class B13 4-6-0 No. 756 was used by the C.M.E.'s Department (though not officially in Service Stock) as a counter-pressure locomotive for road testing of other locomotives. Sister engine No. 761 was then similarly adapted to take its place and was transferred to Service Stock in September 1934. It was normally kept in the Paint Shop at Darlington Works (fig. 38). In October 1946 it was re-numbered 1699 (fig. 125, Part 2B), then in July 1948, after nationalisation, it was sent to the newly-opened Locomotive Testing Station at Rugby and remained there until condemned in May 1951. It went to Crewe Works to be cut up. The full history of these engines will be found in Part 2B.

In August 1925 the N.E. Area Engineer's Department purchased a 40 h.p. petrol tractor of similar type to those inherited by the L.N.E.R. from the N.B.R. and G.E.R. (and which were eventually classified Y11). Like the G.E.R. machine, this latest acquisition was regarded as a piece of miscellaneous equipment. It was known simply as L4 and never figured in any locomotive stock returns during L.N.E.R. days. It spent its career at the Greenland Creosote Works at West Hartlepool. Apparently it must have come to the notice of the C.M.E.'s department at one stage because in the *Railway Magazine* for August 1929 it was listed as class Z6 (Z4 and Z5 were by then in use for the ex-G.N.S.R. 0-4-2T's) with the number 8434, this list having been cleared for publication by one of Gresley's staff. Nevertheless, neither number nor class appears to have been adopted and it sank into obscurity until it was rediscovered by the C.M.E.'s department in 1949, when at last a proper number and classification were given to it (see page 5).

SCOTTISH AREA

The N.B.R. did not maintain a separate stock of service locomotives and the Running Department had to provide the engines for works shunting, and official saloon haulage. At Cowlairs in L.N.E.R. days, four pilots were employed, one each for Erecting Shop, Carriage Shop, Wagon Shop and Stores. They were supplied by Eastfield shed and were usually class Y9 or the small 0-6-0 tanks of class J88. After their transfer to Eastfield from Carlisle in the summer of 1926, ex-North Eastern Nos. 285 and 453 of class J71 were regularly used as works pilots, and in February 1939 (when both had been withdrawn) two J72's Nos. 2192 and 2326 were sent to be used on the same duties and these remained at Eastfield until January 1958. At St. Margaret's, the works shunting was done by the shed's No. 1 Pilot amongst its other jobs, and for many years it was customary to use an old 0-6-0. In L.N.E.R. days this was usually a class J31, and later class J24 and class J36. Eventually, however, a regular assignment of a class N15 to this job was made. (No. 9175 was on this duty at Nationalisation.) Kipps Works continued doing repairs until May 1925 and in its last two years the shunting there was carried out by N.B. No. 1464 of class D51 from Kipps shed. At Burntisland the "Shops Pilot" was usually N.B. No. 836, a J88.

The G.N.S.R. also had no separate stock for service purposes, but was akin to Gorton in using up relics for shunting at Inverurie Works, and the two in use at Grouping were by then 57 years old. These were class D47 No. 45A as the works shunter, and No. 48A for Engineer's ballast trains (figs. 133 and 134, Part 4). This latter engine was equipped with an additional Westinghouse pump to provide compressed air for bridge-riveting apparatus and when No. 48A was withdrawn in June 1925 the extra air pump was carried by a variety of engines, amongst them No. 6894 of class D41 and No. 6835 of class D40 being observed. After No. 45A was withdrawn in 1925 (it was specially prepared for display at the S.&D. Centenary celebrations — see p.46), shunting duties at the works devolved mainly on 0-6-0T's, at first of G.N.S.R. origin and then in later years ex-N.E.R. J72 engines were used. The duty was also undertaken by two 0-4-4T's built by the same companies: by January 1940 eight of the nine ex-G.N.S.R. tanks of class G10 had been scrapped, but No. 6887 (which was renumbered 7505 in 1946) continued to earn its living at Inverurie (fig. 199, Part 7) until August 1947, when class G5 No. 7287 took over the job until in March 1953 it too was withdrawn. By then in its 57th year, it almost paralleled the situation on the G.N.S.R. at Grouping.

Although never officially regarded as departmental locomotives, the Scottish Area possessed two Sentinel-engined self-propelled ash cranes. Despite their mobility and being passed for working independently at up to 24 m.p.h. over running lines between sheds, the L.N.E.R. numbered and regarded them as wagon stock. Even so, they had permission to haul 350 tons at 5 m.p.h. and 50 tons at 24 m.p.h. It is believed that they were obtained chiefly for clearing the ashpits used by engines fitted with drop grates. The first was ordered on 12th September 1929 and delivered in December, the crane and grab being made by Coles at Derby whilst Sentinel at Shrewsbury made the chassis, the boiler and the two engines, one for the crane and the other for movement. Sentinel's works number was 8157 and the L.N.E.R. number was 773044; it worked mainly in Glasgow at Eastfield and Parkhead sheds being known locally as "Stoorie Annie". The other one had a building date of December 1931 and was delivered to Haymarket shed in January 1932, its works number being 8565 and its L.N.E.R. number 773066. An attempt was made to use this machine at St. Margaret's as well as Haymarket, but difficulty was experienced maintaining enough steam to keep it moving throughout the 2-mile journey between these sheds. It was also alleged to have been unreliable at revealing its presence on signal box track circuit diagrams, and so it had a potentially dangerous tendency to become "lost" on an extremely busy main line. Subsequently it is known to have also worked at Thornton and Dundee. The cranes were rated to lift 3 tons at 9 feet radius and 1½ tons at 16 feet. When built, these machines had only a rudimentary shelter for the operator, but latterly No. 773066 had an enclosed cab (figs. 53&54). From 1938, the 700,000 numbers were required for other use and the two ash cranes were allotted numbers 971575 and 971577 (ex-773044/66). However, when No. 773066 arrived at Darlington Works for overhaul in December 1946 it was still so numbered. Both were noted carrying their second numbers when subsequently lettered "BRITISH RAILWAYS". Later, when Scottish Region leaned more towards former L.M.S. ideas, these two cranes were again renumbered in 1953, becoming RS1032/1½ (fig. 55) and RS1033/1½ (RS standing for Rail Steam and 1½ the lifting capacity in tons at maximum radius). Both survived until 1959, No. 1032 being condemned in July and No. 1033 in November.

BRITISH RAILWAYS

At nationalisation, the L.N.E.R. handed over 21 locomotives in Departmental Stock comprising one each of classes B13, J52, J55, J66, Y4 and Y5, three each of classes J92 and Y3, and nine class Y1. In addition, there was the petrol tractor at West Hartlepool known as L4, but which went unrecorded in the locomotive lists.

During B.R. days 45 locomotives of L.N.E.R. origin or type (see table on pages 26-27) were transferred from Running to Departmental Stock, some to replace existing departmental engines which had become worn out and others for new duties. Fresh classes to feature in the departmental lists were B1 (described in Part 2B), J50 and J69 (Part 8A), J72 (Part 8B), Y8 (Part 9B), and EB1 (Part 10B). All of them were put to use at places in the Eastern and North Eastern Regions, and for the most part are conveniently dealt with under these locations.

Before so doing, the renumbering scheme of E.R. and N.E.R. departmental service vehicles must be mentioned. This was implemented in May 1952 and was necessitated because their existing numbers conflicted with the revised numbering for wagon stock adopted by the Railway Executive. Service vehicles for which the Mechanical & Electrical Engineer had responsibility for maintenance were included in the range 1 to 1000 with groups allocated to type of vehicle. For example, sludge carriers were numbered 601 upwards and water carriers took 701 upwards. The departmental locomotives were allocated 1 to 100 and as there were just over twenty of them, this enabled them to be grouped according to the districts in which they were employed. So those maintained at Doncaster were numbered 1 upwards, those at Stratford began at 31 and those at Darlington at 51, but no concentrated effort was made to carry out this renumbering quickly. Stratford started their renumbering in September 1952, whilst Doncaster and Darlington followed in November, but it has proved difficult to obtain actual dates for some items. However, by the beginning of June 1953 it is known that twenty had received their new numbers. Further allocations under this scheme were made as late as February 1966 and it was April 1968 before the last engines with this series of numbers were condemned. It will be noticed by reference to the table on page 26 that some of the later additions to the departmental list (i.e. the B1 class) duplicated the numbers of earlier engines which had by then been withdrawn from service. It may also be mentioned that Departmental Nos. 52/6, 81-8, 91/2 were borne by diesel-mechanical locomotives added to stock by British Railways. Some of these are referred to in the following account.

The display of the departmental numbers on the locomotives varied a great deal, as can be seen from the accompanying illustrations. The words DEPARTMENTAL LOCOMOTIVE usually appeared, but not always. The representative of the Chief Civil Engineer at Lowestoft was apparently determined to leave in no doubt the ownership of the Sentinel locomotives under his control as each one proclaimed CIVIL ENGINEER'S DEPARTMENTAL LOCOMOTIVE.

EASTERN REGION

DONCASTER LOCOMOTIVE WORKS. — At the time of nationalisation there were two shunting engines at the locomotive works, class J52 No. 8782 and class J55 No. 8319 (fig. 39, Part 8A). Both received 60,000 series numbers in July 1948 and were condemned on 23rd June 1950. At the end of the previous month two J52's, Nos. 8816/45, had been taken from Running Stock as replacements. They duly became 68816/45 and were renumbered again as 2 and 1 respectively in the departmental series in November 1952. In March 1956 another J52, No. 8858 (which had been withdrawn in December 1955), took on the identity of No. 2 (fig. 19, Part 8A) and the original engine with that number was broken up. No. 1 was condemned in February 1958, its place being taken by J52 No. 68840, transferred from Running Stock on 27th January 1958. This engine was numbered 9 in the departmental list. Nos. 2 and 9 were withdrawn in February 1961 and replaced by a pair of J50's, Nos. 68911/4, which became Nos. 10 and 11 (fig. 6, Part 8A). Then, in September 1962, five more J50's (all then allocated to Doncaster m.p.d.) were put into departmental stock at Doncaster. These took Departmental Nos. 12-16 (ex-68917/28/61/71/6 respectively). It is understood that the sphere of activity of the seven departmental engines was enlarged to include work at the adjacent Carriage Shops. There was also a need for additional shunting engines to move the large number of steam locomotives arriving for scrapping at the Plant. Except for No. 14, which was withdrawn in

September 1965, all the others were condemned in the previous May, their work being taken over by diesel locomotives.

DONCASTER WAGON WORKS. — Class Y1 No. 8134 had worked here since it was delivered in November 1926. It was laid aside in February 1948 and replaced by Y3 No. 8165, transferred from Running Stock on the 5th of that month. It became Departmental No. 5 in March 1953 and was condemned in November 1958, no immediate replacement being provided.

RANSKILL WAGON WORKS. — This establishment had been built during the 1939-45 War as a Royal Ordnance Factory and was subsequently taken over by the L.N.E.R. for use as a wagon repair shop. Its first permanent allocation of a shunting locomotive was class Y1 No. 8132 on 3rd February 1948. This engine, as recounted earlier, had been stored in the Paint Shop at the Plant since 1940. It became No. 68132, then Departmental No. 4 and remained at Ranskill until withdrawn in June 1959. On 3rd September 1951 it was joined by class Y3 No. 68181, taken from Running Stock at Tyne Dock shed in the N.E. Region. This engine became Departmental No. 3 in November 1952 and was condemned in November 1959 (fig. 36).

PETERBOROUGH ENGINEER'S YARD. — Class Y1 No. 8133 was the regular engine here from November 1926 until withdrawn as Departmental No. 6 in November 1955. It had at least one temporary spell working at Hall Hills Sleeper Depot at Boston, being noted there (as No. 68133) about 1949. By September 1955 No. 6 was apparently unfit for further work because on 29th of that month Y3 No. 68183 arrived from Dairycoates shed to take over its duties. No. 68183 was transferred to Departmental Stock on the above date and was renumbered 8 in the following month. It lasted until January 1959. The replacement this time, which had arrived at Peterborough in June 1958, was Departmental No. 81, a 150 h.p. Andrew Barclay 0-4-0 DM.

HALL HILLS SLEEPER DEPOT, BOSTON. — At nationalisation, class Y3 No. 8166 was the resident engine here, having taken over from class Y1 No. 4991 in February 1940. No. 8166 was renumbered 68166 (in August 1948), then again as Departmental No. 7 (in March 1953 — fig. 32). In November 1961 (or possibly earlier) it was transferred to Lowestoft Engineer's Yard, and Boston thereafter had no departmental locomotive on its books.

STRATFORD WORKS. — At nationalisation, six service engines were in use here, J66 No. 8370, J92 Nos. 8667/8/9 and Y4 No. 8129 at the Locomotive Works, and Y5 No. 8081 at the Carriage Shops. The last-mentioned was withdrawn in April 1948 and Y7 No. 8088 was obtained from the N.E. Region on 27th June to replace it (figs. 103/4, Part 9B). The next loss was crane locomotive 8669, in October 1950, and no replacement was provided. However, when sister engine 8667 was also scrapped in May 1952, J66 No. 68382 was transferred from Running Stock on 30th June as replacement. The Y7 was withdrawn in October 1952 and the original J66 in Service Stock (No. 8370, by then renumbered Departmental No. 32 — fig. 76, Part 8A) became the nominated engine attached to the Carriage Shops, being then recorded as under the jurisdiction of the Carriage & Wagon Engineer rather than the C.M.E. In fact, before that time this engine had usually acted as stand-in whenever the Y5, or Y7 later, was unavailable for work.

The last crane engine, by then renumbered Departmental No. 35, was withdrawn in November 1952 and another J66, No. 68378, was taken from Running Stock on 15th September to replace it. The complement of service locomotives at Stratford had now fallen to four, at which figure it remained until shunting was taken over by diesel locomotives provided by the Running Department in September 1962, except for the class Y4 which hung on until December 1963. Departmental No. 32, the original J66, survived until September 1962, but the other two became worn out and required replacement. The first to go was Departmental No. 36 (ex-68378) which was condemned in January 1959, its place being taken from December 1958 by class J69 No. 68532 (which became No. 43). This engine lasted only until August 1959, when it was replaced by another J69, No. 68498, which became Departmental No. 44 (fig. 102, Part 8A). The other J66, Departmental No. 31 (ex-68382), was scrapped in November 1959 and replaced by J69 No. 68543, which took the number 45 in the Departmental lists. Nos. 44 and 45 were both condemned in September 1962, together with J66 No. 32.

LOWESTOFT. — At nationalisation there were four Sentinel locomotives available to the Civil Engineer for shunting at the Sleeper Depot and at the Engineer's Yard. These were class Y1 Nos. 7773 and 8130 (formerly Nos. 8401 and 8400) and class Y3 Nos. 8177/8 (ex-Nos. 96 and 98), the latter pair then being the usual engines at the Sleeper Depot. Availability of the Sentinels was poor and on 11th July 1948 class Y3 No. 8173 was taken from Running Stock and sent to Lowestoft, followed on 1st January 1950 by another Y3, No. 8168 (see fig. 36 in Part 1 and figs. 72/3 Part 9B).

On 3rd April 1951 class Y1 No. 8131 (ex-7773) was sent to Norwich, for use at the Engineer's Yard at Wensum (where it remained for four years) whilst in July 1952 class Y3 No. 8178 was despatched to Chesterton Junction Permanent Way Depot near Cambridge. Under the 1952 renumbering scheme the remaining four Sentinels at Lowestoft became Nos. 37 (8130), 38 (8168), 40 (8173) and 41 (8177) (figs. 33 & 37). Two new 200 h.p. 0-6-0 DH locomotives, Departmental Nos. 91 and 92, were sent to Lowestoft in June and July 1958 respectively, but

both were moved to Chesterton Junction during the following year. Prior to this, Sentinel No. 37 had been condemned in January 1956, and No. 38 followed it to the scrap heap in February 1959. There were then only two Sentinels at Lowestoft, Nos. 40 and 41. About November 1961 class Y3 Departmental No. 7 (ex-68166) was sent to Lowestoft from Hall Hills Sleeper Depot at Boston to assist the existing pair. No. 41 was condemned in March 1963 whilst the remaining two, Nos. 7 and 40, went in May 1964 when the depot closed. No. 40 was in use right to the end, with No. 7 kept as spare engine.

CHESTERTON JUNCTION P.W.D., CAMBRIDGE. — Prior to the arrival here of class Y3 No. 8178 in July 1952, the yard had been shunted by "the ballast link" from Cambridge running shed. The link consisted of two engine crews, usually using a class J15 0-6-0 (often No. 65379). No. 8178 was renumbered Departmental No. 42 and was joined by class Y1 No. 39 in March 1955 (fig. 75, Part 9B). This engine came from the Wensum Yard at Norwich. Then, in March 1956, class Y3 No. 68162 (which had been withdrawn from Running Stock the previous January and then repaired at Gorton Works) was added to Departmental Stock as No. 21 and sent to Chesterton Junction. By March 1959 Nos. 21 and 42 were derelict and Departmental No. 91 (a 0-6-0 DM, mentioned above) was the yard shunter, backed up by No. 39 which was still workable. No. 92, the other diesel 0-6-0 from Lowestoft, arrived later at Chesterton Junction and Sentinels Nos. 21 and 42 were condemned in July 1960. At that time No. 39 was stored at Cambridge shed but was not withdrawn until April 1963.

ILFORD ELECTRIC CAR SHEDS. — The ex-N.E.R. electric locomotive No. 11 rebuilt by Doncaster in 1942 and which became No. 6498 under the 1946 renumbering scheme was found regular employment when on 25th August 1949 it was sent to Ilford Car Sheds to act as the shunter there. In 1950 it was renumbered 26510, but not until January 1959 was it taken out of Running Stock and transferred to Departmental Stock as No. 100 (fig. 40). It did no work after 4th ·November 1960 because the overhead power lines at Ilford depot were converted from d.c. to a.c. on the following day. Although its duties were taken over by a diesel shunting locomotive provided by the Running Department, No. 100 was put into store at Goodmayes and not withdrawn from service until April 1964, when it went to Doncaster Works for cutting up.

CLASS B1. — As the winter of 1963 approached it became apparent that the complete dieselisation of motive power in East Anglia would result in carriage heating deficiencies. Accordingly, in November 1963 nine B1's were withdrawn from service and transferred to Departmental Stock to act as mobile stationary boilers for the pre-heating of carriage stock. They were allocated Nos. 17 to 25 in the departmental list. Almost immediately, No. 61323 was condemned and its allotted number 24 was taken instead by a further engine, No. 61375. To cover withdrawals from the original nine engines and also for use at new locations, five more B1's were transferred to Departmental Stock in 1965, followed by a final three in February 1966. All had gone by April 1968. Further details will be found on page 150 of Part 2B, and in the table at the end of this chapter (figs. 41, 42 & 43).

There were many other instances of steam locomotives being used for stationary boiler work, often for lengthy periods, and specific mention has been made of this under classes C1, D16, K3, L3 and N1. In none of these cases was the engine concerned transferred to Departmental Stock.

NORTH EASTERN REGION

FAVERDALE WAGON WORKS (DARLINGTON). — Class Y1 No. 44, which had begun work here in August 1927, was condemned on 31st October 1956. It was then known as Departmental No. 51 (fig. 34). Its replacement was class Y3 No. 68160, which was taken out of Running Stock on 29th October 1956 and renumbered Departmental No. 57. This engine was condemned in February 1961. The replacement this time was a Hunslet 204 h.p. 0-6-0 DM, Departmental No. 88. This machine had been built as No. D2612 in January 1961 and was transferred to Departmental Stock and renumbered the following month.

GENEVA PERMANENT WAY DEPOT (DARLINGTON). — Class Y1 No. 59, latterly Departmental No. 54, was here from December 1933 until withdrawn in June 1961 (fig. 35).

Departmental No. 87, an 88 h.p. 0-4-0 DM built by Ruston & Hornsby, replaced it in that same month.

YORK ENGINEER'S YARD. — Class Y1 Departmental No. 53 (ex-No. 45) worked here from September 1930 until it was condemned in March 1959. Departmental No. 84, a similar machine to No. 87 mentioned above, arrived in January 1959 to replace it.

WEST HARTLEPOOL CREOSOTE WORKS. — A request in 1949 by the Civil Engineer for a replacement for L4, the petrol-engined tractor used here since 1925, at last provoked action by the C.M.E.'s department to regularise the position of this machine. It was officially taken into Departmental Stock in May 1949 and re-numbered 15097 (fig. 13), joining the two Running Stock class Y11 engines in that classification. Authority to replace it was granted by the Railway Executive on 12th December 1949 and it was condemned in June 1950. The replacement was No. 11104, a 57 h.p. 0-4-0 DM (supplied by F.C. Hibberd), which became Departmental No. 52 in May 1953.

YORK. — Class Y8 No. 8091, which had been used since May 1943 as the shed shunter, was transferred to Departmental Stock as Departmental No. 55 in June 1954 (fig. 38, Part 1).

NORTH BLYTH. — The final additions to N.E. Region departmental stock were class J72 Nos. 69005/23 which, as Departmental Nos. 58 and 59 (fig. 39), were sent to North Blyth in October 1964 for use in freezing weather to thaw coal in the wagons on the shipping staiths. This was not successful and after periods in store they were withdrawn in October 1967 and September 1966 respectively.

ANALYSIS OF L.N.E.R. LOCOMOTIVES IN DEPARTMENTAL STOCK

Stock at 1/1/23 (17): 1 G.N. 0-4-4T, 1 G.N. 0-6-0T, 1 J66, 1 J71, 2 J78, 1 J79, 1 X1, 1 X3, 1 Y4, 2 Y5, 2 Y7, 3 Z4 (later J92)

	TOTAL at 31st December	DURING YEAR	
		ADDED	DELETED
1923	15 (a)		
1924	17		
1925	20	1 Y1, 3 Petrol Cars	1 J79
1926	17	4 Y1	1 J71, 2 J78, 1 X1, 1 X3, 2 Y7
1927	17	2 Y1	1 G.N. 0-6-0T, 1 Y5
1928	17	1 J54	1 G.N. 0-4-4T
1929	17		
1930	18	1 Y1	
1931	18		
1932	18		
1933	19	1 Y1	
1934	20	1 B13	
1935	20		
1936	21	1 J52	
1937	21	1 M.&G.N. 0-6-0T	1 M.&G.N. 0-6-0T
1938	21		
1939	18		3 Petrol cars
1940	19	1 Y3	
1941	19		
1942	21	2 Y3	
1943	21		
1944	21		
1945	21		
1946	21		
1947	21		
1948	21	2 Y3, 1 Y7	2 Y1, 1 Y5
1949	22	1 Y11 (b)	
1950	21	2 J52, 1 Y3	1 J52, 1 J55 (ex J54), 1 J92 (ex Z4), 1 Y11
1951	21	1 Y3	1 B13
1952	20	2 J66	2 J92 (ex Z4), 1 Y7
1953	20		
1954	21	1 Y8	
1955	21	1 Y3	1 Y1
1956	20	1 J52, 2 Y3	1 J52, 2 Y1, 1 Y8
1957	20		
1958	19	1 J52	1 J52, 1 Y3
1959	15	3 J69, 1 EB1	2 J66, 1 J69, 2 Y1, 3 Y3
1960	13		2 Y3
1961	11	2 J50	2 J52, 1 Y1, 1 Y3
1962	13	5 J50	1 J66, 2 J69
1963	18	9 B1	1 B1, 1 Y1, 1 Y3, 1 Y4
1964	16	2 J72	1 B1, 2 Y3, 1 EB1
1965	10	5 B1	4 B1, 7 J50
1966	5	3 B1	7 B1, 1 J72
1967	2		2 B1, 1 J72
1968	—		2 B1

N.B. This analysis agrees with the Annual Report made each year to the shareholders of the L.N.E.R. and, from nationalisation, by the British Transport Commission and its successors. There were several other locomotives in use from time to time on Departmental Stock.

(a) There was an unexplained drop of two in the total of Departmental Stock at the end of 1923, the original figure being reinstated a year later (see page 15).

(b) In miscellaneous stock from time of purchase in 1925 until 1949.

SUMMARY OF L.N.E.R. DEPARTMENTAL LOCOMOTIVES

Class	No.	To Deptl. Stock	Normal Location	1946 No.	B.R. No. 1948	1952	Withdrawn
B13	761	9/34	Darlington (Stooperdale); Rugby Test Plant 7/48	1699 10/46	(61699)	—	5/51
G.N. 0-4-4T	(a)	At Gpg.	Doncaster Loco. Works	—	—	—	11/28
G.N. 0-6-0T	3470A	,,	Boston Hall Hills Sleeper Depot	—	—	—	4/27
J52	3980	11/36	Doncaster Loco. Works	8782 11/46	68782 7/48	—	6/50
J54(b)	3920(c)	11/28	,, ,, ,,	8319 3/46	68319 7/48	—	6/50
J66	7281	At Gpg.	Stratford Loco. Works; Stratford Carr. Works 10/52	8370 4/46	68370 12/48	32 9/52	9/62
J71	263	,,	Darlington Loco. Works	—	—	—	8/26 (d)
J78	590	,,	Percy Main; Springhead 1/24; York 10/24	—	—	—	8/26 (d)
,,	995	,,	Gateshead Loco. Works	—	—	—	8/26 (d)
J79	1662	,,	,, ,, ,,	—	—	—	9/25 (d)
J92(e)	B	,,	Stratford Loco. Works	8667 6/46	68667 2/49	—	5/52
,,	C	,,	,, ,, ,,	8668 6/46	68668 2/50	35 9/52	11/52
,,	D	,,	,, ,, ,,	8669 6/46	68669 3/50	—	10/50
M.&G.N. 0-6-0T	16A	1/37	Melton Constable Loco. Wks.	—	—	—	10/37
X1	66	At Gpg.	Darlington	—	—	—	8/26(d)
X3	190	,,	Heaton	—	—	—	8/26(d)
Y1	44	8/27	Faverdale Wagon Shops (Darlington)	8136 7/46	68136 11/52	51 11/52(f)	10/56
,,	45	9/30	York Civil Engineer's Yard	8152 10/46	68152 5/51	53 4/54	3/59
,,	59	12/33	Geneva P.W. Depot (Darlington)	8153 10/46	68153 6/51	54 10/54	6/61(g)
,,	4801(h)	11/26	Boston Hall Hills Sleeper Depot; Retford 2/40; Doncaster 4/40; Ranskill Wagon Works 2/48	8132 9/46	68132 5/48	4 12/52	6/59
,,	4802(h)	,,	Peterborough Engineer's Yard	8133 3/46	68133 6/48	6 3/53	11/55
,,	4803(h)	,,	Doncaster Carr Wagon Works	8134 12/46	(68134)	—	2/48
,,	8400(i)	9/25	Lowestoft	8130 1/47	(68130)	37 by 5/53	1/56
,,	8401(j)	12/26	Lowestoft; Norwich Wensum Eng. Yd. 4/51; Cambridge Chesterton Jct. Eng. Yd. 3/55	8131by5/51	(68131)	39 8/53	4/63
,,	8402(k)	8/27	Temple Mills Wagon Wks; Stratford c.3/40	8135 1/47	(68135)	—	8/48

SUMMARY OF L.N.E.R. DEPARTMENTAL LOCOMOTIVES (Continued)

Class	No.	To Deptl. Stock	Normal Location	1946 No.	B.R. No. 1948	1952	Withdrawn
Y3	49	4/40	Boston Hall Hills Sleeper Depot; Lowestoft c.11/61	8166 6/46	68166 8/48	7 3/53	5/64
,,	96	9/42	Lowestoft	8177 6/46	(68177)	41 by 5/53	3/63
,,	98	,,	Lowestoft; Cambridge Chesterton Jct. Eng. Yard 7/52	8178 5/46	(68178)	42 3/53	7/60
Y4	7210	At Gpg.	Stratford Loco. Works	8129 5/46	68129 10/48	33 9/52	12/63
Y5	7230	,,	Stratford Carr. Works	8081 12/46	(68081)	—	4/48
,,	07228	,,	Stratford; Norwich 12/24; Stratford 3/25; Lowestoft 5/26; Stratford 1/27	—	—	—	6/27
Y7	129	At Gpg.	Darlington Loco. Wks.	—	—	—	8/26(d)
,,	898	,,	,,　　,,　　,,	—	—	—	8/26(d)
Petrol Car	3711(l)	-/25	Darlington	—	—	—	2/39
,,	3768(l)	,,	York	—	—	—	2/39
,,	3769(l)	,,	Gateshead	—	—	—	2/39

Miscellaneous operating stock (not in stock totals):—

Class	No.	To Deptl. Stock	Normal Location	1946 No.	B.R. No. 1948	1952	Withdrawn
G.N. 0-4-0T	—	(At Gpg.)	Peterborough Engineer's Yard	—	—	—	-/26 or -/27
(Y11)	—	(At Gpg.)	Lowestoft Engineer's Yard	—	—	—	9/25(d)
(Y11)	L4 (8/25)		West Hartlepool Creosote Works	—	15097 5/49 (m)—		6/50

(a) Lettered "Doncaster Works".

(b) Rebuilt to class J55 in September 1933.

(c) On becoming a service locomotive, No. 3920 was lettered "Service Stock No. 3". It became No. 4800 in April 1930, then 4990 in August 1937.

(d) Transferred to Running Stock at dates shown.

(e) Classified Z4 until April 1927.

(f) Renumbered 68136 on 8/11/52 and then Departmental 51 on 17/11/52.

(g) Purchased in September 1961 by the Middleton Railway, Leeds and still extant.

(h) Nos. 4801/2/3 were un-numbered until April 1930. In 1937 they became 4991 (September), 4992 (March) and 4993 (April) respectively.

(i) Renumbered 7772 in April 1943.

(j) Renumbered 7773 (in error for 8131) in June 1946.

(k) Renumbered 7774 in January 1943.

(l) The petrol cars were renumbered 23711/68/9 in September 1928, March 1928 and March 1927 respectively.

(m) No. L4 was taken into B.R. Departmental Stock in May 1949, numbered 15097, and added to class Y11.

TRANSFERS TO DEPARTMENTAL STOCK BY BRITISH RAILWAYS

Class	No.	To Deptl. Stock	Normal Location	B.R. No. 1948	1952		With- drawn
B1	61059	11/63	Lowestoft; Ipswich -/64	—	17	11/63	4/66
,,	61181	,,	March	—	18	,,	12/65
,,	61204	,,	Yarmouth	—	19	,,	2/66
,,	61205	,,	Norwich	—	20	,,	1/65
,,	61233	,,	Cambridge	—	21	,,	4/66
,,	61252	,,	Ipswich	—	22	,,	5/64
,,	61300	,,	Cambridge	—	23	,,	11/65
,,	61323	,,	,,	—	(24) (a)		11/63
,,	61375	,,	King's Lynn	—	24	,,	4/66
,,	61272	1/65	New England (Hitchin)	—	25	1/65	11/65
,,	61138	,,	Norwich	—	26	,,	10/67
,,	61105	3/65	Parkeston	—	27	3/65	5/66
,,	61194	8/65	Stratford (Thornton Fields)	—	28	8/65	6/66
,,	61264	11/65	Colwick	—	29	11/65	7/67(c)
,,	61050	2/66	Canklow; Rotherham 9/66; Barrow Hill 5/67.	—	30	2/66	4/68
,,	61051	,,	Canklow	—	31	,,	3/66
,,	61315	,,	Canklow; Rotherham 9/66; Barrow Hill 5/67.	—	32	,,	4/68
J50	68911	2/61	Doncaster Works	—	10	2/61	5/65
,,	68914	,,	,, ,,	—	11	2/61	5/65
,,	68917	9/62	,, ,,	—	12	9/62(e)	5/65
,,	68928	,,	,, ,,	—	13	9/62(e)	5/65
,,	68961	,,	,, ,,	—	14	9/62(e)	9/65
,,	68971	,,	,, ,,	—	15	9/62(e)	5/65
,,	68976	,,	,, ,,	—	16	9/62(e)	5/65
J52	8816	5/50	,, ,,	68816 5/51	2	11/52	3/56
,,	68840	1/58	,, ,,	—	9	1/58	2/61
,,	8845	5/50	,, ,,	68845 6/50	1	11/52	2/58
,,	68858	3/56	,, ,,	—	2	3/56	2/61
J66	68378	9/52	Stratford Works	—	36	11/52	1/59
,,	68382	6/52	,, ,,	—	31	8/52	11/59
J69	68498	8/59	,, ,,	—	44	8/59	9/62
,,	68532	1/59(f)	,, ,,	—	43	1/59	8/59
,,	68543	11/59	,, ,,	—	45	11/59	9/62
J72	69005	10/64	North Blyth; Gateshead -/65; Tyne Dock	—	58	10/64	10/67
,,	69023	,,	North Blyth; Heaton -/65; Tyne Dock	—	59	10/64	9/66(c)

Class	No.	To Deptl. Stock	Normal Location	B.R. No. 1948	1952		With-drawn
Y3	68160	10/56	Faverdale Wagon Shops	—	57	10/56	2/61
,,	68162	3/56	Cambridge Dist. Eng. Yard	—	21	3/56	7/60
,,	8165	2/48	Doncaster Wagon Shops	68165 5/48	5	3/53	11/58
,,	8168	1/50	Lowestoft	—	38	by 5/53	2/59(b)
,,	8173	7/48	,,	—	40	by 5/53	5/64
,,	68181	9/51	Ranskill Wagon Shops	—	3	11/52	11/59
,,	68183	9/55	Peterborough Eng. Yard	—	8	10/55	1/59
Y7	8088	6/48	Stratford Works	68088 10/48	34	9/52	10/52(c)
Y8	8091	6/54	York	—	55	6/54	11/56
Y11	L4(d)	5/49	West Hartlepool Creosote Works	15097 5/49		—	6/50
EB1	26510	1/59	Ilford Carriage Sheds	—	100	1/59	4/64

(a) No. 61323 was immediately condemned and its intended number 24 in the Departmental List reallotted to No. 61375.

(b) Ceased work and condemned 29/12/58 but not taken out of stock until 2/59.

(c) Subsequently preserved.

(d) See also table on page 25.

(e) Class J50 Nos. 12-16 were allocated these numbers in September 1962, but continued to run with their old numbers for some time. No. 12 had been renumbered by 3rd March 1963, the other four were still not renumbered on 7th April 1963. The smokebox numberplates showing their old numbers were retained to withdrawal.

(f) No. 68532 was received for use at Stratford Works on 16th December 1958 although not officially taken into Departmental Stock until 1st January 1959.

<h1 style="text-align:center">G.N.R. 0-4-4 CRANE TANK</h1>
<h2 style="text-align:center">STIRLING 5ft. 7in. ENGINE</h2>

ENGINE IN SERVICE STOCK AT GROUPING (Built 1876): "DONCASTER WORKS". TOTAL 1.

Prior to 1872 all G.N.R. passenger tank engines had been of the 0-4-2 type with well tanks. Then, between 1872 and 1881, Stirling built forty-six engines of 0-4-4 wheel arrangement with tanks positioned above the bogie. These became known as "back tanks". One of them, No. 533, was turned out from Doncaster (Works No. 198) in April 1876. Its 4ft. 0½in. diameter straight-back boiler was replaced in October 1891 by a larger one, 4ft. 5 in. diameter and again domeless. In the June 1900 classification No. 533 became class G2 and it was withdrawn from running stock in June 1905.

No. 533 was not scrapped. Instead it was equipped with a crane at the rear end and was set to work in March 1906 at Doncaster Plant where it not only handled heavy materials but also carried out shunting duties for a further twenty-two years. It carried no number and was merely lettered "DONCASTER WORKS" (fig. 23). Official records varied in describing this crane engine; some had it as No. 3 Yard Crane whilst others referred to it as No. 3 Loco Crane. No evidence has been discovered as to the number 3 ever being carried, and what Nos. 1 and 2 were is still only a matter of conjecture. A possible explanation is that these numbers were allotted to the mobile cranes at Doncaster, rather than referring to items on a departmental locomotive list. When repainted by the L.N.E.R. in June 1923, other than displaying its new owner's initials, it was still lettered "DONCASTER WORKS". The engine then continued as works shunter until it was condemned on 23rd November 1928, its replacement being class J54 No. 3920.

G.N.R. Renumbering

There is no evidence that this Departmental locomotive ever carried a number or was placed on the duplicate list. The statement in the original "Locomotives of the L.N.E.R., 1923-37" (Prentice & Proud, published 1941) that this engine was No. 533A (or 3533A on the L.N.E.R.) cannot be substantiated. As it had been withdrawn, it did not appear in the official allocation dated November 1905 and the number 533 appeared as a blank. Nor is there any mention of a 533A in the 1912 allocation (the 0-6-0 No. 533 had been built in December 1911 — L.N.E.R. class J6) or in the Doncaster Works Register made up in 1916.

Dimensions when rebuilt in 1906

No L.N.E.R. engine diagram was issued for this locomotive and the following dimensions have been taken from G.N.R. records.

Cylinders (2 inside)	17½" x 24"
Motion	Stephenson with slide valves
Boiler:	
Max. diam. outside	4' 5"
Barrel length	9' 10"
Firebox length outside	4' 6"
Pitch	7' 2¼"
Heating surface:	
Firebox	83.17 sq. ft.
Tubes (208 x 1⅝")	898.67 sq. ft.
Total	981.84 sq. ft.
Grate area	12.79 sq. ft.
Boiler pressure	140 lb./sq. in.
Coupled wheels	5' 7"
Bogie wheels	3' 1"
Wheelbase	7' 3" + 10' 3" + 5' 0" = 22' 6"

Rebuilding

When built, No. 533 carried a typical Stirling pattern domeless boiler, with a maximum outside diameter of 4ft.0½in. and pitched at 7ft. 0in. above rail level. The heating surface of the firebox was 81 sq. ft. and the tubes 806 sq. ft., giving a total of 887 sq. ft. The large combined tank and bunker over the rear bogie held 1,000 gallons of water and 1½ tons of coal. The total weight in working order was given as 40 tons 15 cwt., with a maximum axle loading (on the rear coupled wheels) of 14 tons 14 cwt. The total adhesive weight was 26 tons 5 cwt.

In October 1891 a boiler 4½ inches larger in diameter, but of otherwise similar size, was fitted and this was the type of boiler carried at the time the locomotive was rebuilt with a crane in March 1906. To accommodate the crane the well-tank beneath the bunker at the trailing end was removed. Water was then carried in a pair of new side tanks about 8 feet long and set well forward over the leading coupled wheels. These tanks projected forward of the smokebox door and were braced at the front by an upward curved bracket joining the tops of the tanks. The bent over sheet hitherto used for the crew's protection was replaced by an Ivatt-style cab. Other modifications included new sandboxes at the front below the running plate necessitated by the addition of the side tanks. This sanding gear was steam-operated instead of gravity as originally fitted, but the rear sanding was removed. A new rear bufferbeam was fitted, made of steel instead of the sandwich pattern which was retained at the front end. The hand crane, which could make a complete revolution on its pivot, could lift up to 5 tons at a radius of 11ft. 6 in.

Compared with the original condition, a number of detail differences were evident on the crane locomotive though it is likely that many of these were incorporated prior to rebuilding, particularly at the 1891 reboilering. For instance, the chimney was cast in one piece rather than being of the earlier built-up pattern, the Stirling brass trumpet casing round the safety valves was replaced by the much smaller Ivatt rectangular iron casing, the whistle was transferred to a position above the cab roof from in front of it on the boiler, the twin slots in the rear coupled wheel splashers were filled in by backing plates, parallel stock buffers took the place of the tapered variety, and boiler feed was no longer by means of clack boxes on the sides of the boiler barrel.

About the time of Grouping the crane fell into disuse, due to the breakage of the large wheel, but it was not removed when the engine was given a general repair, which was completed in June 1923. At this repair a set of 17½ in. x 24 in. cylinders taken from withdrawn 0-4-2 No. 103 were fitted. There seems to be little doubt that until this time the crane engine still carried G.N.R. fully-lined green livery. Following the above mentioned general repair it was repainted black, with "L N E R" on the bunker and "DONCASTER WORKS" on the tank sides.

Until September 1925 the various boilers it carried had all been domeless, but at a further general repair in that month it was fitted with an Ivatt domed boiler made in October 1899 for 4-4-2T No. 1515 (L.N.E.R. class C12) and carried by that engine until March 1919 when it was transferred to No. 1528 of the same class, which kept it until August 1925. The dimensions of this boiler were:—

Max. diam. outside	4' 5"
Barrel length	10' 1"
Firebox length outside	5' 6"
Heating surface:	
Firebox	103 sq. ft.
Tubes (213 x 1¾")	1016 sq. ft.
Total	1119 sq. ft.
Grate area	16.25 sq. ft.

The change to this boiler is most intriguing as it was 15 inches longer than the previous boilers, and makes the absence of any photographs all the more frustrating to see which of the two likely alternatives was adopted. Either the boiler must have been shortened or — and this is more probable — the cab was positioned further back. This would have been possible without fouling the crane which, in any case, had not been used for some years. There was also a third possibility in that with the unshortened boiler the Ramsbottom safety valves could *just* clear the cab frontplate, though a slot would have had to be cut in it for the relieving lever. As the crane was in disuse, presumably its hook would have been removed otherwise this would have been directly over the safety valves.

Brakes

The engine retained its vacuum brake gear which it used for the testing of rolling stock at the Works.

Summary of Class

1924 No.	G.N.R. No.	Maker	Works No.	Built	Rbt. with crane	Withdrawn
—	533*	Doncaster	198	4/1876	3/06	11/28

*Number carried until withdrawn from Running Stock in June 1905.

G.N.R. CLASS J19 0-6-0 TANK
STIRLING 4ft. 0½in. ENGINE

ENGINE IN SERVICE STOCK AT GROUPING (Built 1872): 3470A. TOTAL 1.

Most descriptions of G.N.R. No. 470 have been based on a very inaccurate report contained in G.F. Bird's book "Locomotives of the Great Northern Railway", published in 1910. Surprisingly Bird's description was accepted without question until in more recent times some research revealed the inaccuracies. The detailed story of No. 470's genesis is set out in Volume 1 of the R.C.T.S. "Great Northern Locomotive History", page 88.

Suffice it to state here that in 1863-64 the West Yorkshire Railway purchased two 0-6-0T's from

Manning, Wardle of the maker's standard pattern. They were numbered 5 and 6 in the W.Y.R. list. In June 1865 they were taken over by the G.N.R. and were renumbered 470 and 471 respectively. In 1872 both these engines were sent into Doncaster Works by Patrick Stirling for rebuilding. However, they emerged in completely new guise and were officially recorded as being new engines, except for the wheel centres, and were given Doncaster Works numbers. The engine with which we are here concerned was turned out in September 1872 as works number 92, retaining its running number 470. The change in design was total and included a saddle tank in place of the previous side tanks: its appearance in fact was almost indistinguishable from Stirling's other saddle tank shunting engines of G.N.R. class J19 built in 1874-75.

No. 470 was placed on the Duplicate List on 7th July 1919 and was transferred to Service Stock on 19th December 1921 for use at Hall Hills Sleeper Depot, Boston. By then it was running with the rear section of coupling rods removed. It was withdrawn as L.N.E.R. No. 3470A (fig. 24) in April 1927 on replacement by a class Y1 Sentinel 0-4-0T. No. 3470A was included in G.N.R. class J19 but was never given any classification by the L.N.E.R.

Dimensions

No L.N.E.R. engine diagram was prepared for No. 3470A and the following details are those given on the G.N.R. 1913 diagram, prior to conversion to burn oil.

Cylinders (2 inside)	16″ x 22″
Motion	Stephenson with slide valves
Boiler:	
Max. diam. outside	4′ 10½″
Barrel length	10′ 0″
Firebox length outside	4′ 2″
Pitch	6′ 5″
Heating surface:	
Firebox	74 sq. ft.
Tubes (163 x 1¾″)	772 sq. ft.
Total	846 sq. ft.
Grate area	11.6 sq. ft.
Boiler pressure	160 lb./sq. in.
Coupled wheels	4′ 0½″
Tractive effort (85%)	13,818 lb.
Length over buffers	27′ 5½″
Wheelbase	7′ 3″ + 7′ 0″ = 14′ 3″
Weight (not maximum)	38T 12c*
Max. axle load	15T 0c
Water capacity	900 gallons
Coal capacity	1½ tons

* Maximum weight in working order elsewhere quoted by G.N.R. as 40T 10c.

G.N.R. and L.N.E.R. Renumbering

In July 1919 No. 470 was placed on the G.N.R. duplicate list as 470A when the number was required for a new Gresley 2-8-0 (L.N.E.R. class O1).

Following a general repair at Doncaster Works (which took from October 1924 to January 1925) it emerged painted black with red lining and lettered and numbered "L N E R 3470A."

Details

No. 470 was given a new boiler without dome when reconstructed in 1872 and in July 1889 this was replaced by a similar new one which served the engine to its demise. Originally the working pressure was 160 lb. per sq. in., but this was reduced to 140 lb. about 1919.

In March 1914 No. 470 was equipped to burn oil fuel on the Holden system supplied from a 200 gallon tank. This tank occupied two-thirds of the bunker-space, leaving a section around the hand brake column for storing coke, for which a new shovelling hole had to be provided. At the same time the rear coupling rods were removed, thus making the engine in effect an 0-4-2ST. The volute springs of the rear axle were replaced by coil springs as the troughs for the original springs impeded the oil burner situated at the back of the firebox, in its centre. Although the engine never again ran in six-coupled form, it continued to be described as an 0-6-0ST in the Doncaster records, at least until 1921 when it was deleted from Running Stock.

By the time No. 3470A was withdrawn, buffers with parallel stocks had been fitted in place of the tapered pattern.

Brakes

A hand brake only was provided.

Allocation and Work

For many years the engine was employed as shed pilot at Bradford (Bowling Junction), remaining there until December 1921 when it was sent to Hall Hills Sleeper Depot at Boston, where it spent the rest of its life.

Summary of Class

1924 *No.*	*Maker*	*Works No.*	*Built*	*Withdrawn*
3470A 1/25	Doncaster	92	9/1872	4/27

G.N.R. TRAM TYPE 0-4-0 TANK

In 1892 a steam powered traverser was built for use in the Doncaster Carriage shops of the G.N.R. This was replaced in 1906 by an electrically driven traverser. The original power unit was utilised in the building of a small vertical-boilered locomotive for use as a shunter at the company's Civil Engineer's yard just north of Peterborough station on the east side of the railway, where it was put to work in 1908 and was in regular service until the end of 1926 (fig. 26).

The principal dimensions of this machine were:—

Boiler diam.	3′	6″
Height of boiler	6′	10½″
Cylinders (2)	7″ x 8″	
Coupled wheels	2′	6″
Wheelbase	6′	0″
Length over buffers	16′	0″

The vertical boiler was mounted at one end of the chassis and there were two 6 in. diameter cross tubes in the firebox. The two-cylinder vertical engine stood at the other end, the crankshaft being geared at 1:3 ⅔ to the driving axle. The wheels were coupled and had solid webs, each wheel having four almost circular lightening holes. Sheet metal panelling, waist high, ran all the way round the locomotive, broken by an entrance at either side. There was also an all-over roof with a deep canopy all round. The livery was green with full black and white lining and the letters "G N R" in shaded transfers. No identification number was ever carried and the G.N.R. livery persisted to the end of the locomotive's life.

The official diagram of the locomotive depicts spring buffers at each end supplemented by substantial dumb buffers at the boiler end. However, a photograph taken about 1910 shows dumb buffers to have been substituted at the engine end and it is possible that the set of spring buffers had also been removed from the boiler end of the locomotive. A pair of small capstan sheaves (whether powered or not is unknown) were mounted above the draw hook at the engine end, presumably for rope haulage.

The date that this locomotive was condemned by the L.N.E.R. has not been discovered, but its successor (a class Y1 Sentinel 0-4-0T) took over in November 1926 and the boiler from the displaced machine is known to have been cut up at Doncaster during week ending 5th March 1927. The machine never figured in G.N.R. or L.N.E.R. stock returns, nor did it receive any classification in the locomotive lists. Its lowly status can be gauged by its description in the Divisional General Manager's memorandum concerning a replacement, as "consisting of a coffee pot boiler placed on a trolley".

CLASS J92 (Z4 until 1927) 0-6-0 CRANE TANKS
G.E.R. CLASS 204 — S. W. JOHNSON
4ft. 0in. ENGINES

ENGINES IN SERVICE STOCK AT GROUPING (Built 1868): B, C, D. TOTAL 3.

These 0-6-0T's had the distinction of being the oldest tank engines in service on the L.N.E.R., having been built for the G.E.R. by Ruston & Proctor of Lincoln in 1868. Even more remarkable was the fact that they outlasted the L.N.E.R. company and were not withdrawn until 1950-52.

Originally there were five engines in the class, Nos. 204-8, built to the order of S. W. Johnson, the then Locomotive Superintendent of the G.E.R. In 1881 his successor, Massey Bromley, had most of them rebuilt, at which time they acquired half cabs. Ten years later No. 205 was reconstructed by James Holden with a 3-ton capacity crane at the rear end for use at Stratford Works. Nos. 204/6 were similarly converted during 1893, but Nos. 207/8 were scrapped in August 1889 and October 1892 respectively.

In 1894 the three crane engines lost their running numbers and instead were designated B, C and D in their former numerical order. They ran thus for a further fifty-two years before regaining numbers, 8667/8/9, under the Thompson general renumbering scheme. In passing, it may be mentioned that engine A was a small 0-4-0 saddle tank previously numbered 200. It had been built by Manning, Wardle & Co. in 1872 and was withdrawn from service in February 1922, though it remained on the scrap road at Stratford until mid-1923 before it was cut up.

The three crane engines were at first classified Z4 by the L.N.E.R., the letter Z originally being used for miscellaneous locomotives. In April 1927 they were reclassified J92 at the end of the 0-6-0T series.

Standard L.N.E.R. Dimensions at Grouping

Cylinders (2 inside)	16" x 22"
Motion	Stephenson and slide valves

Boiler:

Max. diam. outside	4' 2"
Barrel length	9' 1"
Firebox length outside	4' 11⅜"
Pitch	6' 3"
Diagram No.	38

Heating surface:

Firebox	84.81 sq. ft.
Tubes (227 x 1⅝")	905.40 sq. ft.
	990.21 sq. ft.

Grate area	13.9 sq. ft.
Boiler pressure	140 lb./sq. in.
Coupled wheels	4' 0"
Tractive effort (85%)	13,962 lb.
Length over buffers	26' 6"
Wheelbase	6' 9" + 7' 9" = 14' 6"
Weight (full)	40T 8C
Max. axle load	15T 5C
Water capacity	780 gallons
Coal capacity	15 cwt.

G.E.R. and L.N.E.R. Renumbering

On 1st October 1894 the four service locomotives at Stratford Works became A, B, C and D, the last three being crane engines Nos. 204/5/6 respectively. The large Worsdell-pattern cast plates on the bunker sides had the former running number changed to the appropriate letter. The new plates then read, for instance, "B" with the words "WORKS ONLY" set in a concave arc beneath with "R & P REBUILT" in smaller letters below that. No date of rebuilding was shown. This conformed to the G.E.R. practice in that, when rebuilt, only Stratford-built engines carried the year of rebuilding — those originally constructed by contractors did not. The only known exception to this rule was the Manning Wardle 0-4-0ST A referred to earlier which carried "REBUILT 1895 M & W" (sic) on its plate.

After Grouping, the L.N.E.R. replaced these plates with their standard small cast pattern, only legible at very close range. Tank locomotives normally, of course, carried their running numbers additionally in transfer numerals on the side tanks, but no such distinction was accorded to the crane engines, only the Company's initials appearing thereon. However, the legend "B WORKS" (for example) did appear on the front bufferbeam (fig. 1).

When the Thompson general renumbering scheme was formulated, B, C and D were allotted Nos. 8667/8/9 and this change was made on 2nd June 1946, the numbers (in shaded transfers) appearing in the usual place on the side tanks and front bufferbeam (fig. 47). No. 8668 received a general overhaul in March 1947 when its lettering and numerals were executed in painted Gill Sans characters, without shading (fig. 48). The other two engines were still running with their old-style transfers at nationalisation.

Development and Rebuilding

When built, Nos. 204-8 were without cabs and had the dome on top of the firebox. The chimney tapered inwards from base to top, a type much favoured by Johnson, and Salter spring-balance type safety valves surmounted the dome. Braking was by hand only, with four wooden brake blocks bearing on the intermediate and trailing coupled wheels. The boiler was somewhat smaller than that carried after the engines had been rebuilt with cranes and had the following dimensions:—

Max. diam. outside	3' 10"
Barrel length	9' 1"
Firebox length outside	4' 4¾"

Heating surface:

Firebox	76.0 sq. ft.
Tubes (124 x 2")	608.5 sq. ft.
Total	684.5 sq. ft.

Grate area	12.5 sq. ft.
Weight of engine (full)	34T 9C
Max. axle load	13T 0C

During 1881-82 Bromley had all these engines, with the exception of No. 206, fitted with open-back cabs and steam-operated brakes on all six wheels. Iron brake shoes were substituted for the wooden ones. The dates of these alterations were:—

Engine No.	*Date*
204	8/1881
205	12/1881
207	9/1881
208	10/1882

No. 206 did not receive the steam brake until converted to a crane engine. After the alterations made by Bromley to the other engines the pitch of the boiler was quoted as being half an inch higher, at 6ft. 3½in., and it is possible that thicker tyres had been fitted to the wheels increasing their diameter from 4ft. 0in. to 4ft. 1in. At this time the weight of these engines was said to be 35 tons 16 cwt. with a maximum axle load of 13 tons 14 cwt.

On 12th August 1889 an order (LM 284) was issued to Stratford Works to fit No. 205 with a crane. Although this engine had lain at the Works since February of that year, it did not enter shops for the work to be done until June 1890.

Fig. 18   Class DES1 No. 8001 at Derby, March 1952.
Angled ends to rain strip, external filler to rear sandbox.

Fig. 19   Class DES1 No. 8002 at March, June 1948.
Curved rain strip, recesses behind hand grips on side panels of engine compartment, shallower
battery boxes on running plate, lower part of fan casing plated over behind front ladder.

Fig. 20   Class DEJ1 (previously DES1) No. 15000 at March, June 1963.
Rain strip and rear sandbox filler altered to correspond with second engine (8001), L.N.E.R.
Group standard buffers, radio aerial on cab roof, B.R. emblem on engine compartment.

Fig. 21   Class DEJ1 No. 15002 at March, April 1959.
B.R. emblem on battery box.

Fig. 22   Class DEJ2 (ex-DES2) No. 15004 in Derby Works yard, October 1956.

Fig. 23   G.N.R. 0-4-4 crane locomotive "Doncaster Works" after conversion in 1906.

Ex-G.N.R. 0-6-0ST No. 3470A shunting at Boston, September 1926.

With rear section of coupling rods removed.

Fig. 25   Class J54 Service Stock No. 3 at Doncaster Works, c.1929.

Fig. 26   G.N.R. 0-4-0 vertical boiler locomotive at
Peterborough Engineer's Yard.

Fig. 27   Class Y1 No. 4803 at Doncaster.
Attached to Carr Wagon Shops.

Fig. 28   Class Y1 No. 4993 at Doncaster, September 1937.
Renumbered from 4803.

Fig. 29   Class J52 No. 3980 at Doncaster Works, c.1937.
Works shunter.

Fig. 30 M. & G.N. 0-6-0ST No. 16A at Melton Constable.
Removable boards in cab cut out for protection.

Fig. 31 M. & G.N. 0-6-0ST No. 16A in the Paint Shop at Stratford Works awaiting
scrap, 1937.

Fig. 32   Class Y3 No. 7 (ex-68166 in Boston
shed, July, 1958.
Attached to Hall Hills Sleeper Depot.

Fig. 33   Class Y3 No.41 (ex-8177) at the
Civil Engineer's yard, Lowestoft,
May 1960

Fig. 34   Class Y1 No. 51 (ex-68136) at
Faverdale Wagon Works,
Darlington, September 1955.

Fig. 35   Class Y3 No. 54 (ex-68153) in the works
yard at Darlington in August 1961 after
withdrawal from service at Geneva P.W.D.

Fig. 36   Class Y3 No. 3 (ex-68181) at Ranskill Wagon Works, July 1957.

Fig. 37   Class Y3 No. 40 (ex-8173) shunting at Lowestoft yard, May 1960.

Extensive reconstruction was necessary and No. 205 did not emerge until May of the following year. It re-entered service in September. To accommodate the 3-ton capacity, 11ft.-radius, steam driven, swivelling jib crane at the back of the locomotive, the rear wheels were set back one foot and the rear overhang became 3ft. 11 ⅞ in. instead of 4ft. 6in. The 16in. x 22in. cylinders were retained together with the four-bar slide bars. The side tanks with their distinctive rounded front corners were kept. The new boiler that was provided was of the same pattern then being used by Holden to reboiler the Bromley class E10 0-4-4T's, with the dome on the front ring of the barrel. At 4ft. 2in. it was 4in. larger in diameter than the original boiler and had a longer firebox, 4ft. 11⅜ in. against 4ft. 4¾in. The barrel, tube arrangement and heating surface of these boilers were the same as in the Holden 0-6-0T's of that period (L.N.E.R. class J66), but the front tubeplate and firebox were shallower. The length of the firebox was intermediate between the J66 (and J67) engines and the later J68 and J69 classes, consequently the boiler was not interchangeable with any of these classes (see Part 8A of this series). However, a number of No. 205's details were made standard with the Holden 0-6-0T's, such as the springing and the 15-spoke cast-iron 4ft. 0in. diameter wheels which replaced the original wheels with wrought-iron centres. Some of the original features were retained, among them being the distinctively raked cab footsteps with the deep valance to the rear of them, but no valance in front, and the small splashers over the leading wheels. The wooden sandwich pattern front bufferbeam was kept, but a steel plate bufferbeam was provided at the back of the engine. Footsteps adjacent to the leading wheels were fitted for the first time. These were of unusual pattern and had boxed-in sides. Although the leading sandboxes below the running plate were at first retained, these were replaced later by the Holden pattern above the running plate thus conforming to the arrangement used on his 0-6-0T's.

On 10th and 13th December 1892 authorities (LM 1132 and LM 1140 respectively) were given to rebuild the two surviving members of the class (Nos. 204/6) in similar fashion and they entered shops in March 1893. Both engines were turned out in the following December but were not shown as re-entering service until May 1894. Unlike No. 205 the cylinders were replaced on these two engines at the time of rebuilding. The new boilers which were fitted had two more tubes than that on No. 205, reflecting a similar change made in the contemporary batch of Holden shunting engines (see page 74, Part 8A). Details are given in the accompanying table.

In June 1907 engine C (ex-205) was reboilered again. The new boiler was the same overall size as before but the barrel was telescopic instead of butt-jointed, the front ring being 4ft. 1in. diameter and the back ring 4ft. 2in. This change followed the contemporary practice with the Holden 0-6-0T's, and resulted in a slight increase in heating surface. Engines B and D were reboilered in March and June 1909 respectively and there was an increase from 225 to 227 in the number of tubes in their new boilers, a like change having been made in the intervening period in the J66 boiler.

With the introduction of the telescopic boiler the working pressure on the Holden 0-6-0T's was raised from 140 to 160 lb. per sq. in. However, all engine diagrams for the crane tanks continued to quote the lower figure. Nevertheless, the Engine Repair Register at Stratford recorded C as having a pressure of 160 lb. per sq. in.

In December 1932 three new boilers were constructed at Stratford and fitted to D in February 1934, B in August 1935 and C in October 1935. It is believed that these were to the 1909 design, but had Ross pop safety valves in place of the Ramsbottom type. The working pressure was 140 lb. per sq. in.

As already mentioned, new cylinders were provided for B and D when they were rebuilt as crane engines in 1893 whereas C had kept its original cylinders. This engine was given a new set in November 1900. In February 1921 B received the second-hand cylinders from No. 0105, a Johnson No. 1 class 2-4-0 withdrawn in 1913, which had carried similar cylinders to the crane engines. The width of the cylinder casting had to be reduced to suit the smaller distance between the frames of B. D was similarly dealt with in May 1923 when it was given the cylinders

BOILER DIMENSIONS

	Butt-jointed barrel		*Telescopic barrel*	
Date introduced	1891	1894	1907	1909
Tubes (1⅝ ")	223	225	225	227
Heating surface (sq. ft.):				
Firebox	84.81	84.81	84.81	84.81
Tubes	881.24	889.24	898.40	905.40
Total	966.05	974.05	983.21	990.21

from No. 0101, a Bromley class E10 0-4-4T withdrawn in 1906. It would seem that Stratford Works had been provident in setting aside these cylinders for future use in the crane engines. The cylinders from the 0-4-4T would have been 16½in. diameter compared with 16in. of the earlier pattern.

The second-hand cylinders did not last long and new cylinders were cast and fitted to B (in May 1928), C (in October 1927) and D (in March 1926). Although the engine diagram continued to record the diameter as 16in., the Engine Register showed a figure of 16½in. for all three engines.

Details

All three engines ran without casings around their Ramsbottom safety valves during L.N.E.R. days, as they had done for a large part of their pre-Grouping existence (fig. 44). When pop valves were fitted at the time the engines were reboilered in 1934-35, the position of the whistle was changed from being beside the Ramsbottom valves to a standpipe in front of the cab (fig. 50). A further alteration made to B and D at that time was to the method of lubrication of the cylinders, the Roscoe displacement lubricator on each side of the smokebox being replaced by a Wakefield sight-feed type in the cab. Engine C had been similarly altered earlier, in September 1931 (fig. 46).

In common with other small-boilered G.E.R. engines, the stovepipe chimney was replaced in L.N.E.R. days by the N.E.R. cast-iron pattern (cf. figs. 44 & 46). In the case of C this was done in September 1931 (before reboilering), but B and D were not dealt with until reboilered, in August 1935 and February 1934 respectively. It will be noticed that, from September 1931 until October 1935, C was unique in that it retained Ramsbottom safety valves but had been given a cast-iron chimney and sight-feed lubricator.

The plain flat-edged pattern of smokebox door was replaced by a heavier door with rounded edge (as used latterly, for example, on other G.E.R. 0-6-0T's), this occurring before Grouping in the case of B and C, but D retained the old type of door much longer and was not altered until September 1941 (cf. figs. 45 & 46).

For the whole of its life as a crane engine, B differed from C and D in that its front guard irons were attached to the main frames whereas the others had theirs bolted to the front face of the bufferbeam (figs. 44 & 45). On all three engines the rear guard irons were attached to the frames.

Toolboxes were at first carried on top of the right-hand side tank. That on D was removed at some time during the early thirties and the other two engines lost theirs somewhat later (figs. 45 & 46).

Buffers of the self-contained type with parallel casing were usually fitted though C at an early period had taper-stock buffers at the rear end.

The cranes themselves were used on stripping work for such tasks as removing smokebox doors. It is understood that these cranes were rendered redundant when tender repairs were transferred to the New Works and the stripping gang moved into the old tender shop which was equipped with its own overhead electric crane. The cranes on the locomotives were, it is believed, never used in L.N.E.R. days and it is probable that they had not seen employment since before the 1914-18 War. Latterly (after 1945), the chains and hooks were removed (fig. 47). In consequence of the disuse of the cranes, the iron framework round the crane supporting storm sheets was replaced by a more permanent close-boarded wooden arrangement to give the enginemen more protection in the open-back cab (fig. 51).

Brakes

Throughout their time as crane engines braking was by steam.

British Railways

All three engines received their new numbers in the 60,000 series. No. 68667 was the first to do so, in February 1949 when it received a light repair at Stratford Works. It retained "L N E R" in shaded lettering on the tank sides and the new number was likewise displayed below (fig. 49). In February 1950 No. 68668 was completely repainted and was given the lion and wheel emblem on the tanks, the number (in unshaded numerals) then appearing on the bunker sides (fig. 50). No. 68669 was similarly treated during the following month.

In September 1952, only two months before it was withdrawn from service, No. 68668 became "Departmental No. 35" in accordance with the B.R. renumbering scheme for Eastern and North Eastern Region Service Stock (fig. 52).

Allocation and Work

Throughout their existence the three crane engines were employed on duties in and around the locomotive workshops at Stratford. Normally, only two were required each day, one in the vicinity of the Engine Repair Shop (or "New Works") and the other in the area around the Stripping and Paint Shops. In addition to moving dead engines in and out of the buildings, they also hauled stripped engines and wagon loads of boilers, wheels and other parts to and from the Old Works adjacent to Stratford passenger station. Tenders were overhauled at the New Works and these had to be taken to the Old Works for re-attachment to engines repaired there. To reach the Old Works it was necessary to traverse running lines between Chobham Farm Junction and Polygon signal box. Engine crews for the Service locomotives at Stratford were provided by the C.M.E.'s department, and a pilotman supplied by the Running Department had to be carried for this movement. The cost of this pilotman was charged to the C.M.E.'s department. When the usual crane engine crews were off sick or on holiday, replacements were provided by the Running Department, who received appropriate payment from the C.M.E.'s department. However, as a pilotman was not then necessary for the above-mentioned movement, the cost of his services was saved. The crews of the service locomotives were ex-Running Department men who had failed their eyesight or medical examinations, but were sufficiently fit for yard work.

The crane engines were housed in a two-road shed in the angle of running lines by Fork Junction. Maintenance was carried out at weekends by a member of the erecting shop gang.

Very occasionally one of the crane engines was seen outside its normal environment. Two such instances were noted during the 1939-45 War when, on 6th August 1940, C was at the head of a breakdown train in the Down Carriage Sidings at Stratford, whilst on the 27th January 1941 one of them was seen in the L.M.S. goods yard alongside the G.E.R. lines at Bow.

Engine Diagram

Section E, 1924. Z4. Reclassified J92 in April 1927.

Classification: Route availability 3; B.R. power class 0F.

Summary of Z4/J92 Class

B.R. No.	1946 No.	1894 Designation	Orig. No.	Built	Date	Rebuilt with crane	With-drawn
68667 2/49	8667 6/46	B	204	Ruston & Proctor	5/1868	12/93 (a)	5/52
68668 2/50	8668 6/46	C	205	”	7/1868	5/91 (b)	11/52 (c)
68669 3/50	8669 6/46	D	206	,,	9/1868	12/93 (a)	10/50

(a) Nos. 204/6 re-entered service in May 1894.

(b) No. 205 re-entered service in September 1891.

(c) No. 68668 became "Departmental No. 35" in September 1952

M. & G.N. CLASS "FOX WALKER" 0-6-0 TANK
3ft. 7in. ENGINE

ENGINE TAKEN OVER 1 OCTOBER 1936 (Built 1877): 16A. TOTAL 1.

This engine was the survivor of two 0-6-0ST's named *Ormesby* and *Stalham* built by Fox. Walker & Co. (maker's No. 333 and 338) and delivered in May and July 1877 respectively to the Great Yarmouth & Stalham Light Railway, which, by an act of 1878, changed its name to the Yarmouth & North Norfolk Light Railway. On 1st January 1883 the Yarmouth & North Norfolk was amalgamated with the Lynn & Fakenham and the Yarmouth Union to form the Eastern & Midlands Railway.

Ormesby and *Stalham* received E. & M.R. numbers 15 and 16 respectively, which numbers they retained when the Eastern & Midlands Railway was vested in the newly-formed Midland & Great Northern Joint Committee in 1893.

No. 15 was replaced by a new 0-6-0T carrying the same number, built at Melton Constable in 1901, and is reputed to have been subsequently sold to a firm in the "North of England" for colliery work. There were nine of these new 0-6-0T's, which became class J93 on the L.N.E.R. (see Part 8B of this series), and the last one was placed in service in 1905. It took the number 16, whereupon old No. 16 was consigned to the Duplicate List as 16A.

When the M. & G.N. stock was taken over by the L.N.E.R. on 1st October 1936, No. 16A was the shunting engine attached to Melton Constable Works and therefore entered the L.N.E.R. service stock list. It neither received any L.N.E.R. classification nor was it renumbered, although a manuscript list headed "Midland & Great Northern Joint Line — Engines Condemned 1936/1937" includes "016A Tank Departmental Shunting". In the event, this double duplicate number was never applied and No. 16A was withdrawn in October 1937 (fig. 31).

Dimensions

No L.N.E.R. diagram was issued for this engine, but a Midland & Great Northern diagram dated November 1919 gives the following dimensions:—

Cylinders (2 outside)	13″ x 20″
Boiler pitch	5′ 3″
Boiler pressure	120 lb./sq. in.
Coupled wheels	3′ 7″
Tractive effort (80%)	7,545 lb.
Length over buffers	22′ 10″
Wheelbase	4′ 10″ + 4′ 10″ = 9′ 8″
Weight (full)	24T 3C
Max. axle load	8T 7C
Water capacity	540 gallons
Coal capacity	1T 3C

An apparently later, but undated, entry on this 1919 diagram gave the following additional details:—

Heating surface:	
Firebox	51.0 sq. ft.
Tubes	393.0 sq. ft.
Total	444.0 sq. ft.
Grate area	6.8 sq. ft.

This later entry repeated the cylinder dimensions and boiler pressure already given above, yet gave "Tractive power" as only 6,300 lb., seemingly indicating that the boiler was working at only 100 lb. per sq. in.

It is possible that this entry on the 1919 diagram was added to cover a new boiler fitted in 1929, since the September 1936 M. & G.N. locomotive stock list shows No. 16A with exactly the same overall weight and heating surface figures as quoted above, but with a slightly reduced grate area of 6.7 sq. ft. Also given in the September 1936 list are the following dimensions and details:—

Boiler:	
Diameter	3′ 4½″
Barrel	11′0½″ (actually combined length of barrel and firebox shell)
Tube length	8′ 5¼″
Tubes	102 x 1¾″
Date new	February 1929
Last general repair	November 1934

Details

The two Great Yarmouth & Stalham engines with their short wheelbase, round saddle tanks, inclined outside cylinders and twin Salter spring balance safety valves mounted on a brass-cased dome were very much typical of Fox, Walker practice. The front end had a distinctive appearance with a stovepipe chimney and sloping-fronted smokebox with wingplates whose contour was followed by curiously shaped sandboxes mounted on the platform above the cylinders, the sandpipes passing between the cylinders and the frames. For backward running, sandboxes were provided behind the cab footsteps. (Quite by coincidence, the Midland Railway had acquired two almost identical Fox, Walker engines in 1879, but the longer surviving of the pair was withdrawn as long ago as 1906.)

As built, the two engines which eventually came to the M. & G.N. had boilers with a barrel length of 8ft. 0in. and a mean diameter of 3ft. 4⅞in. and a firebox 3ft. 6in. long with a grate area of 7.5 sq. ft. No details of replacement boilers have been traced until 1929, when No. 16A received its last new boiler, the customary M. & G.N. boiler date plate being fixed to the front end of the right-hand cab panel.

The original cab appears to have had a cut-away front weatherboard with the circular windows set fairly close together. This was matched by a similar-shaped back weatherboard, also with windows, although it is possible that at first no back weatherboard was fitted. Later, the front weatherboard was extended to the full width of the cab, with upper side sheets added extending back from it in order to give additional protection to the enginemen. Before 1893, new front and back weatherboards were provided in which the circular windows were placed further apart. By 1923 No. 16A had acquired removable boards which fitted into the space between the bunker side sheet and the cab roof (fig. 30). It was usually on the driver's (right-hand) side of the cab, but could be changed to the other side if the wind was in that quarter. In good weather it was often not put up at all.

Other alterations carried out at Melton Constable included the replacement of the original square-ended wooden bufferbeams with new wooden beams having curved ends, possibly influenced by the similar-shaped bufferbeams on the Johnson-designed M. & G.N. engines. New buffers with parallel casings were also fitted, but on the front bufferbeams at least the safety chains, once so characteristic of Great Northern locomotive practice, were retained to the end. In its last few years, No. 16A ran without the lamp irons on the front bufferbeam.

Until No. 16A was given its final shopping in November 1934, its livery was black with fine red and white lining, the white line being inside and touching the red. When No. 16A was repainted in 1934, only the red lining was applied.

Brakes

The only brake was a hand brake acting on the driving and trailing wheels.

In their M. & G.N. days up to about 1901, Nos. 15 and 16 are believed to have been used on yard shunting at Yarmouth. No. 16 was then to spend the remainder of its life as works shunter at Melton Constable where it was affectionately known as "Black Bess". Its last duties were to assist in the removal of material and equipment when the works were closed by the L.N.E.R. It was sent to Stratford via King's Lynn and was condemned on 25th October 1937 and cut up there.

Summary of Class

1937 No. (016A)	1905 No.	E. & M.R. No.	Maker	Works No.	Built	Withdrawn
(016A)	16A	16	Fox, Walker	338	7/1877	10/37

N.E.R. PETROL INSPECTION CARS

VEHICLES AT GROUPING (Built 1908/12): 3711/69 (later 23711/69). TOTAL 2.

VEHICLE BUILT AFTER GROUPING (1923): 3768 (later 23768). TOTAL 1.

None of these vehicles figured in Running Stock returns, but in 1925 they were added to Service Stock.

In March 1908 a small petrol-engined saloon was turned out from York Carriage Shops by the North Eastern Railway. It was intended for inspection journeys carried out by officers of the Company and had seating accommodation for six in a central saloon, with a separate compartment at each end for the driver. The length of the body was 17ft. 0in. and the car weighed 6 tons 12 cwt. It was numbered 3711 in the Carriage Stock lists.

The six passengers were seated on two easy chairs and two settees, whilst two additional passengers could be accommodated on camp stools if required. There was a table for maps and documents in the centre of the saloon, the lower portion covering the engine. Entrance to the saloon was through the end driving compartments. The frame was constructed of light channels and angles carrying a body built of teak, with mahogany panels, the interior being finished in walnut. A clear lookout was obtained in every direction, single pillars only being used to carry the glass of which the sides and ends of the car were chiefly constructed. Drop windows were fitted in each of the four doors and in the centre of each side. Externally the car was painted lake, which was the standard N.E.R. coaching stock livery, and lettered to match.

The engine, of unknown make, had four cylinders and developed an estimated 35 to 40 b.h.p. at 950 r.p.m. It was mounted below the floor, with the centre line of the crankshaft on a level with the driving axle but at right-angles to it. The drive was through a 3-speed gearbox giving speeds of 15, 30 and 45 m.p.h. in either direction, top speed being direct from the engine to the bevel gears on the driving axle. Reversal was carried out by moving two bevels fitted on a sliding sleeve on the driving axle and this was operated by a horizontal reversing screw in one driving compartment. The wheelbase of the car was 10ft. 0in. with disc wheels 3ft. 0in. in diameter. Roller bearings were fitted to all wheels and sand could be fed to either side of the wheels on the driving axle.

Although fitted with electric lighting from a storage battery, the engine does not appear to have had a self-starter and it had to be hand cranked from one end of the vehicle. Heating was by hot water from the engine cooling system, with two supply tanks built into the framing. Petrol capacity was 20 gallons and the average consumption 12 m.p.g. Braking was by hand only and warning of approach, originally provided by a horn worked off the engine exhaust, was later given by an electric horn mounted on the roof in the centre of the car. An emergency coupling was provided for pulling the car in case of failure, but no buffers were fitted and therefore the car could not be propelled. However, buffers were later provided (fig. 56).

During trials when new the car ran 1,200 miles without a mishap of any kind and speeds of upwards of 55 m.p.h. were obtained. The car is believed to have been based initially at Middlesbrough but was latterly at Darlington.

Early in 1911, Raven, the newly-appointed C.M.E. of the N.E.R., suggested that a further two cars should be obtained for inspection duties. On 4th September of that year he reported to the Locomotive & Stores Committee that he had received a tender from the Wolseley Co. amounting to £2,617 for two complete cars. However, he considered this price to be excessive and he suggested that the cars should instead be built in N.E.R. workshops by purchasing a pair of 6-cylinder engines (including clutch and fittings) from White & Poppe of Coventry for £550, and gearboxes and bevel gears from E. G. Wrigley & Co. of Birmingham for £294.

This latter course was adopted and the cars, numbered 3768 and 3769, were put into service in April 1912 (fig. 58). Some official records show that they were built at Gateshead Works but inter-department correspondence shows that the frames were constructed at Walker Gate (the works where the Tyneside electric stock was maintained) and the bodies at York. Where the cars were assembled is not certain.

These two cars followed generally the design of the earlier car, but were much larger, seating being provided for twelve passengers instead of six. The length over body was 23ft. 6in. and the wheelbase was 16ft. 0in. The cars were also higher (13ft. 1in. against 11ft. 9½in.) and wider (8ft. 6in., compared with 7ft. 0in.). The weight was almost double that of No. 3711, at 12 tons 12 cwt.

Unlike No. 3711, entrance to the passenger saloon was gained by two doors, one on each side. Although the saloon was partitioned off from the driving compartment at each end, communication with the driver could be made through sliding windows fitted in the partition above waist level. Each driving compartment had a door on either side. The table was placed in one corner of the saloon, built around the fuel tank which held 60 gallons. Seating was on two settees and eight armchairs, all arranged with their backs to the sides of the saloon. Heating was provided by a hot water radiator worked off the engine cooling system.

All-round visibility was not as good as on the earlier car, a certain amount of panelling obtruding above waist level. A clerestory roof was fitted and this tapered down at each end of the cars so that the engine cooling radiators could be placed on the roof. The cars were painted N.E.R. lake, with the Company's crest on the saloon doors. The interiors were finished in mahogany, with brass fittings.

The 6-cylinder engine was rated at 75 h.p. at 1,150 r.p.m., giving speeds of 15, 22½ and 45 m.p.h. in either direction through a clutch and three-speed gearbox, the drive to the bevel gearing on the rear axle being by means of a propeller shaft and universal joints. Petrol consumption was stated to be 7 m.p.g. Electric lighting was employed and presumably electric self-starters were fitted as no starting handle is visible on photographs of these two cars.

As on No. 3711, braking was by hand only, but Nos. 3768/9 differed in having buffers and drawgear from the start. An electric horn was provided at each end, mounted on the roof adjacent to the radiator. A sandbox was fitted in the centre of each driving compartment.

No. 3768 was normally stationed at York, with No. 3769 at Gateshead (fig. 59). On 22nd October 1921 No. 3768 was almost completely destroyed by fire in one of the roundhouses forming York South shed. The whole of the wooden body and interior fittings disappeared, except for a few portions of charred door posts. It was condemned on 30th June 1922.

A grant of £2,825 was made from the Fire Insurance Fund and a new car carrying the same number, 3768, was built at York, entering service under the L.N.E.R. in December 1923 as 3768Y (fig. 57). It differed from the original in a number of ways. Although the 16ft. 0in. wheelbase was the same, the new car body was a foot longer, at 24ft. 6in. The roof was domed and had no clerestory section — an obvious visual point of difference. The new car seated eleven passengers on wicker chairs and couches instead of on armchairs and settees. An improvement was the fitting of a folding washbasin in the saloon, whilst there were two heating radiators in place of one. Again, the latter were worked off the engine cooling system but the radiators for this were mounted in the end panels of the car below the windows instead of being roof-mounted. The wheels were 3ft. 6in. diameter in place of 2ft. 11in. and there were four sandboxes (one in each corner of the driving compartments) rather than two. The new car was slightly heavier, at 13 tons 17 cwt. It was finished externally in teak livery, adopted also by the L.N.E.R. for the two surviving N.E.R. cars.

The new car was also stationed at York and was kept in a wooden shed built within one of the two remaining roundhouses at Queen Street shed (the third was demolished after the fire mentioned above. When Queen Street ceased to be used by L.M.S. engines in 1932, the petrol car, together with the locomotive-hauled saloons, found a home in the building which had formerly been the boiler shop at York Locomotive Works.

Under the L.N.E.R.'s carriage stock renumbering scheme Nos. 3711/68/9 had 20,000 added to these numbers, in September 1928, March 1928 and March 1927 respectively.

By 1929 the two oldest cars, Nos. 23711/69, were giving a lot of trouble, having run approximately 114,000 and 80,000 miles respectively with their original engines. These mileages were really quite good considering the primitive form of petrol engines at the time the cars were built. In August 1929 a new 80 h.p. Leyland engine was fitted to No. 23769 and the car then returned to work in the Newcastle area. The following October No. 23711 was also sent to York Carriage Works for a new engine to be fitted.

No. 23768 (the York car) was fitted with Raven cab fog signalling apparatus at York in December 1930 and No. 23769 of Gateshead was similarly equipped about the same time. Two of the cars were also fitted with a metal brush arrangement specially to operate the track circuits governing the automatic semaphore signals on the East Coast main line between York and Darlington (fig. 57). Due to a misunderstanding the third car (either No. 23711 or 23769) was not so equipped and on one occasion when returning north from a visit to York Works it failed to operate the signals. A signalman reported this and stated that the signals did not return to danger behind the car with the result that a goods train was following it under the same clear signals!

As already mentioned, No. 23711 was latterly based at Darlington, but in September 1938 it was sent to Gateshead to replace No. 23769 which was out of action having suffered a broken axle on 23rd September near Coldstream. On 5th November the latter went to Darlington Works for repairs to be made but these were not put in hand because enquiries were being made regarding the economics of using these cars. It was found that the cost of running Nos. 23711/68/9 worked out at 4.89d., 5.45d. and 5.42d. per mile respectively compared with 6.74d., 7.76d. and 8.28d. per mile for a steam locomotive hauling a saloon on their respective duties. However, the steam engines could be used on other work, whereas if not required for an inspection run the petrol cars stood idle.

In consequence of this report all three cars were withdrawn from service on 4th February 1939. On 20th March No. 23711 left Gateshead pulled by class A3 No. 2597 *Gainsborough*. This interesting combination travelled up the main line as far as York, where the car was left for entry to the Carriage Works, whilst the Pacific went on to Doncaster for attention at the Plant. No. 23768 had been moved into York Carriage Works on 28th February whilst No. 23769 was sent there from Darlington Works on 24th March. All three cars were then broken up.

Dimensions

Car number (1923)	3711	3769	3768
Date built	1908	1912	1923
Engine: No. of cylinders	4	6	6
Horsepower	35-40	75	—
R.P.M.	950	1150	—
Wheel diameter	3′ 0″	2′ 11″	3′ 6″
Weight	6T 12C	12T 12C	13T 17C
Seating capacity	6	12	11
Length: Passenger compartment	9′ 7½″	15′ 11¾″	16′ 0″
Over headstocks	—	22′ 4″	23′ 4″
Over body	17′ 0″	23′ 6″	24′ 6″
Over buffers	—	25′ 5¼″	27′ 0″
Overall height	11′ 9½″	13′ 1″	13′ 1″
Width over body	7′ 0″	8′ 6″	8′ 6″
Wheelbase	10′ 0″	16′ 0″	16′ 0″
Coach Diagram No.	190	191	244

Summary of Petrol Inspection Cars

Car	Built	Date	Renumbered	Withdrawn
3711	York	3/1908	23711 9/28	2/39
3769	Walkergate/York	4/1912	23769 3/27	2/39
3768Y	York	12/1923	23768 3/28	2/39

LOANS OF LOCOMOTIVES TO AND FROM THE L.N.E.R.

During normal times the L.N.E.R. was self-sufficient in regard to its stock of locomotives and it was only during and after the 1939-45 War that the Company needed to borrow additional engines to cover urgent requirements. This was due not only to extra wartime traffic but also to make up for locomotives requisitioned by the Government. At this time too the L.N.E.R. helped out the other main line companies by loans of suitable locomotives to cover their shortages.

Throughout the existence of the L.N.E.R. there were movements of locomotives to and from the Company for testing and for exhibition at special events. Engines were also frequently hired out to small neighbours and private concerns, such as collieries, and it is proposed to mention here only the most noteworthy loans of this kind. The ex-N.B.R. class Y9 four-coupled saddletanks were particularly popular and there were records of all except two of these that survived Grouping being hired to collieries or other industrial concerns from time to time, occasionally for quite lengthy periods.

Class A1 4-6-2 No. 4472 *Flying Scotsman* was exhibited by the L.N.E.R. at the British Empire Exhibition held at Wembley in April to November 1924, and again in May to November 1925 (when class K3 No. 200 was also present). The G.W.R. exhibit, a Castle class 4-6-0, proclaimed it to be the most powerful passenger locomotive in the British Isles. This resulted in a contest to prove the statement during the last week in April 1925, when Pacific No. 4474 was sent to the G.W.R. to compete against No. 4074 *Caldicot Castle* between Paddington and Plymouth, whilst No. 4475 *Flying Fox* and No. 2545 ran trials against No. 4079 *Pendennis Castle* on the G.N. main line. Full details may be found by reference to Part 2A of this series, pp. 13 & 14.

At the beginning of July 1925 the L.N.E.R. celebrated in grand style the centenary of the opening of the Stockton & Darlington — the first steam-worked public railway in this country. The highlight of the event was the great procession of locomotives and rolling stock representing a century of rail travel. The L.N.E.R. invited the other main line companies to participate in this historic occasion and they willingly sent examples of their locomotives and rolling stock to the North East. A detailed account will be found herein at page 46 et seq.

During its first decade the L.N.E.R. afforded facilities for trials of several interesting locomotives built by British contractors. Some of the locomotives were of distinctly novel and unusual construction.

In 1924 the Graz Works of the Austrian company Simmering - Graz - Pauker constructed their first diesel powered locomotive. This was an 0-4-0 with hydraulic transmission. It was shipped to England where it underwent tests on the G.E. Section of the L.N.E.R. Although of small capacity and therefore more suitable for shunting duties, it was also tried on the main line where it hauled a train of four passenger coaches between London and Cambridge, this being recorded in "The Railway Magazine" for September 1924 (fig. 61).

The first British steam turbine locomotive was built in 1910 by the North British Locomotive Co. to the design of Sir James Reid and W.M. Ramsay. The turbine drove a generator which supplied current to traction motors. This locomotive was purely experimental and after a series of trials was laid up. A second locomotive, known as the Reid-Macleod, appeared in 1923 and was a rebuild of the first machine. In operation it was quite different in that electric transmission was abandoned in favour of pure turbine drive.

A long frame carried the boiler and condenser units. This was carried on two pivoted trucks each having four 4 ft. diameter driving wheels and a bogie at the outer end, giving a 4-4-0 + 0-4-4 wheel arrangement. There were two turbines, working in series, the high- and low-pressure units with their gearboxes being mounted longitudinally at the inner ends of the rear and front trucks respectively. The shafts drove the axles through double reduction spur and bevel gearing with a final flexible quill connection. There were no coupling rods on the wheels. In each turbine casing there was a separate reverse turbine. The boiler was situated at the rear end, the driving cab in the middle and the air-cooled evaporative condenser was at the front. The initial steam pressure was 180 lb. per sq. in. and each turbine developed 500 h.p. at 8,000 r.p.m., or about 950 h.p. at rail. The locomotive was designed to haul loads of 225 tons at 60 m.p.h.

The Reid - Macleod locomotive was exhibited at the 1924 Wembley exhibition, to and from which it was hauled. It then took up trial running on L.N.E.R. metals between Glasgow and Edinburgh (with Eastfield men) in March 1926 and again in April 1927 (fig. 64). The load in each case was two bogie coaches. The first trip ended in failure at Greenhill with trouble in the circulating pumps. Edinburgh was reached on the second occasion, but only after delay caused by hot axleboxes. Turbine failure occurred on the return trip, after which the locomotive was not seen again.

Another bold technical venture was the Kitson-Still combined steam and diesel powered 2-6-2 tank locomotive. This was turned out from the works of Kitson & Co. of Leeds in late 1927 and spent some seven years running trials and in service on the L.N.E.R., based mainly at Leeds and York (fig. 65).

The Kitson-Still locomotive was designed to overcome the task of getting a direct-coupled diesel engine to start under load. The 8-cylinder horizontal oil engine was double acting, the outer ends of the cylinders being diesel whilst the inner ends were powered by steam pressure. Steam alone was used when starting and, when a speed of 4 m.p.h. was reached, fuel began to be injected into the diesel ends. As soon as the diesel ends were firing, steam was shut off and the locomotive was propelled by diesel alone. Drive to the coupled wheels was by jack-shaft through 1.878:1 reduction gearing. Steam was generated in a small boiler, pitched high, by an oil burner. After diesel propulsion had begun, the burner was switched off and heat was then obtained from the diesel exhaust which passed through the boiler, aided by waste heat from the water jackets surrounding the diesel cylinders. Steam was used for the brakes, whistle and other auxiliaries. It could also be used as a booster for acceleration or when climbing gradients as well as for starting. The locomotive could develop about 1,000 h.p. and it weighed 70 tons.

Kitson's spent the best part of ten years and a considerable amount of money on the development of the locomotive. It largely contributed to the downfall of the company, who eventually had to call in a receiver in 1934. At first it worked trials in the Leeds area working from Ardsley and was exhibited at an L.N.E.R. rolling stock exhibition at Leeds in April 1928. Later that year it worked a 400-ton goods train from Darlington to Starbeck and back.

The L.N.E.R., who were clearly interested in this machine, supplied their dynamometer car for some of the trials held later. By 1933 it had reached a state of sufficient reliability to be based at York shed whence it regularly worked the afternoon goods to Dairycoates, outward via Beverley and back by Selby and Church Fenton. After Kitson's went into receivership, it lay idle in York North shed at least until July 1935, after which it disappeared to be disposed of by its courageous but unsuccessful makers.

Among the pioneers in this country of diesel powered locomotives were Armstrong Whitworth & Co. of Newcastle. On 10th June 1932 trials took place at Forth Yard, Newcastle of a 40-ton 0-6-0 diesel-electric shunting locomotive built by the company (fig. 62). Gresley and a number of N.E. Area officials were present. An extended trial of three months was authorised on 28th July by the Locomotive Committee. It was reported in the December 1932 issue of the "Locomotive Magazine" that the locomotive had been working 24 hours per day for six days a week at an L.N.E.R. goods yard in Newcastle and had performed every duty required for the past four months. The yard referred to was probably Blaydon where the locomotive is known to have been seen. The L.N.E.R. did not in the end purchase it and it finished its career owned by Preston Docks.

During 1933 Armstrong Whitworth built a more ambitious diesel-electric locomotive intended for main line work. This was rated at 880 h.p. and had the 2-6-2 wheel arrangement. It worked a demonstration run from Newcastle to North Wylam and back on 6th July (fig. 63). Further testing took place later in the year on trains from Newcastle as far as Berwick and on the Carlisle line. It was officially received on trial by the L.N.E.R. on 19th February 1934. The trial period was quite extensive (a Minute of the Locomotive Committee for 28th June records authorisation for a further four month period) and during its running it covered 26,140 miles. On 7th June it worked a special passenger train carrying members of the Institute of Transport from their conference at Leeds to Darlington Reclamation Depot and return. All other workings were with goods trains, frequently between Newcastle and York. Again the L.N.E.R. did not purchase this locomotive.

There were two small independent railway companies acting as feeders of traffic to the East Coast main line in the N.E. Area of the L.N.E.R. From time to time they hired locomotives from their big neighbour, particularly when their own engines were under repair. The North Sunderland Railway had a 4-mile line from Chathill to the coast at Seahouses. By the thirties the steam locomotives owned by the N.S.R. had been reduced to one (*Bamburgh*, a Manning Wardle 0-6-0ST of 1898) supplemented by a small diesel 0-4-0 named *The Lady Armstrong*. At times of need the L.N.E.R. loaned class J79 No. 407 or 1787 and, after these engines were withdrawn in 1936-37, class Y7's were used, including Nos. 982 and 986 (fig. 107, Part 9B). The Easingwold Railway lay north of York and ran the 2½ miles from Alne on the main line to Easingwold. Class J71 and J72 engines from York shed were the usual replacements for their own Hudswell Clarke 0-6-0T (fig. 12, Part 8B).

A third small company in the York area of the North East, the Derwent Valley, even though 16 miles long had no locomotives (other than a Sentinel shunter) of its own and relied entirely on the L.N.E.R. to work its goods traffic. Ex-Hull & Barnsley 0-6-2T's of class N12 were involved from 1927 to 1938, Nos. 2491, then 2485 (for 7½ years) and lastly No. 2483. After this, class N9 Nos. 1645/50 were used briefly in 1939. Thereafter a class J25 0-6-0 tender locomotive was usually employed on the line (fig. 78). York L.N.E.R. shed was responsible for the maintenance of these engines.

Following successful use by the L.N.E.R. of Sentinel shunting engines of class Y1 and Y3, a new design with four cylinders was tried at Scarborough in 1928 (Sentinel Works No. 6776). It achieved notoriety by setting fire to the roof of the locomotive shed, but it never became L.N.E.R. property although it was included in the rolling stock exhibition at Scarborough in August 1928.

Between December 1934 and February 1935 class P2 No. 2001 *Cock o'the North* was in France for trials to be conducted, both on the test plant at Vitry-sur-Seine and on the road. Details of these trials are given in Part 6B, pp. 176-9.

During 1936-38 the contractors Sir Robert McAlpine & Co. were engaged on the construction of the Ebbw Vale steelworks in South Wales. In December 1936 they purchased four J66 engines from the L.N.E.R. for use on the contract and at the same time hired six more (Nos. 7298, 7301/7/9/10/24) together with class J62 Nos. 5883/5/6. No. 5886 was damaged whilst at work at Ebbw Vale and was withdrawn in November 1937. The remaining hired engines were returned to the L.N.E.R. during May and June 1938.

About June 1939 the L.N.E.R. took on trial a Metro-Vick-Cammell 58-seat diesel railcar based on a design by the Hungarian firm of Ganz, which had supplied similar cars to numerous railways throughout the world. The car had been built in England in 1937 and at one time worked on the L.M.S. from Willesden shed.

In the north east the car was allocated to Hull (fig. 66) and took up the Pontefract, Selby and York duties originally worked by the Armstrong Whitworth diesel-electric railcar *Lady Hamilton,* together with a late evening trip to Withernsea and back. It spent some months at Hull but appears to have been returned to the makers on the outbreak of World War II.

It next appeared in 1951 when, after conversion to the 5ft. 3 in. gauge, it commenced working on the Ulster Transport Authority as No. 5. It was sold for scrap in 1965.

During the 1939-45 War radical changes in traffic requirements throughout the country coupled with Government needs overseas resulted in a large number of loans of locomotives both to and from the L.N.E.R.

An immediate result of the entry of Great Britain into the War was the requisition in September 1939 of locomotives for service in France and the Low Countries. The G.W.R. contributed 100 of their Dean Goods 0-6-0's and to help balance this sudden loss, 40 class J25 0-6-0's were lent in October 1939 - March 1940 by the L.N.E.R. to the G.W.R. (together with a similar number of Midland Railway class 2F and 3F 0-6-0's from the L.M.S.). Ten of these J25's were returned to the L.N.E.R. during 1943 and the remainder in 1946. They were stationed mostly in the Wolverhampton and Worcester Divisions (figs. 71 & 72). Full details will be found in Part 5, pp. 167/8.

During the first part of the War the G.W.R. system saw a larger increase in traffic than elsewhere in the country and locomotives were loaned to them by the other three main line companies to ease the difficulty. The L.N.E.R.'s contribution was 30 class O4 2-8-0's which were sent to the G.W.R. in November 1940. These engines were no strangers to the G.W.R. as this company still possessed 50 of this type which it had purchased from the Government after the 1914-18 War. The O4's were allocated mainly to Wolverhampton Division, with a few going to Southall and Bristol. Two were returned to the L.N.E.R. in April 1941, ten more in July/August 1942 and the remainder during January/February 1943 (see Part 6B, pp. 61/2).

A further demand on the L.N.E.R. for heavy goods engines was made by the Government who required 92 O4's for use in Egypt and Palestine. These were handed over for shipment in September/October 1941. Two were lost at sea. At first these engines were regarded as on loan but were all written off the L.N.E.R.'s books in December 1943. A full account will be found in Part 6B, pp. 62-65.

Earlier, in October 1939, the Government had requisitioned 14 ex-G.E.R. 0-6-0T's (one J68 and 13 J69's) for use initially on the Military railways at Longmoor and Melbourne. These too were written off, in October 1940. After the War some of these engines saw further use in industrial service — see Part 8A, pp. 91 & 99.

During June and July 1940 12 more ex-G.E.R. engines were requisitioned. These were 2-4-2T's of classes F4(11) and F5(1) and were utilised to haul armoured trains on coastal defence duties. Four more F4's joined them in January/February 1941. All received armour plating, which was removed when they returned to the L.N.E.R., twelve in March-July 1943 and the remaining four in February-April 1945 (see Part 7, p. 70).

In March 1940 class Y8 No. 559 was loaned to the Royal Engineers for use whilst fortifications were being constructed on the Spurn Head Railway, a line more used to sail or petrol propulsion rather than steam (fig. 68).

Two ex-N.B.R. class Y9 0-4-0T's (Nos. 9310 and 9610) were loaned to the L.M.S. in December 1940 for use at Motherwell. No. 9610 was returned in May 1941 and No. 9310 in December 1944. The L.M.S. also borrowed a pair of class Y3 Sentinel locomotives in January 1941 for use in Scotland, No. 23 at Greenhill and No. 35 at Bonnybridge. Both were returned to their home shed at Wrexham in December 1944. Class G5 0-4-4T's Nos. 1169 and 1713, fitted with special spark arresters, were sent to R.O.F. Bishopton, near Paisley in January 1941. No. 1713 returned to the N.E. Area in November 1943 and No. 1169 in September 1944.

Between February and July 1942 the War Department hired four class J50 0-6-0T's for use at Military Ports in Scotland. They were returned to the L.N.E.R. in May and June 1945 (see Part 8A, pp. 17 & 18).

During 1941-42 the Southern Railway had a number of engines surplus to requirements because of the wartime reduction in passenger services. The S.R. was thus able to lend engines to the other three major companies and in November 1941 ex-L.B.S.C. class B4 4-4-0's Nos. 2051/68 were despatched from store to Neville Hill shed in the N.E. Area. They were at first used on the Leeds-Hull and Harrogate services, working alongside the native class D20 engines. No. 2051 was at Bridlington for a time before both were transferred in July 1942 to York (fig. 70). Here they were used as assistant engines on the heavy through trains, such as the 10-05 a.m. to Newcastle, returning on the Newcastle-York via Ripon parcels, usually paired with a G.N.R. or N.E.R. Atlantic. By the time that they were returned to the Southern in December 1944 they were worn out and never worked again.

By October 1942 the L.N.E.R. was very short of engines to work the greatly increased volume of goods traffic then passing over the East Coast main line, and the Southern Railway was asked to help. This was quickly answered by the loan of ten Urie N15 "King Arthur" class 4-6-0's (built 1919-23). These were Nos. 739/40/2/4/7-51/4 which were allocated to Heaton, and instructions were issued that they were to be used only on goods trains between Newcastle and Edinburgh, the authorised load being that of the L.N.E.R. K2 class (fig. 69). The procedure at that time was to re-man engines on these duties in the vicinity of Tweedmouth and so, although shedded at Heaton, the engines were worked by men from Gateshead, Heaton, Tweedmouth, St. Margaret's and Haymarket in accordance with the "common-user" principles then in vogue. There was one recorded visit to Glasgow on 14th December 1942 when No. 742 *Camelot* worked a goods from Niddrie to Shettleston via Bathgate and, after turning on the Haghill fork and taking water at Parkhead shed, returned to Edinburgh on a meat train. Although not intended for passenger duties, there were occasional instances of such use. For instance, four days after the above event No. 742 replaced a failed engine on an Edinburgh to King's Cross train at Berwick and worked the 20-coach train forward to Newcastle. The "King Arthurs" were also recorded on goods trains south of Newcastle and were seen off the main line at Starbeck and Hull. Very occasionally they turned up on secondary passenger workings, including York-Selby, Leeds-Harrogate and Newcastle-Darlington trains. In July 1943 with the advent of the U.S.A. 2-8-0's, the "King Arthurs" were returned to the Southern.

In January 1943 the first W.D. 2-8-0 was built and by May 1945 there were 935 of them. They were intended for use overseas, particularly when the Allies invaded Europe, but when they first appeared 450 were loaned to the L.N.E.R., L.M.S. and the Southern for use in the war effort. The L.N.E.R. received 350 between February 1943 and January 1944 and they saw service throughout the system. The United States Army Transportation Corps also designed a 2-8-0 for similar use in Europe and nearly eight hundred were shipped to the U.K. It was agreed that the first 400 were to be put to immediate use in Britain. The L.N.E.R. took delivery of one on 30th December 1942 and four more during January 1943, but it was decided initially to concentrate the class in south Wales so these five were transferred to the G.W.R. at the end of that month. A further 38 were commissioned in L.N.E.R. workshops prior to entering service with the other three main line companies. All of these figured in the L.N.E.R.'s engine transfer sheets showing the allocation of operating stock, between March 1943 and January 1944. During this time the L.N.E.R. acquired 168 of these engines for its own use in all three Areas (figs. 73 & 74).

At the beginning of the War the L.M.S. class 8F 2-8-0 had been adopted by the Railway Executive as the standard heavy goods locomotive for new construction and they were built in the workshops of all the main line companies. The L.N.E.R. turned out 60 engines of this type between June 1943 and September 1945 for use on their system. They were lettered and numbered in the L.M.S. series and were treated as being on loan to the L.N.E.R. (fig. 67). A further 68 were taken into L.N.E.R. stock and were classified O6.

The final type of heavy goods locomotive to see wartime service on the L.N.E.R. was the W.D. 2-10-0, a development of the "Austerity" 2-8-0. During December 1943 and the first quarter of 1944 13 2-10-0's were loaned to the L.N.E.R. However, it was soon decided to concentrate these engines on the L.M.S. and by May 1944 they had left the L.N.E.R.

The Allied invasion of Europe in June 1944 caused immediate changes to the L.N.E.R.'s operating stock of 2-8-0 locomotives. The military authorities now required the use of the W.D. and U.S.A. types on the Continent. All except one of the U.S.A. 2-8-0's were returned to the Americans during August and September. The exception was No. 1707 which had met with a serious accident and, through being in works under repair, remained on the L.N.E.R.'s books until February 1945. Also during August and September 1944 the L.N.E.R. transferred 63 W.D. 2-8-0's to the G.W.R. to ease the loss of their U.S.A. engines. A further eight W.D.'s were sent to the G.W.R. in November and December and at the same time 23 were transferred to the S.R. Beginning in November the remaining 256 W.D.'s on loan to the L.N.E.R. were taken out of operating stock, overhauled and sent to the Continent. The last ones left the L.N.E.R. during February 1945. Full details of all the 2-8-0's and 2-10-0's in these wartime moves are contained in Part 6B of this series.

Although not officially deleted from L.N.E.R. operating stock, during 1944 a number of class B12/3 4-6-0's (which had dual braking facilities) were attached to Westinghouse-braked ambulance trains and were based at Westbury, Newbury and Templecombe to handle casualties returned from the Continent. These engines, with their low axle loading, were able to operate over most routes in S.W. England. (See Part 2B, page 63.)

Two G.W.R. diesel railcars, Nos. 6 and 19, were loaned to the L.N.E.R. for trials during 1944 when consideration was being given to the replacement of the L.N.E.R.'s steam railcars. The G.W. cars were used on local services in the Newcastle area, No. 19 being photographed at Blackhill on 25th April 1944 (figs. 76 & 77).

During 1943-44 the L.N.E.R. loaned a number of small 4-coupled tank engines to the military authorities. In May 1943 class Y9 Nos. 10090/3 were sent to Milford Haven for use in the Royal Navy mine depot, whilst sister engine No. 9042 was lent to the W.D. for use at Bonhill in the following November. All were returned in September 1945. Class Y6 tram engine No. 7134 was borrowed by the U.S.A. Transportation Corps in November 1943 for employment at their depot at Burton-on-Trent. It was transferred in July 1944 to the W.D. for use at the R.A.O.C. depot at Sinfin Lane, Derby and came back to the L.N.E.R. the following October. Between March 1943 and April 1944 the U.S. Army authorities had the loan of class Y7 No. 982. Earlier, from March 1942 it had been hired out to the Ministry of Works and Buildings at Shrawardine near Shrewsbury.

A second batch of W.D. 2-10-0's was constructed in 1945, but as hostilities in Europe ceased in May they were not all needed overseas. Twenty were therefore loaned to the L.N.E.R. during June-August 1945 and were stationed at March shed (fig. 75). They were returned to the W.D. in September-November 1946.

After the war in Europe ended large numbers of W.D. 2-8-0's became surplus and were put in store. In November 1945 they started to come home and the main line companies arranged to take 460 of them. The L.N.E.R. needed them the most and by the end of 1946 had 190 in service. The Company decided to purchase 200 engines of this type and accordingly took the 190 then on loan into stock on 28th December, the remaining ten being obtained in January-February 1947. They were given the classification O7 and are described in Part 6B of this series. A further 210 W.D.'s were received by the L.N.E.R. on loan during 1947, this figure being increased later in the year by 68 (although the final eight did not arrive until after nationalisation on 1st January 1948). The extra engines allowed the L.N.E.R. to part with the like number of class O6 L.M.S.-type 8F 2-8-0's which the Company had built for it during 1944-46. These were sent to the L.M.S. during September-December 1947 except for one which did not leave until after nationalisation, in January 1948. The O6's were still however regarded as in L.N.E.R. stock at 31st December 1947. Earlier, between October 1946 and July 1947 the 60 8F's built by the L.N.E.R. in 1944-45, numbered in the L.M.S. series and regarded as on loan to the L.N.E.R., were sent to the L.M.S. The arrival of W.D. 2-8-0's on the L.N.E.R. facilitated this. The reader is referred to Part 6B for full details of these moves.

In November 1945 one of the W.D. Austerity 0-6-0 saddle tanks, No. 71486, was loaned to the L.N.E.R. for trials, the wartime role of the class having ceased. The trials based on Doncaster shed were successful and this engine together with another 74 were taken into stock as class J94 beginning in May 1946 (see Part 8B).

The final loan to be recorded is of Gresley's electric locomotive No. 6701, the prototype class EM1 for the Manchester/Sheffield-Wath electrification. This engine had been built in 1941 and was put in store for the duration of the War, work on the electrification scheme having ceased. In August 1947 No. 6701, by now renumbered 6000, was sent to Holland in order to undergo extensive trials on the Dutch railways, there being no suitable line in Britain then electrified on the 1500-volt D.C. overhead system (fig. 79). It returned home in March 1952, electrification having been introduced between Wath and Dunford Bridge during the previous month.

L.N.E.R. LOCOMOTIVES PRESERVED

The L.N.E.R. was able to take credit for having established at York the first museum in this country entirely devoted to railways. The idea owed its inception to the N.E.R. where one of its officers, J.B. Harper, had for many years collected together various relics associated with his company. There were no facilities for displaying these items which could only be inspected by a privileged few, so in 1922 a committee was formed by the N.E.R. to consider the possibility of obtaining a suitable building to exhibit the collection. In April of that year the company's staff were requested to make known to the committee particulars of any relics which they considered worthy of preservation and this brought a good response.

At this time the Stockton & Darlington Railway centenary celebrations were in the offing and the collection of relics gathered at York formed the basis of the display at Faverdale in July 1925 as part of this memorable event. Although naturally these items came mostly from N.E.R. territory, after Grouping relics had begun to arrive from all sections of the new L.N.E.R. company.

The L.N.E.R. celebrated the centenary of the opening of the Stockton & Darlington Railway in grand style. A poster issued by the Company proudly proclaimed "L.N.E.R. Our Centenary 1825-1925". It showed *Locomotion* driven by George Stephenson. The official proceedings covered three days, July 1st, 2nd and 3rd. On the first day the Centenary Exhibition at Faverdale Works was formally opened by H.R.H. the Duke of York (later King George VI), accompanied by the Duchess. There were three events on July 2nd: first, the great procession from Stockton to Darlington of locomotives and rolling stock; second, the unveiling of a memorial tablet at Stockton by the Duke; and third, the Centenary banquet at Faverdale. On July 3rd the Exhibition was visited by delegates from all parts of the world who had assembled in connection with the International Railway Congress. The Exhibition remained open for the public until July 18th.

Because of the S. & D. celebrations, some old locomotives were not cut up and instead were restored to something like their original condition in readiness to take part in the Centenary Procession and subsequent exhibition of rolling stock at Faverdale (fig. 83). Probably the most noteworthy of these was No. 1275, the last Bouch long-boiler 0-6-0 of a type which for many years was the mainstay of the mineral and goods traffic on the S. & D. railway. This engine was withdrawn from service in February 1923 and laid aside to be painstakingly restored, as was the ex-N.E.R. Fletcher "901" class 2-4-0 No. 910 withdrawn in January 1925. (Incidentally, No. 910 had taken part in the S. & D. Jubilee celebrations at Darlington in 1875, when the

"LOCOMOTION" driven by George Stephenson

engine was new, and again appeared at the 150th event at Shildon a century later.) The N.B. Section sent an old Wheatley class J31 0-6-0 which they repainted as N.B.R. No. 381. This engine had been withdrawn in April 1925. Also from Scotland came class D47/2 4-4-0 No. 45A which was repainted as G.N.S.R. No. 45. Regrettably both these latter engines were cut up after the close of the exhibition.

From an earlier era the 1822 Hetton Colliery locomotive built by George Stephenson and Hackworth's S. & D. 0-6-0 No. 25 *Derwent* were put into running order for the procession, whilst the famous S. & D. 0-4-0 No. 1 *Locomotion* provided a triumphant finale to it by hauling a replica train with passengers and a band in period costume, preceded by a man on horseback carrying a red flag (fig. 80). Unfortunately, *Locomotion* could not be steamed, but a replica tender was constructed in which a petrol engine was installed in order to propel the locomotive and haul the train of eleven vehicles. To heighten the effect smoke came from the engine's chimney by means of burning oily waste in the firebox.

Other locomotives in the procession spanned development up to 1925 and included the enormous L.N.E.R. Garratt No. 2395, newly built and still in shop grey livery (fig. 81). The other three main line companies were invited to take part and a list of all the locomotives involved will be found in the accompanying table which shows the order that they ran in the procession.

After the conclusion of the S. & D. Centenary celebrations *Locomotion* and *Derwent* were put back on display on the platform beside the buffer stops of the south end bays at Bank Top station, Darlington where they had been since 1898 (figs. 84 & 85).

At York work was resumed on the establishment of a permanent museum in which to include not only the original N.E.R. collection but also many of the extra items which had come to light. The one-time First Class Refreshment Room at the Old Station was utilised for documents, prints and small items and was known as the Small Exhibits section of the museum. The Large Exhibits, including locomotives, were displayed in the former machine shop of the York & North Midland locomotive works at nearby Queen Street. This works had closed in 1905. The first three engines to enter the Queen Street museum were the Hetton Colliery locomotive, 0-6-0 No. 1275 and 2-4-0 No. 910. These were joined on 23rd March 1927 by G.N.R. 4-2-2 No. 1, followed by L.B.S.C.R. 0-4-2 No. 214 *Gladstone* on 31st May. The latter was at that time the property of the Stephenson Locomotive Society and was the first instance in this country of privately sponsored preservation of a steam locomotive. The Tennant 2-4-0 No. 1463 was added to the collection in mid-1928.

For a time during 1927 and 1928 the museum exhibits were open for inspection by application to the Curator. Later in 1928 (the exact date is unknown) the collection was opened fully to the public. Being the only railway museum in the country meant that objects began to arrive from all parts of Britain, and thus the display was enlarged although the majority of items were still from the N.E.R. system. In March 1931 the G.W.R. 4-4-0 No. 3717 *City of Truro* was placed in the museum, followed on 1st June 1934 by L.N.W.R. 2-2-2 No. 45 *Columbine* and the N.E.R. 2-2-4T No.66 *Aerolite* (L.N.E.R. class X1). In 1937 the Shutt End Railway 0-4-0 colliery locomotive *Agenoria* (built by Foster & Rastrick in 1829) arrived on loan from the Science Museum, whilst on 21st January 1938 the pioneer G.N.R. Atlantic No. 990 *Henry Oakley* (L.N.E.R. class C2) arrived at York and at the same time a City & South London electric trailer car was placed on exhibition.

On 13th June 1938 the famous Stirling 8-foot "single", G.N.R. No. 1, was taken out of the Museum and sent to Doncaster Works to be overhauled and put into working order prior to taking part in a demonstration run to publicise new rolling stock built for the "Flying Scotsman" train. Subsequently it and its train of old 6-wheel G.N.R. coaches were chartered by the R.C.T.S. for the first ever Society rail tour, from King's Cross to Peterborough and back on 11th September 1938 (figs. 88 & 89). During the remainder of that year No. 1 visited many parts of the L.N.E.R. system and is known to have reached Manchester, Liverpool, Edinburgh, Harrogate, Scarborough, Cambridge, Norwich and other towns before returning to the Museum on 25th January 1939.

The Museum was closed for the duration of the 1939-45 War and because of the risk of damage from German air raids, in July 1941 some of the locomotives were evacuated. *Agenoria, Columbine, Gladstone* and the Hetton Colliery locomotive were stored at Reedsmouth, whilst G.N.R. No. 1, N.E.R. Nos. 910 and 1275 were sent to Ferryhill (Co. Durham) and *City of Truro* went to Sprouston. *Aerolite, Henry Oakley* and N.E.R. No. 1463 appear to have remained at York. Incidentally, *Locomotion* and *Derwent* were similarly evacuated from Darlington station and put in the disused engine shed at Stanhope.

The Museum was reopened on 18th July 1947 by Sir Ronald Matthews. There was one change in the locomotive collection in that the place of the Tennant 2-4-0 No. 1463 was taken by class D17/1 4-4-0 No. 1621, which following its withdrawal in July 1945 had been restored to N.E.R. livery (fig. 87). This engine had taken part in the famous 1895 Races to the North.

On 1st January 1948 the Museum passed into the hands of the British Transport Commission. Soon afterwards, a national committee was set up

**STOCKTON & DARLINGTON
CENTENARY PROCESSION
2nd JULY 1925.**

Tablet No.

1	Hetton Colliery 0-4-0
2	S. & D. 0-6-0 25 *Derwent*
3	L.N.E.R. J31 N.B.R. 381
4	L.N.E.R. "1001" 0-6-0 N.E.R. 1275
5	L.N.E.R. J26 517
6	L.N.E.R. B16 934
7	L.N.E.R. K3 203
8	L.N.W.R. 4cc 0-8-0 1881
9	L.M.S. (L.N.W.R.) 0-8-0 9446
10	L.N.E.R. O2 3501
11	G.W.R. 47XX 2-8-0 4700
12	L.N.E.R. P1 2393
13	L.N.E.R. electric loco 9 (hauled by J71 317)
14	G.W.R. replica 2-2-2 *North Star* on wagon (hauled by J71 181)
15	L.N.W.R. 2-2-2 3020 *Cornwall*
16	G.N.R. 4-2-2 1
17	L.M.S. (M.R.) 4-2-2 679
18	L.N.E.R. X4 5972
19	N.E.R. "901" 2-4-0 910
20	L.N.E.R. E5 1463
21	L.N.E.R. D17 1620
22	L.N.E.R. D15 8900 *Claud Hamilton*
23	L.N.E.R. C2 3990 *Henry Oakley*
24	L.N.E.R. C1 3251
25	L.N.E.R. C11 9902 *Highland Chief*
26	L.N.E.R. C7 2207
27	L.N.E.R. B13 2006
28	L.N.E.R. B3 6169 *Lord Faringdon*
29	L.M.S. 4-6-0 5900 *Sir Gilbert Claughton*
30	L.N.E.R. A1 2563 *William Whitelaw*

Tablet No.

31	Did not run (N.B.L. turbine condensing locomotive)
32	L.N.E.R. electric loco 13 (hauled by J71 1163)
33	L.N.E.R. X1 66 *Aerolite*
34	L.N.E.R. J61 6469
35	L.N.E.R. Y6 7133
36	L.N.E.R. G6 949
37	L.N.E.R. G5 1334
38	L.N.E.R. H1 2151
39	L.N.E.R. A5 5088
40	L.M.S. (L. & Y.) 4-6-4T 11112
41	G.W.R. 42XX 2-8-0T 5225
42	L.N.E.R. U1 2395
43	L.N.E.R. petrol railbus 130Y
44	L.N.E.R. petrol autocar 2105Y
45	Sentinel Cammell steam railcar
46	L.N.E.R. Q7 904 and train of mineral wagons
47	L.N.E.R. Q5 130 and tableau train
48	L.N.E.R. D47/2 G.N.S.R. 45 and train of 4-wheel coaches
49	L.M.S. Hughes 4-6-0 10474 and train of L.M.S. stock
50	G.W.R. Castle 4-6-0 4082 *Windsor Castle* and G.W.R. Royal Train
51	G.W.R. Castle 4-6-0 111 *Viscount Churchill* and G.W.R. articulated stock.
52	S.R. N15 4-6-0 449 *Sir Torre* and train of S.R. stock
53	L.N.E.R. A2 2400 *City of Newcastle* and Flying Scotsman stock
54	*Locomotion* No. 1 hauling replica train of S. & D. stock

47

to consider what should be done about the various railway relics scattered throughout the country. One recommendation in its report, produced in 1951, was that a Curator of Historical Relics should be appointed. This post was filled from 2nd July 1951 by J. H. Scholes, formerly Curator of the Castle Museum at York. Later, when the end of the steam locomotive on B.R. became evident, a further national committee was given the task of formulating a list of suitable additional locomotives to be preserved as part of a national collection.

Meanwhile, the centenary of the Plant Works at Doncaster brought about the removal from York Museum on 21st July 1953 of G.N.R. No.1 and *Henry Oakley*. The latter, together with the large G.N.R. Atlantic No. 251 which had been restored and preserved at Doncaster following withdrawal from service in July 1947, were put into running order to haul the Plant Centenarian special trains.

On 6th January 1957 *City of Truro* left York to go to the new museum at Swindon. The subsequent rearrangement of the York Museum allowed N.E.R. 2-4-0 No. 1463 (fig. 86) to be put on display again — for some years it had been stored at Doncaster Works — whilst G.N.R. No. 251 made an imposing addition to the collection.

During this period the Museum was closed. It was reopened on 20th April 1957 when, for the first time, a charge was made for admission. On 17th September 1966 the Small Exhibits section in the Old Station building was closed and some of the items were put on display in the Queen Street section.

By a Bill enacted by Parliament in 1968, responsibility for the museum at York (also that at Clapham) passed to the Department of Education and Science, with the intention of combining the exhibits in a single new museum at York under the jurisdiction of the Science Museum. Resulting from this, on 31st December 1973 York Railway Museum was closed to enable the exhibits to be prepared for moving mostly to the new National Railway Museum at the former locomotive depot in Leeman Road, opened on 27th September 1975, exactly 150 years to the day since the inaugural run of *Locomotion* from Shildon to Darlington and Stockton on the opening of the world's first steam worked public railway.

Also in 1975, a small local museum was opened in part of the old North Road station at Darlington. Naturally the theme of this museum concentrates on the S. & D. Railway. The locomotives exhibited there are *Locomotion, Derwent*, the long-boiler 0-6-0 No. 1275 and the Tennant 2-4-0 No. 1463. Previously the first two had been on display at Bank Top Station, Darlington whilst the last two were from the old York Museum.

As is well known, the National Collection has been complemented by many privately sponsored locomotive preservation schemes. It is not proposed to recount these in detail — many current books and periodicals are devoted to this subject — and it will suffice to tabulate the forty-seven engines of L.N.E.R. ownership or design still in existence. It may be mentioned that in comparison with the other main line companies the percentage of L.N.E.R. locomotives that have been preserved was not high. This was due mainly to the fact that when the private preservation movement really got under way the only source of condemned locomotives was Woodham's Yard at Barry, the content of which had come largely from the London Midland, Western and Southern Regions of B.R.

Fig. 38   Class B13 No. 761 in the old shed at Faverdale, Darlington, July 1946.
For use as counter pressure locomotive.

Fig. 39   Class J72 Nos. 58 and 59 (ex-69005/23) stored in Heaton shed, September
1965.

Fig. 40   Class EB1 electric locomotive No. 100 (ex-26510) stored at Goodmayes yard, June 1962.

Fig. 41   Class B1 No. 20 (ex-61205) at Norwich.
Used for carriage heating.

Fig. 42   Class B1 No. 22 (ex-61252) at Ipswich, February 1964.

Fig. 43   Class B1 No. 25 (ex-61272) at New England, March 1965.

Fig. 44 Class J92 B Works at Stratford, July 1933.

Stovepipe chimney, uncased Ramsbottom safety valves, Roscoe lubricator on side of smokebox, front guard irons attached to frame.

Fig. 45 J92 D Works at Stratford, 1935.

Retaining plain smokebox door, front guard irons attached to bufferbeam, toolbox removed.

Fig. 46   Class J92 C Works at Stratford, June 1932.

Cast-iron chimney, Roscoe lubricators removed, retaining Ramsbottom safety valves and toolbox on top of side tank, heavier pattern of smokebox door.

Fig. 47   Class J92 No. 8667 at Stratford, June 1947.

Crane disused with hook and chain removed, shaded lettering and numerals.

Fig. 48   Class J92 No. 8668 at Stratford, about April 1947.
Gill Sans lettering and numerals.

Fig. 49   Class J92 Nos. 68667 (and 8669) at Stratford, about March 1949.
B.R. number in L.N.E.R. style shaded numerals.

Locomotives of L.N.E.R. Type Preserved

Co. of origin	Original No.	First L.N.E. No.	Last L.N.E. No.	B.R. No.	L.N.E. Class	Type	Built	Designer	Described Part & Page number	Location (as at June 1988).
BR(E)	—	—	(532)(a)	60532	A2(e)	4-6-2	1948	A.H. Peppercorn	2A/191	I.C.I., Wilton
LNE	1472N	4472*	103	60103	A3(e)	,,	1923	H.N. Gresley	2A/88	Steamtown, Carnforth
,,	—	4464(g)	19	60019	A4(e)	,,	1937	,,	2A/134	National Railway Museum
,,	—	4468*	22	60022	A4(e)	,,	1938	,,	2A/133	,, ,,
,,	—	4488	9	60009*	A4(e)	,,	1937	,,	2A/134	Markinch, Fife
,,	—	4489	10	60010*	A4(e)	,,	1937	,,	2A/133	Montreal, Canada
,,	—	4496	8	60008*	A4(e)	,,	1937	,,	2A/133	Green Bay, Wisconsin, U.S.A.
,,	—	4498*	7	60007	A4(e)	,,	1937	,,	2A/133	Steamtown, Carnforth
,,	—	—	1264*	61264	B1	4-6-0	1947	E. Thompson	2B/(f)	G.C.R., Loughborough
BR(E)	—	—	(1306)(a)	61306	B1(e)	,,	1948	,,	2B/126	,, ,,
LNE	—	8572	1572	61572*	B12/3	,,	1928	J. Holden/ H.N. Gresley	2B/64	North Norfolk Railway
GN	251*	3251	2800	—	C1	4-4-2	1902	H.A. Ivatt	3A/44	National Railway Museum
,,	990*	3990	—	—	C2(e)	,,	1898	,,	3A/164	,, ,,
GC	506*	5506	2660	62660	D11(e)	4-4-0	1919	J.G. Robinson	3B/99	G.C.R., Loughborough (N)
NE	1621*	1621	—	—	D17/1	,,	1893	W. Worsdell	3C/69	National Railway Museum
NB	256*	9256	2469	62469	D34(e)	,,	1913	W.P. Reid	4/47	Glasgow Transport Museum
GNS	49*	6849	2277	62277	D40(e)	,,	1920	T.E. Heywood	4/63	,, ,,
LNE	—	246*	2712	62712	D49/1(e)	,,	1928	H.N. Gresley	4/111	Scottish R.P.S., Bo'ness
GE	490*	7490	2785	62785	E4	2-4-0	1895	J. Holden	4/142	Bressingham Gardens (N)
NE	910*	910	—	—	"901"	,,	1875	E. Fletcher	4/151	National Railway Museum
,,	1463*	1463	—	—	E5	,,	1885	H. Tennant	4/147	Darlington Nth. Road Museum (N)
GE	564*	7564	5462	65462	J15	0-6-0	1912	T.W. Worsdell	5/93	North Norfolk Railway
,,	1217	8217(b)	5567	65567	J17	,,	1905	J. Holden	5/104	National Railway Museum
NE(S&D)	1275*	1275	—	—	"1001"	,,	1874	W. Bouch	5/116	Darlington Nth. Road Museum (N)
NE	876*	876	5033	65033	J21	,,	1889	T.W. Worsdell	5/138	Beamish Open Air Museum
LNE	—	2392(c)	5894	65894	J27	,,	1923	W. Worsdell	5/(f)	North Yorkshire Moors Railway
NB	673*	9673	5243	65243	J36(e)	,,	1891	M. Holmes	5/(f)	Scottish R.P.S., Bo'ness

LOCOMOTIVES OF L.N.E.R. TYPE PRESERVED (Continued)

Co. of origin	Original No.	First L.N.E. No.	Last L.N.E. No.	B.R. No.	L.N.E. Class	Type	Built	Designer	Described Part & Page number	Location (as at June 1988)
BR(E)	—	—	(2005)(a)	62005	K1	2-6-0	1949	A.H. Peppercorn	6A/164	North Yorkshire Moors Railway
LNE	—	3442*	1994	61994	K4(e)	,,	1938	H.N. Gresley	6A/151	Severn Valley Railway
GC	102	5102	3601	63601*	O4	2-8-0	1911	J.G. Robinson	6B/74	Dinting Railway Centre (N)
NE	2238*	2238	3395	63395	Q6	0-8-0	1918	V. Raven	6C/53	North Yorkshire Moors Railway
,,	901	901	3460	63460*	Q7	,,	1919	,,	6C/62	,, ,, (N)
LNE	—	4771*	800	60800	V2(e)	2-6-2	1936	H.N. Gresley	6C/114	National Railway Museum
GN	1247*	4247	8846	68846	J52	0-6-0T	1899	H.A. Ivatt	8A/31	,, ,,
GE	87*	7087	8633	68633	J69	,,	1904	J. Holden	8A/91	,, ,,
BR(E)	—	—	—	69023*	J72(h)	,,	1951	W. Worsdell	8B/27	North Yorkshire Moors Railway
LNE	—	—	8077	68077*	J94	,,	1947	Min. of Supply	8B/93	Keighley & Worth Valley Railway
,,	—	—	8078	68078*	,,	,,	1946	,, ,,	8B/93	Derek Crouch & Co., Widdrington
GN	1744	4744	9523	69523*	N2	0-6-2T	1921	H.N. Gresley	9A/58	G.C.R., Loughborough
LNE	999E(d)	7999	9621	69621	N7	,,	1924	A.J. Hill	9A/103	Stour Valley R.P.S.
NE	66*	66	—	—	X1	2-2-4T	1869	W. Worsdell	9B/58	National Railway Museum
LNE	—	59*	8153	Dep. 54	Y1	0-4-0T	1933	Sentinel Co.	9B/80	Middleton Railway
,,	—	985	8088	68088*	Y7	,,	1923	T.W. Worsdell	9B/98	G.C.R., Loughborough
NE	1310*	1310	—	—	,,	,,	1891	,,	9B/98	Middleton Railway
NB	42*	10094	8095	68095	Y9	,,	1887	Neilson & Co.	9B/106	Lytham Motive Power Museum
NE	1*	1	6480	26500	ES1	Bo-Bo electric	1905	W. Worsdell	10B	National Railway Museum
BR(E)	—	—	—	26020*	EM1	Bo+Bo electric	1951	H.N. Gresley	10B	,, ,,
S&D	1	—	—	—	-(e)	0-4-0	1825	G. Stephenson	—	Darlington North Road Museum (N)
,,	25	—	—	—	-(e)	0-6-0	1845	T. Hackworth	—	,, ,,
GNR	1	—	—	—	—	4-2-2	1870	P. Stirling	—	National Railway Museum
GER	229	—	—	—	(Y5)	0-4-0T	1876	Neilson & Co.	9B/87	North Woolwich Museum

These four locomotives were owned by constituent companies of the L.N.E.R. but had been withdrawn from service before Grouping.

* Indicates the running number currently displayed.

(a)   Class A2 No. 532, B1 No. 1306 and K1 No. 2005 were built after nationalisation but have been painted in L.N.E.R. livery and carry the numbers shown.

(b)   The class J17 carries its pre-1924 L.N.E.R. number 1217E.

(c)   Although built by the L.N.E.R., class J27 No. 2392 has been finished in N.E.R. livery.

(d)   Class N7 No. 999E was built after Grouping but has been painted in G.E.R. colours as No. 999.

(e)   The following locomotives carry the names shown:—

A2	532	*Blue Peter*
A3	4472	*Flying Scotsman*
A4	19	*Bittern* (but see footnote g below)
A4	4468	*Mallard*
A4	60009	*Union of South Africa*
A4	60010	*Dominion of Canada*
A4	60008	*Dwight D. Eisenhower*
A4	4498	*Sir Nigel Gresley*
B1	1306	*Mayflower* *
C2	990	*Henry Oakley*
D11	506	*Butler-Henderson*
D34	256	*Glen Douglas*
D40	49	*Gordon Highlander*
D49	246	*Morayshire*
J36	673	*Maude*
K4	3442	*The Great Marquess*
V2	4771	*Green Arrow*
X1	66	*Aerolite*
S.&D.	1	*Locomotion*
S.&D.	25	*Derwent*

* Name bestowed following restoration.

(f)   Class B1 No. 61264, J27 No. 65894 (2392) and J36 No. 65243 (673) were preserved after publication of the Part in which the description of their class can be found and therefore do not receive individual mention.

(g)   Class A4 No. 4464 has temporarily taken on the identity of No. 2509 *Silver Link*.

(h)   Class J72 No. 69023 was named *Joem* following restoration, but the nameplates have now been removed.

(N)   Part of the National Collection but on loan to the location shown.

ADDITIONAL NOTES ON LOCOMOTIVE POLICY

In Part 1 of this series the chapter covering Locomotive Policy and Construction contained details of the new designs introduced by the L.N.E.R. together with major rebuildings and policy decisions. The origins of the new designs have been discussed at length under their respective class headings in later published Parts, but there were also several proposals which never materialised and these are outlined here.

There were also a number of interesting standardisation proposals made from time to time during the Company's life affecting not only locomotives but also their components. The first of these proposals was an abortive scheme covering boilers in 1923.

Despite the fact that Gresley was in command of locomotive affairs from Grouping until his death in 1941, his eventual successor, Thompson, was pursuing his own ideas from 1930 onwards whilst successively in charge of Stratford, Darlington and Doncaster Works where he had a degree of autonomy over the renewal of stock. The following notes draw attention to his work during that time. It will be noticed that even before Thompson became C.M.E. he was a protagonist of standardisation and of up-dating older locomotives by major rebuilding. When at last he succeeded Gresley he was able to give full rein to his ideas for new construction and standardisation, particularly in the immediate post-war years.

Peppercorn too was active in promoting his own ideas before he actually became C.M.E. in 1946 and these are also discussed, as is the unusual situation whereby the Board of Directors instructed the C.M.E.'s department to implement the introduction of main line diesel traction.

Finally, there is an appraisal early in 1948 when the standardisation cycle was about to be repeated.

Boiler Standardisation 1923

In June 1923 the principal Chief Locomotive Draughtsmen of the L.N.E.R. met at Darlington to agree a policy of boiler standardisation. As related under class J50 (see Part 8A, page 16, of this series), discussions led to a proposal to design a modified version of the N.E.R. class P1 boiler (L.N.E.R. class J25) which could then be fitted to 967 existing engines. This scheme was followed up for the application to class J50, but had to be dropped later when it was realised that the boiler would be too heavy. The list of proposals considered at the time included:

B13 boiler, fit to 75 K2's, also 135 N.E. and 125 G.C. engines.

C7 boiler, fit to 10 O1's, 11 O2's and 26 N.B. engines.

D20 boiler, fit to D9's, D10's, D11's and 251 G.E. engines.

E4 boiler, fit to 440 G.N. engines.

F8 boiler, fit to 222 N.B. and 210 G.E. engines.

J25 boiler, fit to J50's, also 504 G.C. and 440 G.E. engines.

Q2 boiler, fit to 141 G.C. engines.

Q6 boiler, fit to 61 G.C. engines.

Nothing came out of these proposals, nor of ideas to standardise certain components, such as firebox hand-holes instead of wash-out plugs, probably because of the realisation that this would lead to difficulties at sheds which would need to maintain a higher level of spares. (A similar situation presented itself after nationalisation on 1st January 1948, see later.)

Gresley's Proposed 2-8-2T, 4-6-0 and 4-8-2 Designs

Throughout this series reference has been made to proposed locomotive designs where these were refined and developed into eventual construction. Some of these schemes took many years to come to fruition, the earliest proposals often coming to nothing at the time. A notable example was the 2-6-4T which although mooted in 1925 did not materialise until 1945 as Thompson's L1 class.

In addition to the schemes that have been noticed, there were others which never progressed beyond the suggestion or design stage. Details of three of these are given below.

4ft. 8in. 2-8-2T

At about the time the ageing Ivatt 0-8-2 tank engines were being withdrawn from colliery trip working in the Nottingham District (see Part 9B, class R1), various schemes were being considered for their replacement by three-cylinder 2-8-2 tank engines. Twelve engines were initially authorised in 1929 for construction at Doncaster against the 1930 building programme and were allocated numbers 2875-86. Three schemes were drawn out in November 1929 for consideration (see accompanying table and drawings), which showed that it was intended to make full use of standard components, in particular from classes O2 and V1 (then also at the design stage) with the third variant taking the K2 boiler. The tractive effort would have been 36,470 lb., perhaps rather high in consideration of their intended role, and this was reduced to around 30,000 lb. when three new schemes were considered in 1931 based on the smaller class J39 or V1 boilers. The order on the works was cancelled on 4th December 1930.

Design work was sufficiently advanced by April 1932 for Engine Order 329 to be issued at Doncaster on the 28th of that month for the construction of ten 2-8-2T's, to be classified P10, based on scheme No. 6 but with 17½ in. diameter cylinders. This was at a period of uncertainty in industry when orders were being cut back or delayed and so just two months later the order was cancelled on 25th June 1932, before any running numbers were allocated. The scheme was never revived as by the time this could have been possible, class R1 was already extinct and its work taken over by existing engines.

SUMMARY OF CLASS P10 SCHEMES

Scheme No.	1	2	3	4	5	6
Date	11/1929	11/1929	11/1929	1/1931	1/1931	7/1931
Cylinders (3):	18½"x 26"	18½"x 26"	18½"x 26"	16"x 26"	17"x 26"	17"x 26"
(Pattern)	O2	O2	O2	V1	V1 altd.	V1 altd.
Coupled wheels	O2	O2	O2	O2	O2	O2
Motion	O2	O2	O2	O2	O2	O2
Boiler	O2	O2	K2	V1	J39	V1
Pony truck	O2	O2	O2	O2	O2	O2
Trailing truck	V1	V1	V1	V1	V1	V1
Tractive effort (85%)	36,470 lb.	36,470 lb.	36,470 lb.	27,277 lb.	30,794 lb.	30,794 lb.
Water	2,000 gals.	2,500 gals.	2,500 gals.	1,500 gals.	1,500 gals.	2,000 gals.

6ft. 8in. 4-6-0

When the 1937 locomotive building programme was discussed at the Joint Locomotive and Traffic Committee meeting held on 29th October 1936 it included thirty-two new B17's, including twenty for the G.C. Section both to replace old 4-4-0's and to reduce double-heading. However, it was announced at the same meeting that Gresley was contemplating substituting the B17's on the programme by an improved type. In November 1936 there appeared the first outline drawing of an improved 4-6-0 (see drawing). The boiler tapered from 6ft. at the firebox end to 5 ft. 9 in. at the smokebox, and the working pressure was 220 lb per sq. in. The standard three-cylinder arrangement of the class A3 Pacifics was applied, so that the proposed design was in effect a 4-6-0 equivalent of the former. The leading particulars are set out in the accompanying table.

At the meeting of the Locomotive Committee held on 26th November 1936 reference was made to the new type of engine being contemplated, but it was then considered that the urgency for new engines did not justify the design of a new type. It was decided that the need for a more powerful type than the B17 for the G.C. Section should be met by substituting V2's on the building programme. As a result of this decision the thirty-two B17's on the programme were replaced instead by twenty-eight new V2's, and the proposed improved 4-6-0 design was dropped. Presumably, had it materialised, it would have taken the classification B18.

Cylinders (3)	18½" x 26"
Motion	Walschaerts/Gresley with 8in. piston valves
Boiler:	
Max. diam. outside	6' 0"
Distance between tubeplates	12'11¾"
Firebox length outside	10' 0"
Pitch	9' 4½"
Grate area	31.5 sq. ft.
Boiler pressure	220 lb./sq. in.
Heating surface:	
Firebox	198 sq. ft.
Tubes	1291 sq. ft.
Flues	571 sq. ft.
Total evaporative	2060 sq. ft.
Superheater	441 sq. ft.
Total	2501 sq. ft.

Leading wheels	3′ 2″
Coupled wheels	6′ 8″
Tender wheels	3′ 9″
Tractive effort (85%)	31,200 lb
Length over buffers	62′ 10″

Wheelbase:
Engine 6′ 3″ + 5′ 6″ + 7′ 3″ + 9′ 0″ = 28′ 0″
Tender 7′ 3″ + 6′ 3″ = 13′ 6″
Total 52′ 7″

Weight (full):
Engine	84т 0c
Tender	51т 0c
Total	135т 0c
Adhesive	66т 0c
Max. axle load	22т 0c
Water capacity	4,200 gallons
Coal capacity	7т 10c

6ft. 8in. 4-8-2

Following the success of the class A4 Pacifics, particularly on the lighter loaded trains, attention was then directed towards increasing the average speed of the heavy express passenger trains, which could best be achieved by faster uphill running. Reference is made in Part 2A of this series to the proposal in January 1938 to enlarge the firebox of the class A4, whilst in August 1938 appeared a scheme to increase the boiler pressure to 275 lb. per sq. in. Meanwhile the solitary 4-6-4, No. 10000, had been rebuilt in November 1937, but none of these ideas could overcome the limitation of 66 tons maximum adhesive weight imposed by a six-coupled design. The logical step forward was to design a 4-8-2. The work appears to have been carried out in secrecy in the King's Cross drawing office during 1939, and the drawing which was published in a paper read by Gresley's former assistant, Bert Spencer, before The Institution of Locomotive Engineers in March 1947 was retraced at Doncaster from the original in January 1947. The principal details are set out in the accompanying table. In the paper, Spencer recorded that but for the intervening war there was every prospect of the design being proceeded with.

In passing, it is interesting to speculate as to which class letter would have been allotted to the 4-8-2 design if it had been built. The letters A to T (with the exception of I) and X to Z had all been brought into use to cover wheel arrangements existing, or proposed in the case of P, in 1923. The L.N.E.R. had later added U (for the Garratt), V (2-6-2) and W (4-6-4), which completed the alphabet. By 1939 R (0-8-2) and X (single-drivers) had become vacant and it is possible that one of these would have been reintroduced to cover the 4-8-2 wheel arrangement, most probably R because this was in the sequence of eight-coupled classes O to U.

Cylinders (3)	21″ x 26″
Motion	Walschaerts/Gresley

Boiler:
Max. diam. outside	6′ 5″
Distance between tubeplates	19′ 0″
Firebox length outside	11′ 9″
Pitch	9′ 4½″
Grate area	50 sq. ft.
Boiler pressure	250 lb./sq. in.

Heating surface:
Firebox	252.5 sq. ft.
Tubes (121 x 2¼″)	1354.2 sq. ft.
Flues (43 x 5¼″)	1122.8 sq. ft.
Total evaporative	2729.5 sq. ft.
Superheater (43 x 1.244″)	776.5 sq. ft.
Total	3506.0 sq. ft.
Leading wheels	3′ 2″
Coupled wheels	6′ 8″
Trailing wheels	3′ 8″
Tender wheels	4′ 2″
Tractive effort (85%)	45,700 lb.
Length over buffers	77′ 0⅝″

Wheelbase:
Engine 6′ 3″ + 5′ 6″ + 7′ 0″ + 7′ 0″ + 7′ 0″ + 9′ 6″ = 42′ 3″
Tender 5′ 3″ + 5′ 6″ + 5′ 3″ = 16′ 0″
Total 67′ 4⅝″

Weight (full):
Engine	115т 0c
Tender	60т 7c
Total	175т 7c
Adhesive	80т 0c
Max. axle load	20т 10c
Water capacity	5,000 gallons
Coal capacity	9т 0c

Thompson 1930-40

Edward Thompson became Mechanical Engineer at Stratford when C.W.L. Glaze retired on 31st March 1930. Thompson had been his assistant since 1927 and so was familiar with the situation on the G.E. Section. He quickly made his presence felt, until January 1934 when he moved to a similar position at Darlington. During this period a start was made on rebuilding the B12's with larger diameter boilers (see Part 2B), a scheme which seems to have originated early in 1930 and has Thompson's hallmark on it. He seems to have kept his drawing office busy investigating his ideas, one of the most interesting being a scheme for a 4ft. 8in. 0-8-0 tank engine with condensing gear. The drawing first appeared in May 1930, was amended slightly in June (see accompanying drawing) and finally revised in

54

August 1930. No official reference has been found in the L.N.E.R. papers of that period and its origin must remain pure speculation.

The design presents an outward appearance of being typically Great Northern, with flared bunker top, cab profile and half-rounded beading on bunker, cab and side tanks. Class N2 was a Group Standard design and there were examples on the G.E. Section at that time, but here the similarity ended. The condensing apparatus layout was the modified G.E.-style, as applied to certain N2's.

The boiler had a Belpaire firebox, which would not have met with Gresley's approval and was anathema to Thompson anyway. The drawing is endorsed to the effect that class B12 flanged boiler plates were to be used, which strongly suggests a use being found for discarded B12 boilers as part-justification for Thompson's intention to modernise the G.E. 4-6-0's and 4-4-0's. Other features depicted on the drawing included inside Walschaerts valve gear, two inside cylinders with 8 in. diameter piston valves and oval-headed buffers.

The principal dimensions are summarised in the accompanying table.

Cylinders (2 inside)	20" x 26"
Motion	Walschaerts with 8in. piston valves
Boiler:	
Max. diam. outside	5' 0"
Barrel length	10' 1"
Firebox length outside	7' 0"
Pitch	8' 6"
Heating surface:	
Firebox	123 sq. ft.
Tubes (165 x 1¼")	788 sq. ft.
Flues (21 x 5¼")	297 sq. ft.
Total evaporative	1208 sq. ft.
Superheater (21 x 1³⁄₃₂")	170 sq. ft.
Total	1378 sq. ft.
Grate area	21 sq. ft.
Boiler pressure	180 lb./sq. in.
Coupled wheels	4' 8"
Tractive effort (85%)	28,415 lb.
Length over buffers	36' 0"
Wheelbase	6' 0" + 5' 6" + 5' 6" = 17' 0"
Weight (full)	66T 8C
Max. axle load	18T 11½C
Water capacity	1,500 gallons
Coal capacity	3T 5C

The Stratford Drawing Office diary contains other proposals instigated by Thompson, such as a suggestion in December 1930 that the intended B12 5ft. 6in. diameter boiler should be used on class J20. Sketches were shown to Thompson which showed little room for firing. Thompson ordered that when a boiler became available it was to be placed in a J20 for him to see what room there was. In the event, the scheme was abandoned. Apparently it would seem that the total engine weight of such a J20 rebuild would exceed 60 tons and that the maximum axle load was likely to be not less than 20 tons 8 cwt., such figures exceeding those for classes J37 and J38 and so, like those classes, would have been graded as Route Availability 8 as against RA5 with the original size of boiler.

Also in December 1930 came the first proposal to fit classes D15 and D16 with new cylinders having overhead long travel piston valves. This was rejected by Gresley in February 1931 and an alternative scheme to use J39-type cylinders and motion was then pursued. The result was the rebuilding of No. 8900 in February 1933, a success story for which Gresley afterwards gave Thompson full credit. It will be particularly noted that the first rebuild was No. 8900 *Claud Hamilton* itself, in the same way that Thompson's prototype express passenger Pacific in 1945 was No. 4470 *Great Northern*. What better way could there be to publicise his intentions?

Thompson clearly believed that standardisation of boilers was a promising field. In January 1931 the Drawing Office was instructed to investigate the possibility of fitting class N7 boilers to the F4, F5 and F6 2-4-2 tank engines. It was pointed out that the firebox was too wide for the distance between frames. The following September the question of standardising "tank engine boilers" if possible in the following groups was looked into.

1. E4, J15, F3 (160 lb.); F4 (160 lb.); F5, F6 (180 lb.)
2. J65, J66, J67 (160 lb.); J68, J69 (180 lb.)
3. N7 (180 lb.)
4. Scrap F7, F9, G4.

It was decided that in groups 1 and 2 the boilers were already virtually standard and no action was needed. There was no action in group 3 until 1943, when Diagram 101 boiler became standard. In group 4 it may be noted that class F9 had already become extinct, in 1930.

Clearly Thompson believed in standardisation and his period at Stratford was but a foretaste of what was still to come.

Thompson succeeded A. C. Stamer at Darlington as Mechanical Engineer (N.E. Area) in January 1934. A small start had already been made redesigning N.E. boilers from traditional three-ring butt-jointed to single plate, with a few examples of Diagram 63A (class A8 in 1929) and Diagram 69 (class G5 in 1930). Thompson continued with this work, introducing Diagram

59A (class D20 in 1935), Diagram 56B (class Q5/1 in 1936) and Diagram 67B (class J21 in 1937). It was at this point that the Drawing Office at Darlington was run down and the majority of staff transferred to Doncaster in January 1937. Redesign work continued at Doncaster resulting in the later introduction of Diagrams 49A, 50A and 57A in 1938-39 on classes B16, Q6 and J26/J27 respectively, with in their cases the fireboxes given sloping throatplates and barrel shortened to suit. This followed Doncaster practice, though it should also be noted that Thompson had become Mechanical Engineer (Southern Area Western Section) at Doncaster from July 1938 in succession to R.A. Thom, who retired, and so simply carried on his process of modernising the boilers on the N.E. Area locomotives.

Whilst at Darlington Thompson rebuilt class D20 No. 2020 without seeking Gresley's approval in advance, and earned a severe rebuke after he had given details to the technical press (see Part 4). Shortly afterwards class B16 No. 2364 was rebuilt at Darlington, strictly in accordance with Gresley tradition, in particular the fitting of his conjugated valve gear which Thompson would never have introduced (see Part 2B). Then, in 1938 a scheme was considered at Darlington to rebuild a number of J21's for the Tebay line. This was probably Thompson inspired and would have lapsed after the more cautious Peppercorn took over from Thompson in July 1938 (see Part 5).

Thompson 1941

Thompson took over from Gresley at a critical period in the 1939-45 War when normal standards of locomotive maintenance were low and there was an even greater need for the simplification and standardisation of locomotive types and parts. It was not long before Thompson's first proposals were made known, which covered new designs, rebuilding of existing classes and the retention of certain types for specialised needs. Most of the proposals have already been dealt with in earlier Parts of this series, but it is convenient here to set out the salient features of the whole scheme, so that it may be appreciated that a good deal of thought had been applied to the whole philosophy and it was not necessarily a case of destroying the foundations laid by a predecessor.

Two Pacific types were proposed, identical in all respects except for the diameter of the coupled wheels. There would be a 6ft. 8in. variety for high speed main line passenger services, based on the A4 class as regards boiler and cylinder dimensions, but without streamlining. The intention was to fit A4 boilers and cylinders to the A1's and A3's as they became due for renewal, so eliminating the 180 and 220lb. boilers. The 6ft. 2in. version was for new construction to replace classes P1, P2 and V2, and the heavier

work performed by classes B7, B16 and K3. The 4,200-gallon Group Standard tender would be attached. See Part 2A for further details.

Three main types of 4-6-0 were envisaged: two for immediate use and one for new construction on a long term basis. The 6ft. 8in. type comprised class B17 converted to two-cylinder engines to cover express passenger work on the G.E. Section, and also any need for large six-coupled engines elsewhere. The engines would have standard 20in. by 26in. cylinders and the B17 boiler pressed to 220lb. per sq. in. See Part 2B for further details. The 5ft. 8in. type was to be formed by converting class B7 to two-cylinder engines, with cylinders and boilers standard with the B17 class rebuilds. These engines were intended to cover the work of the K2's and some of the K3's. In the event, class B7 was not rebuilt. For new construction there would be a 6ft. 2in. type, to replace in service eventually "all the 4-6-0's not covered by the 6ft. 2in. Pacifics, to replace the D11's, D49's and all heavy 4-4-0 engines, the C1's and other passenger Atlantics, the K2's and K3's not already covered, the J39's and J6's together with other 0-6-0 tender engines at present subject to fairly high speeds." The new engines would have standard cylinders and boilers, whilst the tender would be either the large or small Group Standard tender as required. 410 of these engines were eventually built between 1942 and 1952 (see class B1, Part 2B).

It will be seen that only the B17's and B7's were considered suitable for retaining as standard classes, once they had been fitted with standard cylinders and boilers. The B16's were a special case as they were being rebuilt at Darlington under a Gresley modernisation plan, though none had been dealt with since March 1940. Rebuilding was resumed in 1944 and it is interesting to observe that there was no intention on the part of Thompson to fit his standard cylinders to this class. (Standard boilers could not be fitted to class B16 because of the closer spacing of the engine frames in Darlington practice.)

The B12's were exempt from rebuilding and were "considered as special engines due to their weight". It was stated that a number of B12's would have to be retained for service on the Spey Bridge line (Keith to Elgin, via Craigellachie), though it was anticipated that the restrictions would be relaxed within the period necessary to complete the building programme and that the new 4-6-0's would then be allowed over this line.

All the other existing 4-6-0 classes not already mentioned would be fitted with standard cylinders and boiler when their condition warranted alteration. In fact the only 4-6-0 class affected was the B3. One of the two Caprotti members of the class, No. 6166, was rebuilt in 1943, but the official verdict was : "6166 rebuilt. Remaining five engines to be scrapped in due course. Rebuild not satisfactory".

Three 4-4-0 types figured in the scheme. The first was a heavy type based on the D11 "Director" class, but the prototype selected was class D49 No. 365 *The Morpeth*, which was rebuilt in September 1942 (see Part 4). The rebuild was not a success and none of the D10's or D11's was fitted with a D49 boiler, and the order to rebuild a further four D49's was eventually cancelled in August 1948.

The second 4-4-0 proposal was for a light-weight design with an axle load limited to 18 tons. The basis was the D15 "Claud Hamilton" class, but with 6ft. 8in. instead of 7ft. coupled wheels. Altogether there were seventeen existing classes considered suitable for rebuilding into this one lightweight class. Later it was decided to replace the "Claud" boiler by an entirely new design, as also proposed for the new lightweight 0-6-0 type, with the following heating surface figure:

Tubes and flues	1110 sq. ft.
Firebox	126 sq. ft.
Superheater	264 sq. ft.
Total	1500 sq. ft.
Grate area	22 sq. ft.
Boiler pressure	200 lb./sq. in.

No engines were rebuilt and Stratford Works were left to carry on rebuilding the D15's and D16's with the round-topped firebox boilers introduced by Thompson to the class in 1933 (see Part 3C).

The third 4-4-0 scheme was intended for new construction, which seems quite remarkable for a period as late as the 1940's. The basis was once again class D15, but with 6ft. 2in. wheels. The boiler was finally settled on the J11-type, pressed to 200 lb. per sq. in. Although nothing came of the proposal, it was still actively under consideration as late as the second half of 1943. Unlike the majority of the schemes illustrated in this book, no registered drawing was prepared, but a full engine diagram was completed instead (see accompanying illustration).

Two 0-6-0 goods engine types figured in the standardisation plans. A heavy type was based on class J39, using a boiler standard with the heavy 4-4-0. This would replace all the existing 0-6-0's having an axle load in excess of 18 tons. It was not anticipated that the need for new construction would be great once the standard 4-6-0 (class B1) had become established. It should be noted that Darlington were building J39's at this time. A lightweight 0-6-0 type was proposed to cover the twenty 0-6-0 classes with an axle load less than 18 tons. This was based on class J11, fitted with a new boiler pressed to 200 lb. per sq. in. Between July 1942 and 1953 thirty-one J11's were rebuilt with piston valves, but the ordinary J11 boilers were retained (see Part 5).

The J21's were mentioned as being a special case as several would be retained for service on the Tebay line, there being no standard class suitable to replace them.

Only one 2-6-0 design featured in Thompson's scheme, this being the existing class K4, retaining its three-cylinder arrangement. The decision to rebuild class K3 with two cylinders came later, in June 1943, whilst the intention to rebuild class K4 came later still, in February 1945.

One heavy 2-8-0 goods engine class was proposed, to replace the four classes of 2-8-0, four classes of 0-8-0, the J19, J20 and J38 classes, plus any other small-wheeled engines not covered by the standard 0-6-0's. The O4 was a natural choice and it was planned to gradually reboiler the O1's, O2's and O4's with the standard boiler (carried out in the case of certain O2's and O4's) and to fit standard cylinders when renewals were necessary (applied in the case of certain O4's). See also Part 6B.

Two standard shunting tank engines were considered necessary and the existing J50 and J72 classes would form the basis for heavy and light duties respectively. Fifteen J50's were ordered in July 1941, but these were cancelled in 1942 when it was decided to substitute an 0-8-0T as the standard heavy shunting engine (see class J50 Part 8A and class Q1 Part 9B). For light duties twenty-eight J72's were built after nationalisation, which is remarkable for a class which first saw the light of day in 1898 (fig. 97) (see Part 8B).

Only one 0-6-2T class was considered necessary and it was thought that the N7 was the most suitable as its axle load was limited to 18 tons. It was envisaged that any post-war electrification would be likely to release a number of N7's from the London area and these would be retained in preference to the N5's and N15's. The N7's would replace the whole of the lighter 0-6-2T's, the 4-4-2T's and the 2-4-2T's. It should be noted that a further twenty years elapsed before they were displaced fully by electrification, by which time there was no alternative work to be found for them.

The class V3 2-6-2T's were to be retained, to replace the various 4-6-2T engines, the N2's and the heavier work performed by the N5's. The proposal for the new 2-6-4T design did not appear until January 1943 (see Part 9A).

Five Year Plan 1946-50

At a meeting of the Emergency Board on 26th April 1945, proposals were agreed to adopt ten classes as standard, afterwards identified as being A1, A2, B1, J11, J50, J72, K1, L1, O1 and Q1. A five year building programme to 31st December 1950 was agreed in principle and details were given of the 1,000 locomotives in the programme, as follows:—

Classes	No.
A1, A2	75
B1	400
O1	160
J11	115
L1	110
J50	75
*	65
Total	1000

* Light shunting engine of type to be decided. (This turned out to be class J72).

It was also stated at the meeting that it was proposed to maintain for some considerable time the Pacific locomotives and eight other classes of comparatively new construction, afterwards identified as B2, B16, D49, K5, N7, V1, V2 and V3, although class N7 is omitted on one quoted list. The programme was revised several times before it was completed, for example the order for J50's was replaced by the purchase in 1946 of seventy-five surplus 0-6-0ST's from the Ministry of Supply (see class J94, Part 8B).

Peppercorn 1946-48

In the immediate post-war period a team was sent to the United States to report on current American practice. Peppercorn (who was to succeed Thompson in June 1946) covered steam locomotive design and maintenance aspects and in the ensuing report, dated March 1946, gives the impression that he is more enthusiastic over the New York Central Railroad's latest 4-8-4 Niagaras than the diesel-electric locomotives. The report considers the introduction of a 4-8-4 type for high speed passenger service on the East Coast main line, and for a start suggests the trial construction of one locomotive having 6ft. 8in. diameter coupled wheels, and an additional set of 6ft. 4in. diameter coupled wheels and axles which could be substituted for separate trials on express freight trains. Two outline drawings were prepared at Doncaster, in February and April 1946 respectively, to give an impression of their outward appearance. The 4-8-2 proposal of 1939 was redrawn also in February 1946 in the light of modern thinking. Thompson was still C.M.E. at Doncaster and would no doubt have disliked the front-end appearance, had he seen this drawing. It should be remembered though that the Chief Draughtsman at Doncaster was directly responsible to the Mechanical Engineer, Peppercorn and not to Thompson. This new 4-8-2 scheme is also illustrated in the accompanying drawing and should be compared with the 4-8-4 scheme prepared at the same time. No details were worked out and the scheme was not pursued.

In 1947 there was a proposal to build a light-weight 5ft. 2in. 2-6-0, the most interesting feature of which was perhaps the tender cab, suggesting employment on the line from Barnard Castle to Kirkby Stephen over Stainmore. The first drawing prepared in May 1947 differed from the succeeding August scheme (here illustrated) in having an eighteen-element superheater, whereas by substituting a smaller twelve-element superheater the heating surface figure for the smoke tubes could be increased from 533 to 718 sq. ft. The boiler pressure was to have been 200 lb. per sq. in., but raising this to 225 lb. and reducing the diameter of the cylinders from 17in. to 16in. was also considered. The scheme was being pursued too close to nationalisation to be put into fruition as the L.M.S. already had a similar type in production and indeed Darlington Works built forty engines to this design in 1951-52.

The leading particulars of the August 1947 scheme are set out in the accompanying table.

Cylinders (2 outside)	17" x 26"
Motion	Walschaerts
Boiler:	
Max. diameter	4' 6"
Pitch	8' 3"
Heating surface:	
Firebox	102.60 sq. ft.
Tubes	717.87 sq. ft.
Flues (12)	175.20 sq. ft.
Total evaporative	995.20 sq. ft.*
Superheater (12)	160.00 sq. ft.
Total	1155.20 sq. ft.*
Grate area	19.4 sq. ft.
Boiler pressure	200 lb./sq. in.
Leading wheels	3' 2"
Coupled wheels	5' 2"
Tender wheels	3' 9"
Tractive effort (85%)	20,603 lb.
Length over buffers	52' 9"
Wheelbase:	
Engine	8' 6" + 6' 6" + 7' 0" = 22' 0"
Tender	6' 6" + 6' 6" = 13' 0"
Total	43' 6"
Weight (full):	
Engine	50T 5C
Tender	39T 6C
Total	89T 11C
Adhesive	42T 15C
Max. axle load	14T 5C
Water capacity	3,000 gallons
Coal capacity	5T 0C

* These totals, shown thus on the drawing, do not agree in the decimal places.

Eve of Nationalisation

Almost on the eve of Nationalisation, schemes were being prepared for internal combustion power. By June 1947 schedules had been formulated for the introduction of diesel-mechanical railcars capable of being worked singly, in multiple units with or without trailers or alternatively two units with a standard coach between them. Each car would have two 105 b.h.p. engines with preselective electro-pneumatic gear change, with a maximum speed of 65 m.p.h. In July 1947 consideration was being given to the provision of twenty-five diesel-electric locomotives in replacement of thirty-two Pacifics, to work between London and Edinburgh, and approval was given to invite builders to submit designs and quotations. In October 1947 a recommendation to purchase 181 350 h.p. diesel-electric shunting locomotives to replace 217 steam locomotives was approved, though the number was reduced to 176 (see class J45 in this Part). Meanwhile the L.N.E.R. had already arranged to take delivery of a 200 h.p. diesel-mechanical locomotive for trials (see page 3).

British Railways 1948

Immediately following Nationalisation, a Locomotive Standards Committee was appointed on 8th January 1948 to deal with all matters affecting standardisation of locomotive types and details. There was an urgent need to formulate the 1950 building programme, by selecting for general use the most suitable existing type in each of the six traffic categories. Thereafter the classes selected would continue to appear in future programmes until such time as the new British Railways standard designs were introduced. The traffic categories and the suggested prototypes quoted by the Railway Executive were as follows:—

Mixed Traffic Tender (large wheels), L.N.E.R. class B1

Mixed Traffic Tender (medium wheels), L.M.S. "3000" class 2-6-0

Heavy Mixed Traffic Tank, L.N.E.R. class L1

Light Mixed Traffic Tank, G.W.R. "4575" class 2-6-2T

Light Freight Tender, L.M.S. "6400" class 2-6-0

Dock Shunting Tank, no prototype quoted.

Following their investigation, the Committee recommended that the proposal to build for general use in 1950 (and subsequently until new British Railways designs were evolved) one of the existing designs in each traffic category should be abandoned and that each Region should continue to build engines to its existing designs. Otherwise some, if not all, of the Regions would have had to build, and for many years afterwards maintain and operate, engines which conformed to neither their own existing regional standards nor the future British Railways standards. The Committee also considered the standardisation of parts, but were of the opinion that where the change from existing type of component to a new standard would involve large numbers of engines in the same class being differently equipped over a long period of years, the benefits of attempting to achieve standardisation would be lost.

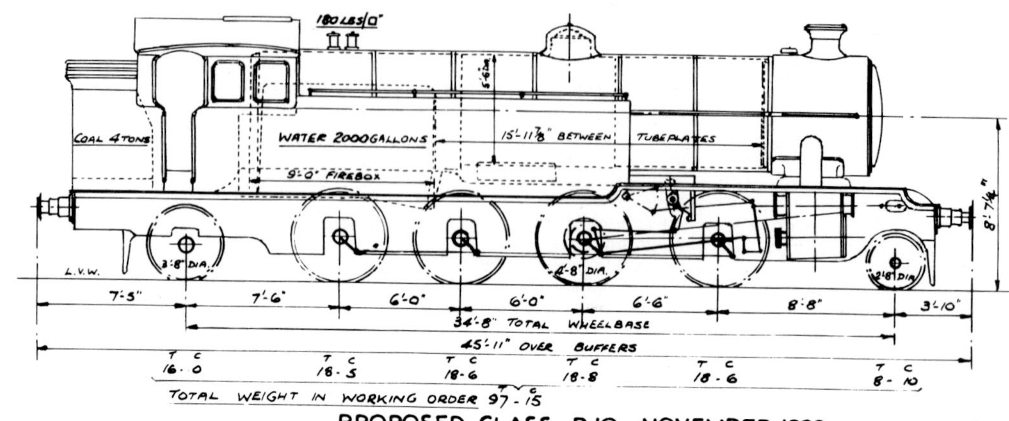

PROPOSED CLASS P 10 - NOVEMBER 1929

1

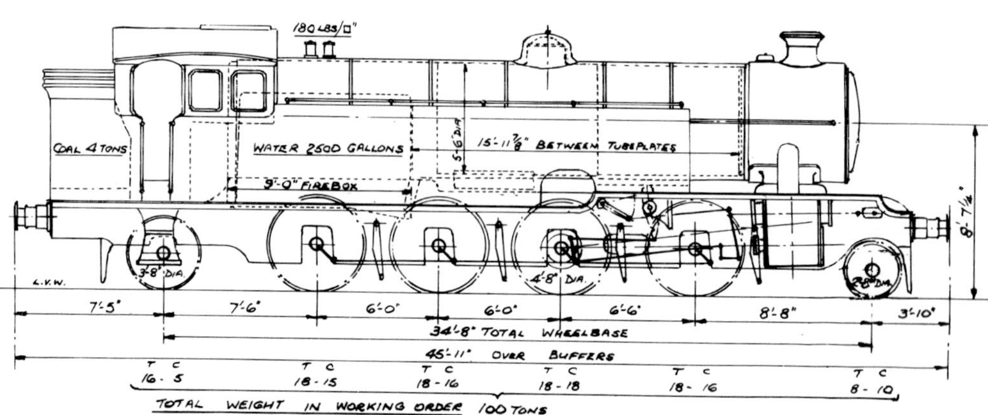

PROPOSED CLASS P 10 - NOVEMBER 1929

2

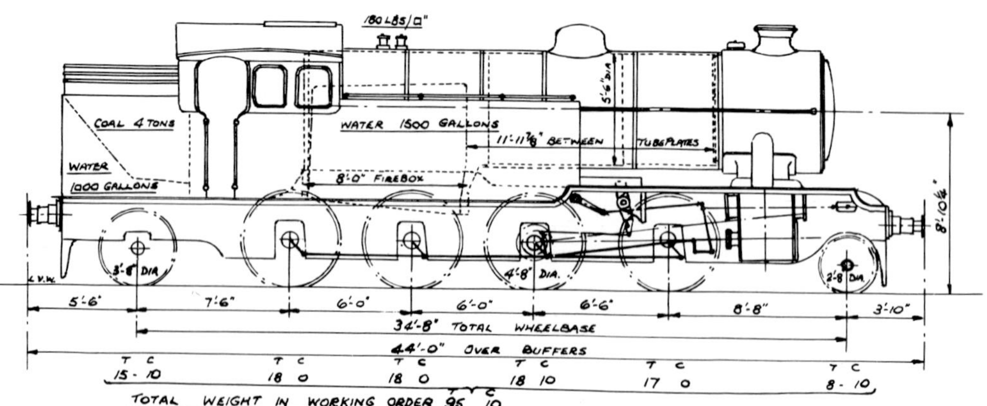

PROPOSED CLASS P 10 - NOVEMBER 1929

3

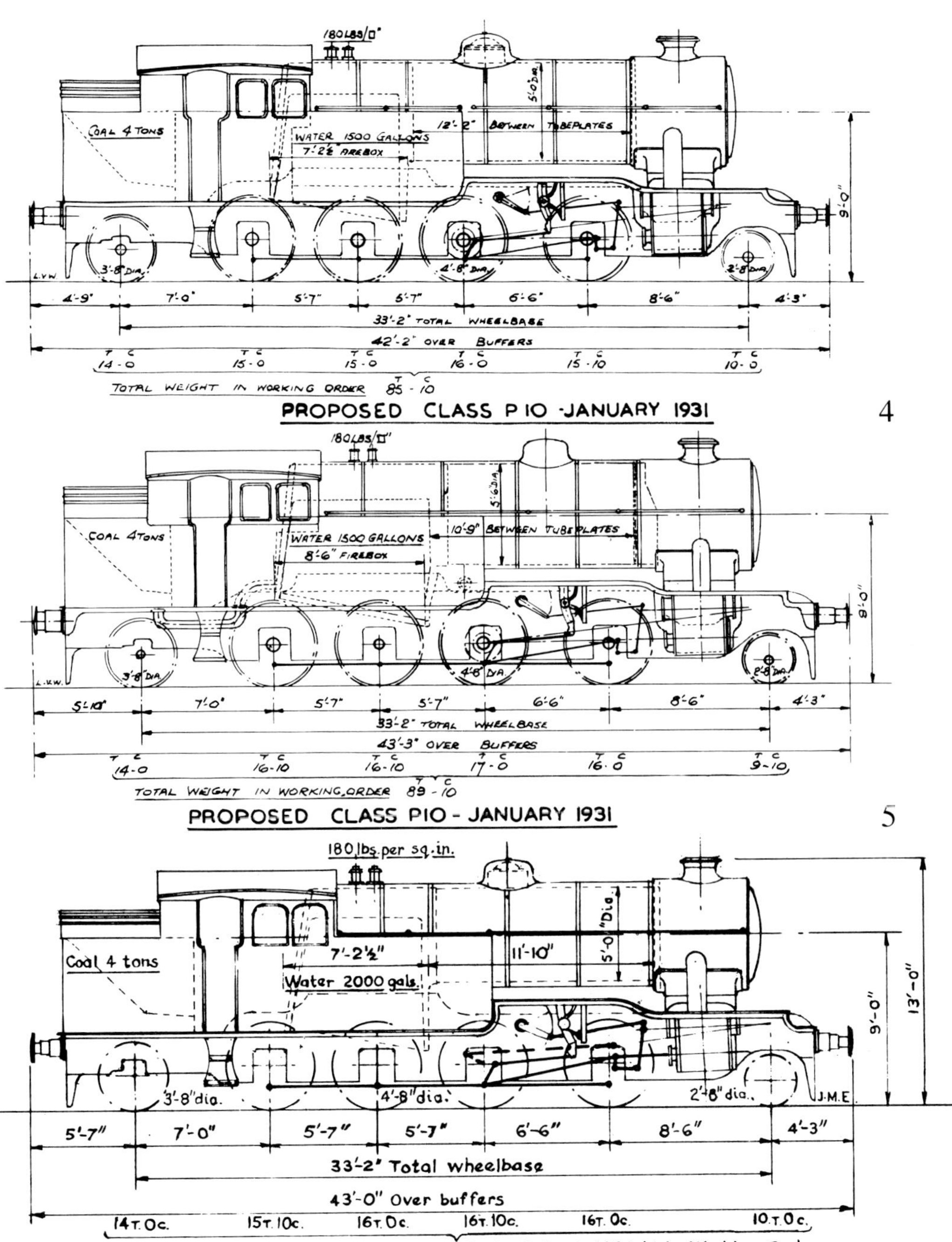

180 LBS/☐"
COAL 4 TONS
WATER 1500 GALLONS
7'-2½" FIREBOX
12'-2" BETWEEN TUBEPLATES
5'-0" DIA
L.V.W.
3'-8" DIA
4'-6" DIA
2'-8" DIA
9'-0"
4'-9"
7'-0"
5'-7"
5'-7"
6'-6"
8'-6"
4'-3"
33'-2" TOTAL WHEELBASE
42'-2" OVER BUFFERS
T C 14-0
T C 15-0
T C 15-0
T C 16-0
T C 15-10
T C 10-0
TOTAL WEIGHT IN WORKING ORDER T C 85-10
PROPOSED CLASS P10 - JANUARY 1931
4

180 LBS/☐"
COAL 4 TONS
WATER 1500 GALLONS
8'-6" FIREBOX
10'-9" BETWEEN TUBEPLATES
5'-6" DIA
L.V.W.
3'-8" DIA
4'-6" DIA
2'-8" DIA
9'-0"
5'-10"
7'-0"
5'-7"
5'-7"
6'-6"
8'-6"
4'-3"
33'-2" TOTAL WHEELBASE
43'-3" OVER BUFFERS
T C 14-0
T C 16-10
T C 16-10
T C 17-0
T C 16-0
T C 9-10
TOTAL WEIGHT IN WORKING ORDER T C 89-10
PROPOSED CLASS P10 - JANUARY 1931
5

180 lbs. per sq. in.
Coal 4 tons
7'-2½"
Water 2000 gals.
11'-10"
5'-0" Dia.
3'-8" dia.
4'-8" dia.
2'-8" dia.
J.M.E.
13'-0"
9'-0"
5'-7"
7'-0"
5'-7"
5'-7"
6'-6"
8'-6"
4'-3"
33'-2" Total wheelbase
43'-0" Over buffers
14 T. 0 c.
15 T. 10 c.
16 T. 0 c.
16 T. 10 c.
16 T. 0 c.
10 T. 0 c.
88 T. 0 c. Estimated Weight in Working Order
PROPOSED CLASS P10 - JULY 1931.
6

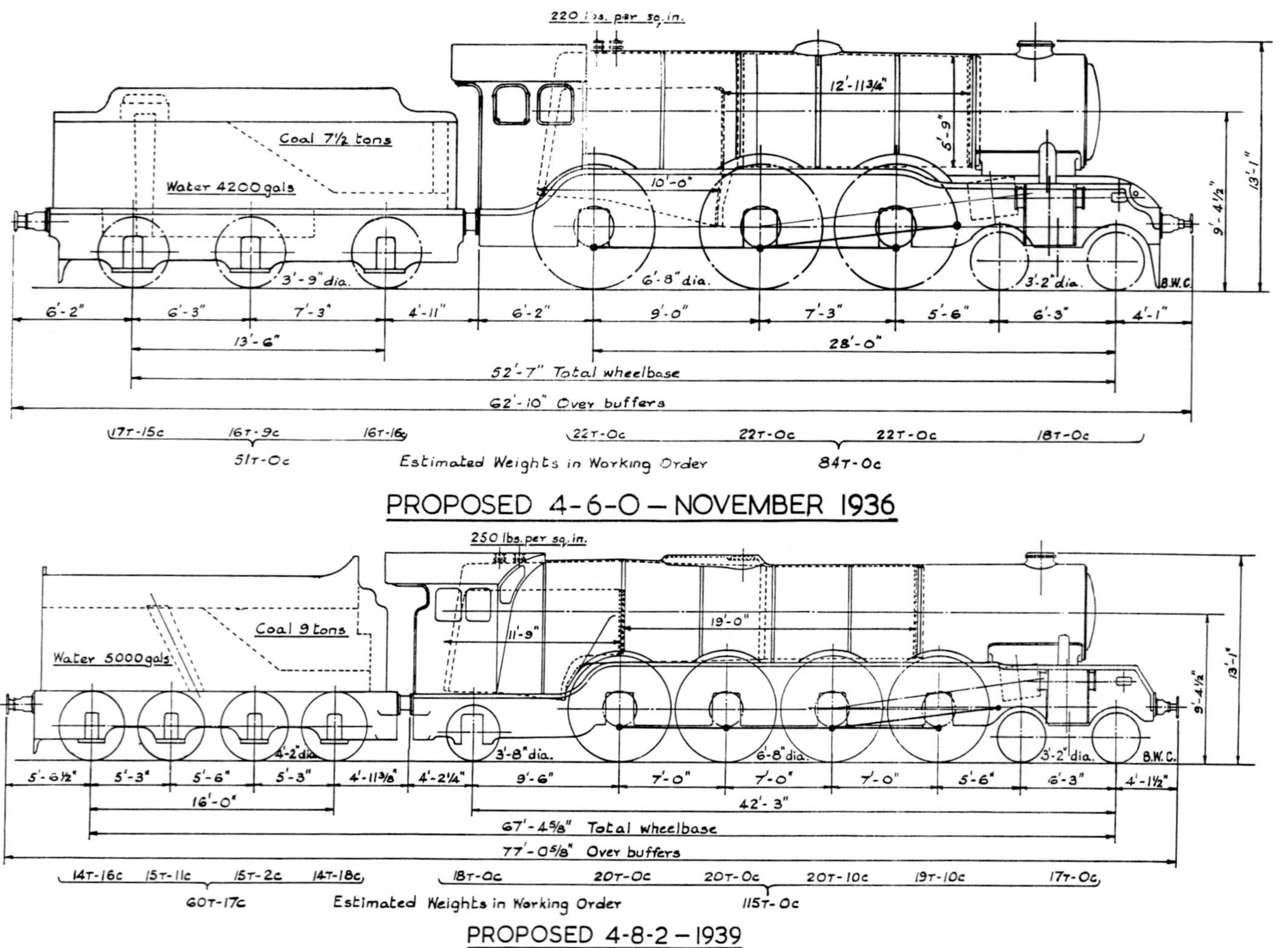

220 lbs. per sq.in.
12'-11¾"
5'-9"
13'-1"
9'-4½"
Coal 7½ tons
Water 4200 gals
10'-0"
6'-8" dia.
3'-9" dia.
3'-2" dia.
B.W.C.
6'-2"
6'-3"
7'-3"
4'-11"
6'-2"
9'-0"
7'-3"
5'-6"
6'-3"
4'-1"
13'-6"
28'-0"
52'-7" Total wheelbase
62'-10" Over buffers
17T-15c
16T-9c
16T-16c
22T-0c
22T-0c
22T-0c
18T-0c
51T-0c
Estimated Weights in Working Order
84T-0c
PROPOSED 4-6-0 — NOVEMBER 1936
250 lbs. per sq.in.
19'-0"
11'-9"
13'-1"
9'-4½"
Coal 9 tons
Water 5000 gals
3'-8" dia.
6'-8" dia.
4'-2" dia.
3'-2" dia.
B.W.C.
5'-6½"
5'-3"
5'-6"
5'-3"
4'-11⅜"
4'-2¼"
9'-6"
7'-0"
7'-0"
7'-0"
5'-6"
6'-3"
4'-1½"
16'-0"
42'-3"
67'-4⅝" Total wheelbase
77'-0⅝" Over buffers
14T-16c
15T-11c
15T-2c
14T-18c
18T-0c
20T-0c
20T-0c
20T-10c
19T-10c
17T-0c
60T-17c
Estimated Weights in Working Order
115T-0c
PROPOSED 4-8-2 — 1939

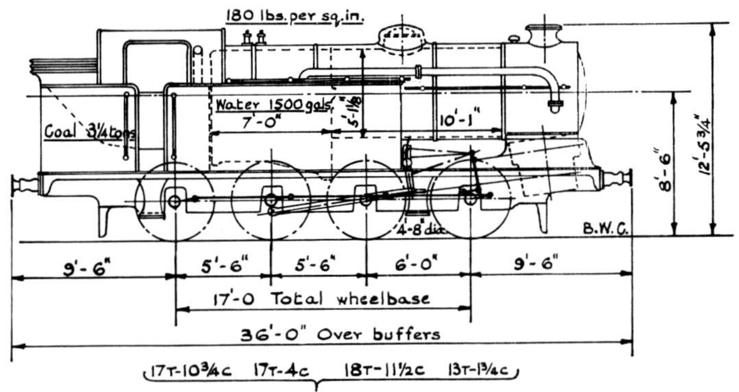

PROPOSED CLASS Q – JUNE 1930

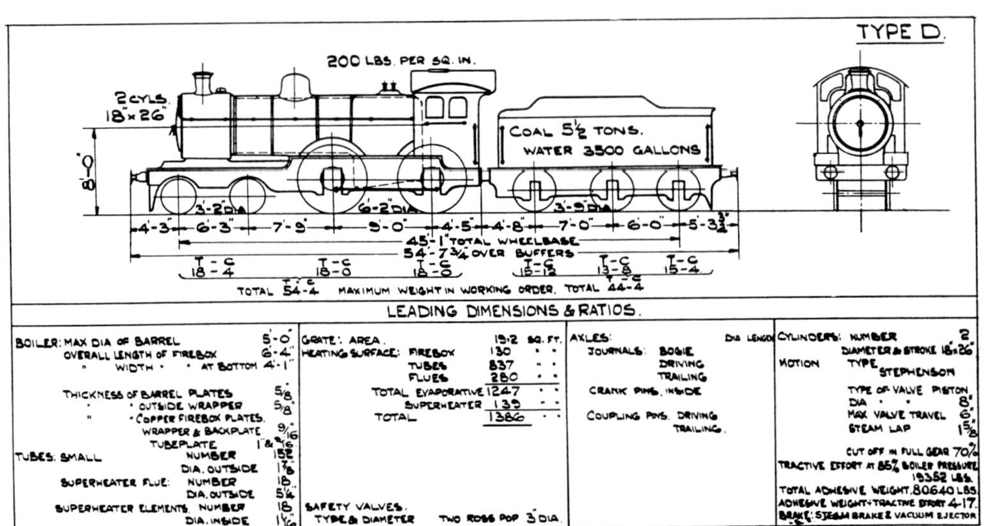

LEADING DIMENSIONS & RATIOS.

BOILER:			GRATE:		AXLES:			CYLINDERS:	
MAX DIA OF BARREL	5'-0"	GRATE: AREA	19·2 SQ. FT.	AXLES:	DIA LENGTH	CYLINDERS: NUMBER	2		
OVERALL LENGTH OF FIREBOX	6'-4"	HEATING SURFACE: FIREBOX	130	JOURNALS: BOGIE		DIAMETER & STROKE 18 x 26			
" WIDTH " " AT BOTTOM	4'-1"	TUBES	837	DRIVING		MOTION TYPE STEPHENSON			
		FLUES	280	TRAILING		TYPE OF VALVE PISTON			
THICKNESS OF BARREL PLATES	5/8"	TOTAL EVAPORATIVE	1247	CRANK PINS. INSIDE		DIA 8"			
" OUTSIDE WRAPPER	5/8"	SUPERHEATER	139			MAX VALVE TRAVEL 6"			
" COPPER FIREBOX PLATES.		TOTAL	1386	COUPLING PINS. DRIVING		STEAM LAP 1 5/8"			
WRAPPER & BACKPLATE	9/16"			TRAILING.		CUT OFF IN FULL GEAR 70%			
TUBEPLATE	1 & 9/16"					TRACTIVE EFFORT AT 85% BOILER PRESSURE 19352 LBS.			
TUBES: SMALL NUMBER	152					TOTAL ADHESIVE WEIGHT 80640 LBS.			
DIA. OUTSIDE	1 7/8"					ADHESIVE WEIGHT ÷ TRACTIVE EFFORT 4·17.			
SUPERHEATER FLUE: NUMBER	18					BRAKE: STEAM BRAKE & VACUUM EJECTOR			
DIA. OUTSIDE	5¼"								
SUPERHEATER ELEMENTS. NUMBER	18	SAFETY VALVES.							
DIA. INSIDE	1 1/16"	TYPE & DIAMETER	TWO ROSS POP 3" DIA.						

PROPOSED 4-4-0 — 1943

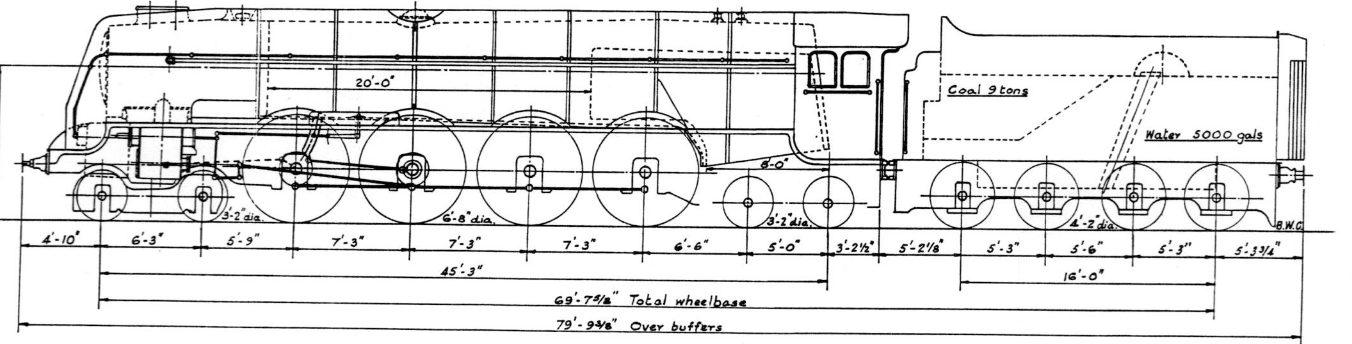

20'-0"
Coal 9 tons
Water 5000 gals
9'-4½"
6'-0"
3'-2" dia.
6'-8" dia.
3'-2" dia.
4'-2" dia.
B.W.C.
4'-10"
6'-3"
5'-9"
7'-3"
7'-3"
7'-3"
6'-6"
5'-0"
3'-2½"
5'-2⅛"
5'-3"
5'-6"
5'-3"
5'-3¾"
45'-3"
16'-0"
69'-7⅝" Total wheelbase
79'-9⅞" Over buffers
PROPOSED 4-8-4—FEBRUARY 1946

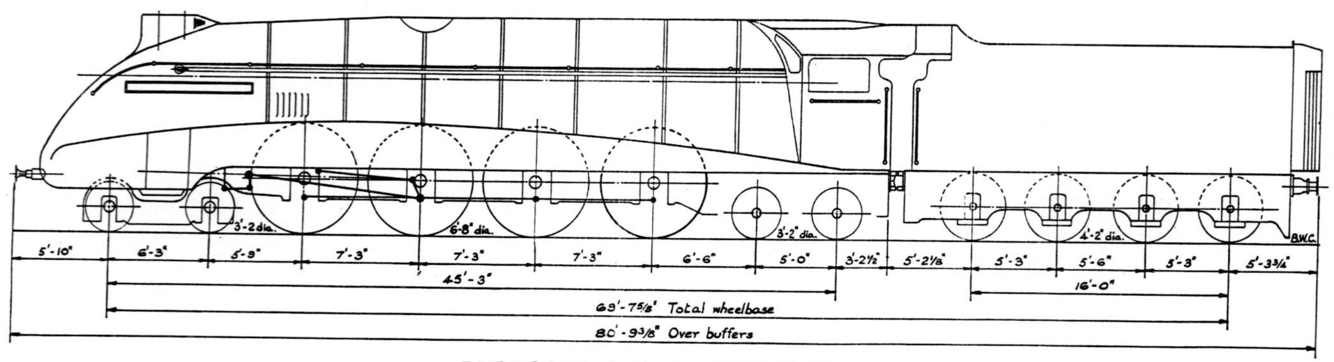

3'-2" dia.
6'-8" dia.
3'-2" dia.
4'-2" dia.
B.W.C.
5'-10"
6'-3"
5'-9"
7'-3"
7'-3"
7'-3"
6'-6"
5'-0"
3'-2½"
5'-2⅛"
5'-3"
5'-6"
5'-3"
5'-3¾"
45'-3"
16'-0"
69'-7⅝" Total wheelbase
80'-9⅜" Over buffers
PROPOSED 4-8-4—APRIL 1946

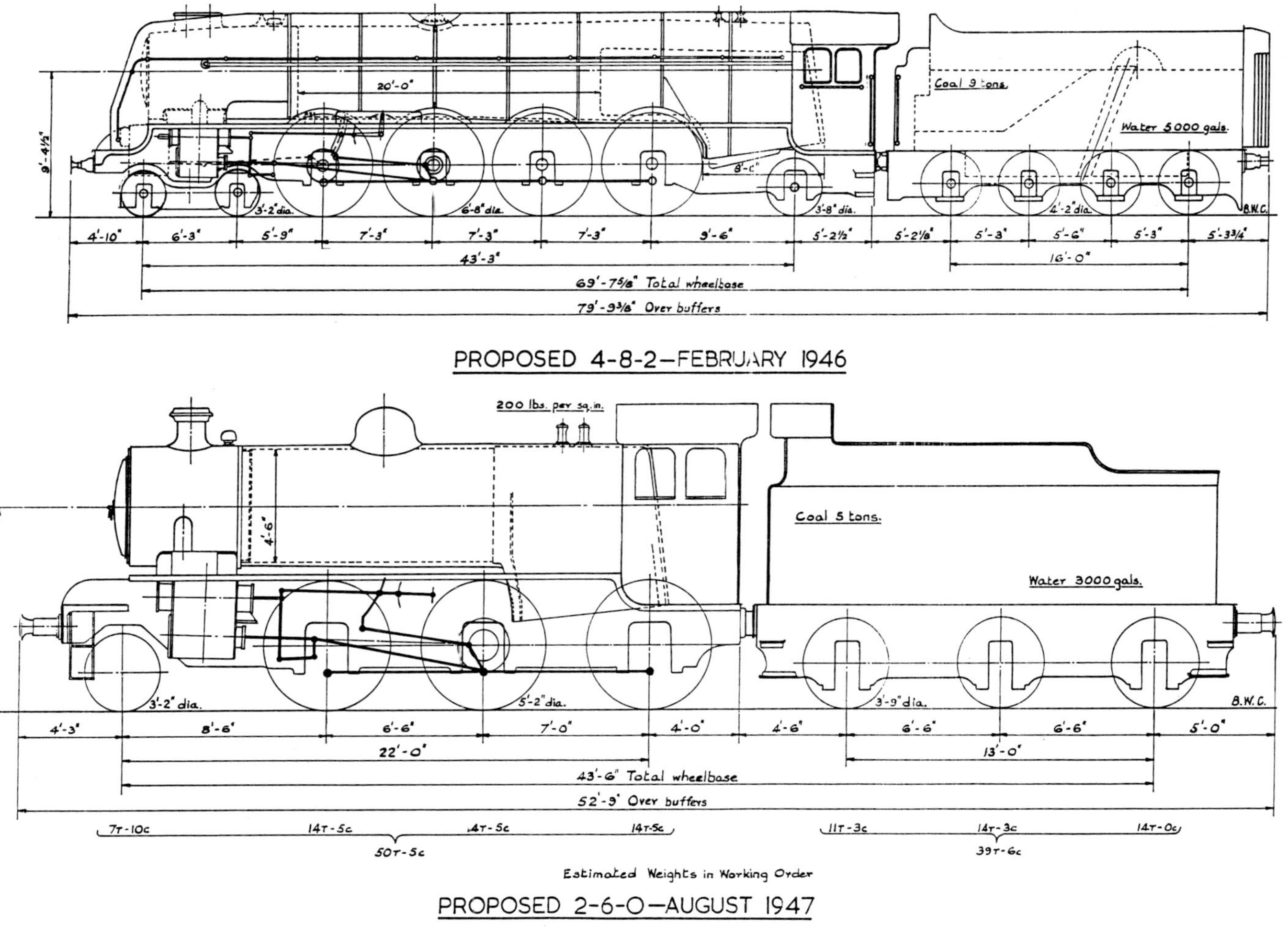

Coal 9 tons.
Water 5000 gals.
20'-0"
8'-c"
9'-4½"
3'-2" dia.
6'-8" dia.
3'-8" dia.
4'-2" dia.
B.W.C.
4'-10"
6'-3"
5'-9"
7'-3"
7'-3"
7'-3"
9'-6"
5'-2½"
5'-2⅛"
5'-3"
5'-6"
5'-3"
5'-3¾"
43'-3"
16'-0"
69'-7⅝" Total wheelbase
79'-9⅜" Over buffers
PROPOSED 4-8-2—FEBRUARY 1946
200 lbs. per sq. in.
Coal 5 tons.
Water 3000 gals.
4'-6"
8'-3"
3'-2" dia.
5'-2" dia.
3'-9" dia.
B.W.C.
4'-3"
8'-6"
6'-6"
7'-0"
4'-0"
4'-6"
6'-6"
6'-6"
5'-0"
22'-0"
13'-0"
43'-6" Total wheelbase
52'-9" Over buffers
7T-10c
14T-5c
14T-5c
14T-5c
11T-3c
14T-3c
14T-0c
50T-5c
39T-6c
Estimated Weights in Working Order
PROPOSED 2-6-0—AUGUST 1947

BOILER NUMBERINGS

The Boiler Explosions Act of 1882 provided for the registration and regular inspection of pressure vessels. Although the Act did not specifically state that individual boilers should be numbered, the railway companies as the largest users of boilers were apparently advised that this would be wise. The number was usually displayed either on a plate attached to the back of the boiler above the firehole door or was stamped on a nut attached to the end of a stay in a similar position. From 1925 the L.N.E.R. adopted a standard boiler plate which gave the number, maker, date new, working pressure, dates of last hydraulic and steam tests with pressure to which tested (fig. 98).

Constitutent companies of the L.N.E.R. took differing views on the series of numbers to be used, but they fell into three broad divisions, viz: the same number as the running number of the locomotive; an individual number for each boiler having no correspondence with the locomotive number; a maker's works — or job — number which was usually concerned with boilers bought from outside contractors. It was not until almost three years after the demise of the L.N.E.R. that its boilers were brought into a homogenous series, each of the main workshops having hitherto continued to use their pre-Grouping method (with certain slight variations). So the most convenient way to examine the L.N.E.R. boiler numbering system is to look at those of each works.

Doncaster

To meet the legal requirements, it was Stirling's custom to use the same number for the boiler as for the engine on which it was mounted. This presented no difficulty as there was no interchanging, and the boiler papers could be kept with those appertaining to the engine, all being filed under the number of the locomotive. There was thus no need for the boilers to be numbered, but from January 1896 the system was changed. By then, steel boilers were replacing the wrought-iron type, their life was appreciably longer, and they could usefully be interchanged. Starting with No. 234 in January 1896, new boilers (which were only fitted to engines in the Capital List) were given numbers the same as the engine to which they were first fitted. When a second-hand boiler was re-used, it was given the number of the engine to which it was next fitted. For some time, few boilers were re-used, because Doncaster were busy on the replacement of wrought-iron boilers, which were usually scrapped. Not until mid-1901 was an already numbered, and used, boiler considered for putting into another engine. The first example seems to have been the 1891-built boiler from No. 566 which became spare in December 1900 and then was ex-works in July 1901 on engine No. 29, both 566 and 29 being 0-4-2's of G.N.R. class F2. About this time Doncaster were building new 4-2-2 No. 263, the boiler for it being stamped with that number, but in April 1900 a new boiler had been built (and numbered 263) and was already installed in the old 2-4-0 No. 263, which had come from the West Yorkshire Railway Co. in 1865. To avoid duplication in this and similar cases Ivatt instituted a duplicate boiler list, starting at 1701, and the 1900-built boiler changed from 263 to 1710. This list ultimately ran from 1701 to 1757, reached by November 1904. It was used for boilers not so far numbered, which then got a number coincident with that of the engine on which it was currently fitted (provided that boiler number was vacant) and for boilers of engines on the A list, because no boiler number was to have a suffix. Engines on that list which had a boiler already numbered were allowed to keep their number, if acceptable, otherwise a 17XX number was given to them.

Stirling Single No. 1 (still happily operative) provides a useful example of Doncaster boiler numberings. Its original boiler of 1870 had been replaced in December 1880 and both these were wrought-iron boilers. Its third boiler, put on in July 1889, was a steel one and served until September 1900. None of these was numbered but their records were kept in No. 1's file. The engine then acquired a second-hand boiler which had started work in July 1896 on No. 664 and which, from September 1900, was numbered 1. This boiler and the engine were taken out of stock on 23rd September 1907 and, apart from participation in the Imperial International Exhibition of 1909, were then stored in King's Cross shed until November 1924, when it was sent to Doncaster. So that No. 1 could be steamed to run in the Stockton & Darlington Centenary procession, its 1896-built boiler was changed by Doncaster to a similar one which had started work in August 1900 on No. 778 and had been stamped with that number. Engine 778 had lost it in June 1904 and it then lay spare until July 1910 when it went to engine 668 which had it until June 1912, and three months later it became Stationary Boiler No. 268 at Doncaster Carr engine shed, the 778 number being removed. Its absence caused perturbation to the N.R.M.'s Chief Mechanical Engineer when, in 1980, he was assessing its suitability for steaming again. Fortunately the records maintained by two of our authors came to his rescue, by providing the building date, and where, and how long it had been in service.

Until the 1896 change running and boiler numbers coincided and there was a practically continuous series from 1 to 1270, plus 1301-85 on Ivatt's 4-4-0's built October 1897 to January 1901, and 1501-30 on his 4-4-2 tanks built February 1899 to November 1901. Below 1270, the only boiler numbers never used were 945-948 and 1174-80. After boiler 1270, the next thirty built (and numbered 1271 to 1300) were all renewals on older engines with widely varying running numbers. For example, when 0-6-0T No. 153 (built in October 1880) had its original boiler replaced in August 1902, it got 1280 which served it until August 1926. Further boilers — both for spares and new engines — took boiler numbers 1386 to 1500, thus closing that gap, and 1531 to 1687 were used similarly. In November/December 1901 there was a minor variation with boiler numbers 1428 to 1430 being allocated to second-hand boilers. Boilers 1658 to 1687 built in 1905 all went to new engines, twenty to Atlantics and ten to 0-6-0 tanks but 1688 to 1700 were never allocated, the duplicate boiler numbers 1701 to 1757 impeding further progress. Amongst the latter were 43 boilers (with former numbers ranging from 2 to 999) taken from engines which had been cut up, but which were capable of further use, interspersed with fourteen recently built boilers. These latter included some quite interesting items, because in 1902 new boilers 1743 and 1748 were put into small Atlantic No. 271 and the original large Atlantic No. 251. There was also a curious use of three low numbers, 60 being allocated to the boiler of the Doncaster-built compound Atlantic No. 292 and 98 to that put in the Vulcan-built Atlantic No. 1300, whilst for some obscure reason the boiler from 1054 was renumbered 67 when it was fitted to engine No. 970 in February 1903.

During 1905 the authorities at Doncaster took a fresh look at numbering systems, not only for new boilers, but also for new tenders. For the latter it was decided to start a new series from 5001 upwards, whereas on boilers 5000 was simply added to the next new boiler after 1757. So boiler 6758 began work in October 1905 on 0-8-2 tank No. 127. Henceforward a continuous series had taken the numbering to 7661 as the last one constructed by the Great Northern Railway, although this was part way through Boiler Order No. 655 and orders already placed in the works would absorb numbers up to 7704. For an unknown reason, 7705 was never used, but the L.N.E.R. then continued the series and, by the time of its demise 25 years later, boiler number 9910 had been reached. There were a few gaps due to changes of intentions and these are shown in the accompanying list.

After nationalisation, Doncaster continued its own series of boiler numbers consecutively and by February 1949 had reached 9996. Prior to that (in 1946) a purchase of seventy-five class J94 shunting tanks had been made from the War Department, and their boiler numbers were the same as their works numbers which, coming from six different manufacturers, ranged from 1755 to 7295. Doncaster brought order to this state of affairs by changing their boiler numbers to 10001 to 10078, which included three spare boilers for the class. They also allocated boiler numbers 10079 to 10150 in their series to allow for any further class J94 which might be purchased, but none was and these numbers remained blank. Similarly, Doncaster allocated numbers 10151 to 10500 to boilers used on the Austerity class 2-8-0 engines which were purchased or maintained by L.N.E.R. workshops. Boiler numbers 10151 to 10371 were actually applied but were subsequently renumbered into the BR10 series 1 to 757.

Having accommodated these newcomers, Doncaster from June 1948 continued its own series from 10501 and early in 1952 finally reached number 10849, which was affixed to the boiler of North British Loco. Co.-built class B1 No. 61399, but from August 1950 the British Railways comprehensive boiler numbering system began to take effect, although it was well into 1954 before the last Doncaster number plate was supplanted. For instance, Doncaster boiler number 10847 applied to class B1 No. 61397 was not changed to B.R. number 28705 until July 1954.

DONCASTER BOILER NUMBERS NOT USED BY L.N.E.R.

7905-7922 Although made to Doncaster Boiler Order Nos. 693/4, they were built by Darlington and were given numbers by that works between D1873 and D1910. They were spare boilers for use by classes D2, D3, J1, J3 and N1.

8130-8132 Originally intended for three class N2 additional to an order for twenty placed with Hawthorn Leslie & Co., but subsequently cancelled.

8613-8616 Included in an order for ten class V1 placed 28/1/32, but order cut to six on 8/7/32 and the remaining four were cancelled.

8617-8621 Allocated to order placed 28/4/32 for five new class A3 engines. Order for engines and boilers cancelled 1/3/33.

8622-8629 Allocated to order placed 23/2/32 for eight new class O2 engines 2430-7, but boiler order transferred to Gorton which used Stratford series numbers for them.

8630-8639 Diagram 102 boilers intended for ten new 2-8-2 tank engines class P10 ordered 28/4/32 and cancelled 27/6/32.

8887-8896 Intended for ten class V1 for N.E. Area ordered 11/3/35, but cancelled 12/7/35.

9077-9098   For new class V2 engines 4776-4803. Building order transferred to Darlington who numbered the boilers between D2892 and D2937.

9289-9298   For ten class V2 ordered 25/1/40, but transferred to Darlington 9/6/41.

9299-9303   Intended for five class V3 for G.E. Section. Order placed 25/1/40, but not proceeded with and cancelled 25/1/43.

9367-9371   For five class V2 ordered 7/6/41, but transferred to Darlington 15/10/42.

9400-9409   Intended for ten class V3 for G.N. Section. Order placed 23/10/41, but not proceeded with and cancelled 25/1/43.

9455-9457   Not used and no details whatever entered into Boiler Order book.

9517   Not used and no details.

9595-9609   Boilers built by Darlington for Thompson A2/3 class engines 500/11-24 and given Darlington boiler numbers before despatch to Doncaster Works.

Gateshead

North Eastern Railway practice was entirely opposite to that at Doncaster; that Company's boilers were entered consecutively in the Boiler Register quite independent of the engine's running number as soon as each boiler completed its pressure test. When the consecutive numbering was started has not been established, but possibly stems from the total number of boilers in stock when requirements of the 1882 Act were put into effect. There were separate Registers for Gateshead and Darlington-built boilers, the prefixes G and D being used to differentiate between them, and York too had its own series. The earliest Gateshead number located is G793, built in October 1884 and by November 1887 this series had reached G1000. That same month Gateshead began a new list starting at G1 again as presumably the low numbered boilers in the previous list had by then been taken out of stock. As many of them would have been iron boilers, their working lives were appreciably shorter than more modern steel boilers, especially when the latter were favoured with treated feed water. By June 1900 this second list had also reached G1000 and again there was reversion to G1. No boiler from either of these lists survived to become L.N.E.R. property, the last one (G901) ceasing its working life with a class "398" 0-6-0 engine in June 1920. The third list had reached G983 in July 1911 and this was the final boiler constructed at Gateshead. The majority of these boilers saw running service in L.N.E.R. days and G979 was in regular use until September 1933. It served J24 class No. 1855 from May 1912 to January 1917 and then another J24 No. 1940 from February 1917 to September 1933.

York

The workshops there had facilities for building small boilers, almost all being for stationary use on cranes, swing bridges, pumping stations and workshops heating. However, amongst them was a batch of eight locomotive-type boilers constructed in 1888 for six new 0-4-0 tanks which ultimately became class Y7, and two for the 0-6-0 crane tanks which took class J78, all these boilers being identical. They were numbered Y31 to Y38 and the last one went out of service in December 1911. The stationary boilers had a YA prefix and the top number reached was YA181 constructed in December 1898 when boiler building at York ceased. Some of these boilers survived well after Grouping. For example, YA166 and YA169 started work in December 1898 at Hull Oil Gas Works and were not taken out of service until November 1928. Another, YA147, was newly installed in December 1900 as Pumping Boiler at Stockton where it served fifteen years. It was put up for sale in May 1916, but the sale order was withdrawn and the boiler was re-used for heating York Motor Garage where it survived until January 1934.

Darlington

The date from which this works numbered the boilers built there is not known, but to comply with the 1882 Act presumably those then in stock were numbered consecutively about that time. The earliest one discovered is D238 which was built in April 1881, and it is on record that the first 0-6-2 tank No. 14 (which became class N8) came out new in June 1886 with boiler No. D456. It was in that month that Darlington also changed over to steel for its boilers. Consecutive numbering in that list was continued until June 1911 when boiler number D2111 had been reached. This was the last boiler of a batch of ten built as replacements for the 0-4-4 tanks which became class G5. However, in the previous month the first of another batch of ten started work on some 0-6-0 tanks (class J71 later) and for them there was reversion to D1. The new list then started was continued to D4080 constructed in November 1950, subsequent Darlington-built boilers being given B.R. series numbers. Until the final Gateshead-built boiler ceased work in 1933, Darlington had used the prefix D to its boiler numbers, but was then able to discard the prefix. The need for it can be illustrated in that in the early months of 1933 class J24 No. 1940 had boiler G979 (as mentioned under Gateshead) and boiler D979 was in class J72 No. 1720, and this was by no means a lone example of duplicated numbering.

Fig. 50   Class J92 No. 68668 at Stratford, about March 1950.
Ross pop safety valves, whistle mounted on standpipe, lion and wheel
emblem, unshaded numerals.

Fig. 51   Class J92 No. 68669 at Stratford, September 1950.
Additional protection provided for enginemen as a result of disuse of crane.

Fig. 52   Class J92 No. 35 Departmental dismanted for scrap at
Stratford, February 1953.

Fig. 53   Sentinel ash crane No. 773044 at Eastfield shed.

Fig. 54   Sentinel ash crane No. 773066 at Dundee shed, October 1946.
Enclosed cab for operator.

Fig. 55   Sentinel ash crane RS1032/1½ (ex-773044) at Parkhead shed, July 1954.

Fig. 56   Petrol inspection car No. 23711 at Darlington shed, c.1935.

Fig. 57   Petrol inspection car No. 3768Y at York, c.1924.
Showing rail brushes fitted to facilitate operation of track circuits.

Fig. 58   Petrol inspection car No. 23769.

Fig. 59   Petrol inspection car No. 23769 at Low Fell, about 1936.

Fig. 60   Class D51 No. 10471 at Port Carlisle, August 1926.
The highest number carried by an L.N.E.R. locomotive.

Fig. 61   Diesel-hydraulic 0-4-0 locomotive built by Graz of Austria on trial at Broxbourne, 13th July 1924.

Fig. 62   Armstrong Whitworth diesel-electric 0-6-0 at work in the L.N.E.R.'s yard at Blaydon in 1932.

Prior to June 1934, boilers built by outside contractors retained the identification number applied by their makers. Then, to facilitate machine accountancy and to eliminate possible duplication, some of these boilers were renumbered 1 to 129. Darlington extended this series by giving boiler numbers 130 to 145 to sixteen on J39's built by Beyer Peacock & Co., these engines having running numbers between 1532 and 1587. At that time only four of the boilers in the numerical range 1 to 145 which Darlington had built in 1911-12 were still in service, but as these had the D prefix, duplication was avoided. D35 and D122 were cut up during 1936, but D128 survived until May 1944. Only the accountants were likely to be confused because D128 was a small boiler used on classes J71 and J72, whereas 128 served all its seventeen years on D49 class engines.

This renumbering from June 1934 of boilers carrying outside contractors' numbers needs some elaboration to understand the position fully. Class Q6 engines 2253 to 2302 had originally carried boiler numbers E4/1 to E4/50 and ten had already been scrapped. Renumbering was achieved by simply dropping E4 and retaining their numbers, which therefore covered 1 to 50 in the new list. Armstrong Whitworth had also built class J72 numbers 2313 to 2337 and given them boiler numbers E21/1 to E21/25; they were renumbered (in sequence) 51 to 75. This firm also built class K3 engines 1100/1/2/6/8/17/8/9 for use in the N.E. Area, and numbered their boilers 1111 to 1118, the same as their works numbers; they were renumbered 76 to 83. New boiler numbers 84 to 87 were not used for two sufficiently good reasons: (i) boiler D84 built in 1912 continued in service until 1940 and (ii) starting at 88 made the treatment of the next batch much simpler. Boilers built by Hawthorn Leslie & Co. in 1929-30 as replacements for classes J71 and J72 had been given maker's numbers 888 to 902, so alteration to 88 to 102 was very convenient. This firm had built another ten boilers in 1929-30 for replacements on classes B15 and Q6, giving them maker's numbers 982 to 991; they were renumbered 103 to 112. Five boilers built in April 1930 by N.B. Loco. Co. as replacements on class H1 had hitherto been 1D/689 to 5D/689, the 689 being the order number; they took 113 to 117. In 1931, ten boilers were supplied by Robt. Stephenson & Co. for Darlington to use on class J39 engines they were building, and these boilers arrived numbered 1D/3176 to 10D/3176. The first four engines Nos. 2977 to 2980 went to the Scottish Area and Cowlairs subsequently numbered them into the system they used. The remaining six (used for engines 1453/69/71/80/2/3) remained on Darlington maintenance and so were renumbered 118 to 123. Five similar boilers followed from Stephenson's for Darlington to put into new class D49 Nos. 283/8/92/7/8 and arrived as 1D to

5D/3177, and these became 124 to 128. Stephenson's then constructed another twenty boilers for class J39 engines, and these carried 1D/3077 to 20D/3077. New engines 2962 to 2976 took the first fifteen boilers and as they were destined for the Southern Area, they duly acquired Doncaster boiler numbers 8580 to 8594. The next four were sent to Cowlairs as spares to facilitate repairs, thus 16D to 19D/3077 changed to Cowlairs numbers. The remaining boiler, 20D/3077, was used by Darlington for new J39 No. 1412 for use in the N.E. Area and at a November 1935 repair this boiler was renumbered 129. The extension from 130 to 145 has already been described.

This list could readily have been extended from 146, because as far as D350, all numbers were then blank except D197 and D230, but Darlington did not take advantage of the opportunity to tidy up a wide variety of other boilers which carried makers' numbers. The thirteen class A5 4-6-2T's, which they maintained, carried boilers H.L. 3616 to 3628 and Gorton had supplied their number 152 to Darlington as a spare to facilitate interchanging at shoppings of these engines. As replacements on classes J71 and J72, there were boilers carrying H.L. 8085 to 8114, and the J72 engines built at Doncaster in 1925 carried that works' boiler numbers 7953 to 7962. With somewhat lofty disdain the N.E. Area accountants specified that "all these boilers may retain their present number as they do not correspond with any other Darlington built boiler." This blithely ignored the fact that Doncaster boiler numbers 8085 to 8114 applied to boilers built in 1928, all the more when numbers 8090 to 8109 were on boilers also built by Hawthorn Leslie for class N2 numbers 2662 to 2681. This clearly illustrates that even after more than ten years of Grouping, Darlington still ploughed its own furrow, and that integration into one L.N.E.R. Company still had a very long way to go.

There was a lot more logic in the accountants' next stipulations. Boilers H.L. 4581 to 4594 had been supplied for replacement purposes on classes J71 and J72 and the instructions stated "These boilers may retain their present number as they do not correspond with any other boiler." On class G5 were ten boilers built by Kitson & Co., which had numbers K2740 to K2749. It was stated "These boilers may retain their present number and when Darlington Works reach these numerals they can be omitted and resumed after 2749." This action was duly taken in January 1936.

In 1929 Doncaster built twenty class K3 engines numbered between 1300 and 1398 for the N.E. Area, and subsequent Darlington maintenance, giving the boilers numbers 8110 to 8129 in the Doncaster register. The N.E. Accountants found that 8110 to 8114 duplicated Hawthorn Leslie numbers on J71/J72 class boilers, and so stipulated that the K3 boilers be renumbered 8130 to 8134, "which would then keep these K3 boilers all in one series." Fortuitously, Doncaster numbers 8130 to 8132 were blank, having been allotted to three N2 class for which the order had been cancelled, but 8133/4 were already in use on class N2 Nos. 2682/3 and this was completley ignored. Then in June/August 1934 the N.E. Area received new class K3 Nos. 1302/4/8/10/24/06 from Armstrong Whitworth carrying that maker's boiler numbers 1156 to 1161. Dating from 1920, Darlington boilers were still in service with these numbers, so in February 1935 instructions were given for these K3 boilers to be altered to 8135 to 8140, which again ignored the existence of Doncaster boilers with the same numbers on class N2 Nos. 2684-9. Whilst Darlington accountants could confidently discount their having to deal with class N2 boiler numbers, one wonders what head scratching there was amongst their counterparts at Doncaster when, in 1944-5, five of these six K3's underwent general repairs there.

One other renumbering at accountants' behest concerned ten boilers for D49 class engines which were built by Cowlairs against Darlington order No. 803 of 9th December 1929. For some obscure reason, Cowlairs numbered them 7947 to 7956 which did not fit into any series used on the L.N.E.R. When these boilers were built, in July to October 1931, Cowlairs register had no higher number than 1803, and Darlington numbers had only reached 2416. The numbers Cowlairs used looked like Doncaster series, but the latter register had already reached 8539 by October 1931, and Doncaster had used 7947 to 7956 some six years earlier, putting 7953 to 7956 on to the first four class J72 engines Nos. 500/12/6/24 of the batch of ten they built for the N.E. Area. Thus in 1934, the N.E. accountants found they had two sets of boilers each numbered 7953 to 7956.

To remove this duplication, they stipulated that the D49 boilers should be changed to 7963 to 7966, to follow the J72 boilers numbered 7953 to 7962 by Doncaster. This completley ignored that there were Doncaster boilers already carrying 7963/5/6, the first one on the Garratt and the other two on a couple of class J50 boilers. Thus, for the remainder of its existence, the L.N.E.R. had two boilers each numbered 7965/6, and it was not until December 1952 that British Railways cleared one of the two 7963 numbers, when the Garratt received its B.R. series boiler number 27098.

Springhead

All Hull & Barnsley Railway boilers were built by outside contractors and until December 1911 their numbers were the same as the engine number. In that month Kitson's delivered the first of five 0-6-0 engines which ultimately became L.N.E.R. class J28 numbers 2408/9/11/6/23 and their boilers were numbered 4705-9, which were the maker's construction numbers for them.

Similarly, the five engines Kitson's supplied in January/February 1915 (which became L.N.E.R. Nos. 2412/3/4/8/20) carried and retained boiler numbers 5010-14. A further five engines of the same class which Yorkshire Engine Co. supplied late in 1914 however had boiler numbers which coincided with the 138 to 142 running numbers of the engines. When replacement was made, which had been necessary on most of the engines built before 1901, the new boiler took over the same number. In the few cases where the older boiler could be repaired for further service, the suffix A was added to its number. This was also done to boilers of engines put on to the duplicate list, but no boiler with A suffix survived to run in L.N.E.R. days. On the engines which became L.N.E.R. class J23, boiler renewal continued to be made by the H. & B. until December 1921 and it would seem that these replacements would have carried their maker's construction numbers. Scrutiny of boiler history cards only brought one example to light — a boiler numbered 5335, bought from Kitson in January 1920, which started work on H. & B. No. 96 in June 1921, was transferred to engine No. 2435 from January 1926 to January 1929 and then served No. 2517 from March 1929 until engine and boiler were withdrawn in July 1937. Other contemporary domeless boilers brought into L.N.E.R. stock from the H. & B. did not have any boiler number recorded on their L.N.E.R. boiler history cards. After the merger, first into the N.E.R. and then into L.N.E.R., Darlington took over the maintenance and built many new boilers (most of them with domes) for ex-H. & B. engines. These were given numbers in the Darlington register as customary, and they ranged from D1488 of April 1923 to D2454 built in August 1932 which started work on class N13 No. 2535 in October 1933 and survived to be given a B.R. series boiler number in September 1950.

Gorton

One almost needs the wisdom of Solomon to follow the series of boiler numbers on this workshop's register. When complying with the 1882 Act, the M.S. & L.R. presumably totalled the boilers which they had and then numbered them from 1 upwards. It would seem that the numbers were applied in the order in which engines went to works for repairs, because such records of those which survived when our research began show no sign whatsoever of regular sequence, either by date of construction or grouping by type. A few examples will demonstrate the irregularity which was found:—

Boiler 120 built 1876 lasted to June 1914 when cut up with engine 102B.

Boiler 141 built 1862 lasted to 1904 when cut up off engine 28.

Boiler 186 built 1874 lasted to December 1916 when cut up off engine 336B.

Boiler 255 built 1871 lasted to June 1913 when cut up off engine 17.

Boiler 294 built 1882 lasted to February 1906 when cut up off engine 230B.

Boiler 399 built 1884 lasted to July 1909 when cut up off engine 48B.

Boiler 505 built 1880 lasted to May 1922 when cut up with engine 456B.

It is estimated that at the end of 1882 the M.S. & L.R. would have around 500 boilers needing registered numbers, plus any spares then still serviceable but not actually installed in engines, but no reasonable explanation can be offered why boilers built prior to the Act should have reached as high a number as 730 and this was not the only example as these numbers show:—

Boiler 703 built 1874 lasted to June 1916 when cut up with engine 390B.

Boiler 713 built 1883 was used by engine 63B until October 1921 and was cut up in June 1923.

Boiler 730 built 1872 lasted to January 1910 when cut up with engine 286B.

Capital stock numbering reached 500 in May 1883 and it seems incredible that there would be almost half as many more on the duplicate list so explanations for inclusion in the original list for boiler numbers 511 (built 1874), 516 (1877), 555 (1883), 599 (1874), 630 (1879), 636 (1874), 637 (1875), 662 (1877) and those in the 700's cannot be given. The spread of these numbers seems to indicate that no large gaps were left in the list.

By June 1901, Gorton had started another boiler list beginning again at 1, working upwards as boilers were completed, but jumping over numbers in the original list which were still occupied, of which there were a good number. Boilers which came in with new engines from outside contractors were numbered in the Gorton list as they were taken into stock. It was a Gorton tradition to minimise gaps in their lists, so when a boiler was scrapped and its number became vacant, the earliest opportunity was taken of giving that number to a new boiler. For example, in the original list a gap at number 125 was filled in February 1894 by giving that number to the new boiler built with 0-6-2 tank No. 539. This boiler was scrapped in April 1906 and in January 1907 boiler number 125 was used again for a new replacement put on 0-6-0 No. 830, and that boiler was in use to July 1934, serving four engines of class J10. Thus the list had no regularity about it, as shown by picking (at random) boilers 253 to 255. When 254 was used again in September 1912 to fill a gap, it divided 253 built in 1899 from 255 built in 1871. There was just as much difference in the types of boiler. Using the L.N.E.R. locomotive classes for easier identification, boiler 253 was of D6, 254 was M1 and 255 was J58 type.

Until the end of the Great Central's existence, Gorton continued to fill gaps and to extend this list when necessary. By Grouping, it had reached boiler number 1955, but the last engine built by that Company (which became class D11 No. 5511) came out with boiler 342, a gap-filling number. Together with the 125 R.O.D. 2-8-0 engines which the L.N.E.R. purchased in 1923 (the boilers of which took random blank numbers in the Gorton register) were thirteen spare boilers which had only been built in 1922. Gorton numbered these boilers 1956 to 1968, and used them during 1924 on class O4 engines. They also allocated their boiler numbers 1969 to 1980 to the 1924 Kitson-built class D11/2 engines, but Cowlairs subsequently used their boiler numbers 1477 to 1488 for them instead and the Gorton numbers remained blank. No more extensions were made to the Gorton list until 1930 when the boilers of ten class Y3 shunting engines and twenty Sentinel railcars on Gorton maintenance were given boiler numbers 1971 to 2000. In true Gorton tradition, allocation to cars and engines was well mixed, and the numbers also included the four railcars which were C.L.C. owned, because Gorton had responsibility for their repairs.

Having reached the round number of 2000, that list was finalised and on new boilers built until the end of 1934 only gap-filling numbers were used. Then the complications ceased, and a tidier mind took over. All subsequent Gorton boilers were grouped according to type and numbered progressively in each group as they were completed. As was the case at Darlington, no cognisance was taken of numbers used by other L.N.E.R. workshops, so the case could — and did — arise where Gorton was repairing different boilers carrying the *same* number. For example, in May 1942 Gorton fitted their new boiler number 3035 to class B7 engine 5483, and in the following October made heavy repairs to boiler 3035 carried by class J69 No. 7383, the latter boiler having been so numbered in the Stratford register when first used in January 1926. Before leaving the list which ended in 1934, it is interesting to point out that boiler No. 24 built in June 1930 which started work on class J62 No. 5882 in November 1932 remained in active service until January 1955 and was then spare until cut up in December 1956 when its registered number was still 24. It was the last unrenumbered Gorton boiler despite nine full years of British Railways ownership.

From 1935 to the end of 1950, Gorton continued to give numbers in its own register, the grouped numbers it used being shown on the following page.

Diagram	Boiler Nos.	Built	Engine Classes to which fitted
13	3001-50	2/1935- 3/1947	B2(B19), B3, B7, B8
14	3101-37	6/1935-12/1949	D10, D11, L1(L3)
15	3201-3444	7/1935- 6/1941	C4, C5, O4, S1
15A	3651-5	6/1939-10/1939	O4/5
15D	3656-98	10/1939- 8/1943	O4/7
15B	3699, 3700	3/1941	B6, O5
17	3721-42	2/1935-11/1942	B5, B9, Q4
17A	3743-66	8/1943- 5/1948	Q1
17	3767-78	11/1946- 6/1948	B5, B9, Q4
18	3841-74	1/1936- 8/1947	A5, D9
19	3941-4094	6/1935-10/1952(a)	J11
19A	4131/2	9/1937	M1
21	4181-4346	5/1935-12/1950(b)	D7, J10, N4, N5
22	4501-38	12/1934-12/1950	C13, C14, D6
97	4901-44	2/1938- 8/1948	D49, J39
97	4965-96	11/1948- 8/1950	,, ,,
100A	5004-5146(c)	12/1943- 6/1950	B1, B2, B3/3, B17/6, O1, O2/4, O4/8

(a) Although Nos. 4073 onwards built from October 1949 got Gorton numbers, none started work before being renumbered into the B.R. scheme operative from August 1950.

(b) Despite boilers 4343 to 4346 being completed after the B.R. scheme became operative, they did not receive B.R. boiler numbers until shopped in January-June 1953.

(c) Gorton Boiler numbers 5147 to 5193 (all of Diagram 100A pattern) were renumbered B.R. 28800-46 before starting work.

Stratford

Until March 1914 it was standard practice at Stratford Works to number a boiler the same as the running number of the engine to which it was first fitted. Indeed this principle was continued in a number of instances until 1928, as boiler numbers 1571 to 1580 were allotted to the Beyer, Peacock-built class B12 engines with L.N.E.R. running numbers 8571 to 8580 which, if built earlier by the Great Eastern, would have been 1571 to 1580. The ten class D16 engines which Stratford built in 1923 did originally have coincident boiler and running numbers 1780 to 1789.

Early in 1914, Stratford decided that boilers should be capable of being interchanged on to other engines of the same class, and in April 1914 0-6-0 engine (class J15 later) 895 was fitted with boiler 905 which had run with the engine of that number from July 1903 to December 1913. The replacement on engine 905 was a new boiler numbered 2501, Stratford having adopted the system of numbering boilers according to types and in number progression as built, which Gorton adopted just over twenty years later as has just been described. Because Stratford continued its 1914 system through to April 1950 on L.N.E.R. type boilers it built or was responsible for maintaining, it is convenient to describe them by using the L.N.E.R. engine classifications and boiler diagram numbers, although it was 1923 and 1928 respectively before these took effect.

The highest engine running number on the G.E.R. in 1914 was 1900, and as the total stock did not exceed two-thirds of that figure (giving ample scope for numbering future construction) Stratford evidently felt safe in starting their individual boiler numbering at 2000. The first group only covered three boilers, but the big gap to the start of the next group was to prove exceedingly convenient in L.N.E.R. days. The number groups Stratford used can be summarised as follows:

Diagram	Boiler Nos.	Built	Engine Classes to which Fitted
33	2000/1/2	9/1914- 6/1915	F4
98	2005-2121	1/1926-10/1930	N7
34	2200-96	5/1914-10/1931	F4, F5, F6
31	2300-97	3/1914- 2/1932	J15
34	2400-49	1/1932-10/1947	F4, F5, F6
32	2500-80	5/1914- 4/1931	E4, F3, J15
32	2650-2799	7/1914- 3/1933	,, ,, ,,
39	2800-2919	11/1914- 6/1938	J65, J66, J67
37	2950-3105(a)	7/1914- 3/1938	J68, J69
29	3100-52	5/1914- 3/1930	D13
37	3153-99(b)	9/1944- 2/1950	J68, J69
35	3200-26	3/1914- 9/1929	G4
28	3250-63	12/1914-12/1931	D14, J16
32	3300-88	3/1933- 1/1947	E4, F3, J15
32	3394-8	3/1948- 5/1948	,, ,, ,,
27	3400-3542(c)	10/1915-12/1950	D15, J17, J18, J19
27	3550-3685	3/1914- 6/1928	,, ,, ,, ,,
46	3700-17	5/1922- 3/1950	J70, Y6
25	3800-61	7/1919- 1/1931	B12, J20
26	3900-36	3/1923- 7/1932	D16
100	4000-36(d)	12/1928- 2/1931	B17
99A	4100-64	5/1932- 8/1941	B12/3
28A	4200-4344	1/1933- 7/1950	D16/3, J19/2
2	4401-8(e)	10/1932- 4/1933	O1(O3), O2, O4/4
25A	4465-79(f)	8/1946- 9/1947	B12/4, J20/1
100	4720-30(g)		B17

(a) The overlap from 3100 to 3105 was possible because boilers in the next group with those numbers had been scrapped.

(b) This group was continued to 3207 of August 1950, scrapping having cleared 3200 to 3207.

(c) Boilers 3536 to 3542 were actually completed in 1949 with those numbers but did not start work until after being renumbered by B.R. to 23201/2/4/5/6/8/10.

(d) Boiler Nos. 4037 and 4047 to 4050 were never allocated and 4038 to 4046, also 4051 to 4058 of Diagram 100, were built under, and retained, Darlington numbers.

(e) These eight boilers built at Gorton were originally given Doncaster boiler numbers 8622 to 8629 but were transferred to the Stratford register as 4401 to 4408.

(f) This allocation had begun with 4450 to 4464, but those fifteen boilers were entered into the Doncaster register under their numbers 9410 to 9424.

(g) Stratford allocated boiler numbers 4701 to 4719 to the Diagram 100 boilers put on to new class B17 engines 2843 to 2861 (not in that order), but these Darlington-built boilers were given, and retained, numbers in the Darlington register. On the other hand, the boilers of 2862 to 2872 built by Robt. Stephenson & Co. in 1937 always had Stratford numbers 4720 to 4730.

It just remains to describe how Stratford dealt with boilers from outside sources, but which were maintained at that works. Soon after the formation of the L.N.E.R. it absorbed two small railways in the Eastern Counties, the Colne Valley & Halstead and the Mid-Suffolk Light. The former had five and the latter had three locomotives, and Stratford took over responsibility for their maintenance. In their boiler register Nos. 1300 to 1311 were occupied by the 2-4-2 tanks of class F7, which had hitherto carried these numbers both for boilers and engines. Numbers were then free from 1312 to 1500 and in L.N.E.R. days, Stratford made a variety of uses of this facility.

Two of the five Colne Valley engines were worn out and were quickly withdrawn by their new owners. In 1924 the other three were given L.N.E.R. numbers 8312 to 8314 and their boilers became 1312 to 1314. Room for a spare, if required later, was provided by leaving boiler number 1315 vacant. A similar situation arose with the Mid-Suffolk locomotives, one of their three being considered worn out, so was withdrawn. The other two were allocated engine numbers 8316/7 and boiler numbers 1316/7; again the next engine number was left unallocated. Then in 1929/30 Stratford built two new replacement boilers for use on class F7 engines. By then boiler 1314 and its ex-Colne Valley engine had been cut up, so boiler number 1314 was re-used in 1929 and the 1930-built boiler filled the hitherto unused 1315. Further F7 replacement boilers were built during 1932-35 and were given 1319 to 1322. Curiously, boiler number 1318 was still left blank, a possible reason being that the Mid-Suffolk boiler off the engine withdrawn in August 1924 had remained spare (but not used) until it was cut up in October 1930 at the same time as the last surviving Mid-Suffolk engine, but the new boilers which became 1319 to 1322 could just as readily have taken the numbers 1316 to 1319 as those were then available.

In 1932 Stratford built three boilers for replacement on the crane tanks of class J92. Since July 1894 these engines and their boilers had only been identified by the letters B, C and D. The engines continued to be known as such until 1946, but Stratford gave boiler numbers 1330 to 1332 to the 1932 boilers.

For use on the G.E. Section in 1936, nine class J39 engines were supplied by Beyer, Peacock and were numbered between 1803 and 1870; Stratford affixed their boiler numbers 1350 to 1358 to them.

In 1925-27 three Sentinel shunting engines were purchased for G.E. Section departmental use and they acquired running numbers 8400 to 8402. Although their boilers carried Sentinel identification numbers, Stratford entered them into its register as boiler numbers 1400 to 1402, and the same procedure was adopted for the two class Y10 Sentinels purchased in 1930, their boilers getting Stratford numbers 1403/4. From 1930, Stratford also assumed responsibility for the maintenance of three Sentinel railcars and nine class Y3 Sentinel shunting engines. They all had boiler identification numbers on them already, but Stratford entered them under its boiler numbers 1405 to 1407 for the cars and 1408 to 1416 for the locomotives.

On 1st November 1937 three classes totalling eighteen engines were taken over from London Passenger Transport Board and they became Stratford responsibility for maintenance. Their boilers had hitherto had registered numbers between 2 and 37 in the London Transport list, but Stratford put them into its register as 1417 to 1434, together with 1435 on the spare boiler which came with them.

This completes the account of Stratford boiler numbering, because that works took no action on renumbering the boilers on the engines absorbed from the M. & G.N. on 1st October 1936. Their boilers were numbered between 1 and 100 in accordance with the engine number to which they were first fitted. Although an 0 prefix was added to the running numbers of the engines, Stratford did not find it necessary to extend this to the boiler numbers.

Cowlairs

The series of boiler numbers used by Cowlairs at Grouping had commenced at No. 112 in 1889 and applied only to new boilers constructed at Cowlairs itself. In the list were included twelve other 1889 boilers but no numbers were shown against these, and there was no mention at all of the preceding ninety-nine boilers which had apparently been taken into account. Nor was there any indication of a numbering scheme for the several hundred Cowlairs-made boilers in existence before the commencement of this list.

At the formation of the L.N.E.R., Cowlairs boiler numbers had reached 1243, but boilers which had been built by outside contractors had retained the number given to them by their makers. The majority had N.B. Loco. Co. numbers, but there were also Beardmore, Hawthorn Leslie, Robt. Stephenson and Yorkshire Engine Co. numbers. From March 1925, Cowlairs renumbered them all from 1 to 314, although for some undiscovered reason, the number 162 was never used (see accompanying table). It seems possible that the boiler intended for that number became 311 instead. At the time of this renumbering the lowest Cowlairs number still in use was 525, although one numbered 245 was in service on class J36 No. (9)250 until it was rebuilt in June 1923.

Cowlairs continued adding to its list as it built further boilers and also as boilers came on to its maintenance, irrespective of whether they were already numbered. The first from elsewhere were 1362 to 1373, applied to the boilers of class N2 engines 2583 to 2594, and similar engines 892

Boiler Nos.	Diagram	Maker
1-20	81 (Sat.)	Beardmore
21/2	78 (Sup.)	,,
23/4	77 (Sup.)	,,
25-50	76	N.B. Loco., Stephenson, Hawthorn Leslie (not in sequence)
51	78 (Sup.)	N.B. Loco.
52-6	78 (Sat.)	,,
57/8	78 (Sup.)	,,
59-93	77 (Sat.)	,,
94-161/3	77 (Sup.)	,,
164-93	81 (Sat.)	Yorkshire Engine
194-215	81 (Sup.)	N.B. Loco.
216-74	81 (Sat.)	,,
275-84	81 (Sat.)	Stephenson
285-310	81 (Sat.)	N.B. Loco.
311	77 (Sup.)	,,
312	81 (Sat.)	,,
313	78 (Sat.)	,,
314	81 (Sat.)	,,

Note. — The boilers under the above diagram numbers fitted the following classes of locomotive: Diag. 76 C11; 77 (Sat.) J35; 77 (Sup.) J35, J37; 78 (Sat.) D29, D33; 78 (Sup.) D29, D30, D33, D34; 81 (Sat.) C15, G9, J36, N14, N15; 81 (Sup.) C16.

to 897 became 1380 to 1385, Doncaster (unusually) having given them the latter Scottish register numbers when they built them. The six Darlington-built K3 engines for the Scottish Area had boiler numbers in that workshop's register, but Cowlairs renumbered them 1421 to 1426 and applied the same procedure to the whole of class J38. They too had Darlington boiler numbers, which ranged from D1819 to D1866, but Cowlairs dubbed them 1427 to 1461 consecutively after they had arrived in Scotland. When ordering the twenty Pacifics from N.B. Loco. Co., Doncaster specified 2563 to 2582 for their running numbers and 7785 to 7804 for their boiler numbers. The first five of these engines were allocated to the Scottish Area and until 1930 were maintained by Cowlairs who gave the boilers their numbers 1462 to 1466, but there was reversion to 7785-89 when Doncaster took over maintenance from 1930 onwards. Cowlairs had better success with their boiler numbers 1467 to 1476 which they applied on the class O4 R.O.D. engines sent to the Scottish Area in 1924. Despite most of these boilers being transferred to Gorton maintenance in the 1930's, the Cowlairs numbers continued in use although they duplicated Gorton numbers also in use on class O4 engines.

Numbers 1477-1500 in the Cowlairs range were given to the boilers on class D11 6378-6401 built for use in the Scottish Area. The next thirty-three boiler numbers were used for new replacements for N.B.R. classes, as were numbers 1535-1629. No. 1534 was applied to a spare Diagram 7 boiler sent from Doncaster to Cowlairs for use on class D1, the entire fifteen engines of which class had been transferred to Scotland after Grouping. This boiler had carried number 8692 in the Doncaster series. Nos. 1630-49 at first remained blank but were subsequently allocated to new boilers for classes J83 and J88, although only the number 1630 was used.

Cowlairs numbers from 1650 to 1831 (apart from 1805 to 1809) were applied to boilers which had already been numbered elsewhere and, until cleared by the B.R. scheme in 1950, were to be the cause of constant confusion when the engines carrying them were transferred to other areas. Someone then decided that enough was enough, and from boiler number 1832 of March 1937, the Cowlairs register was used entirely for boilers of types which were used only in the Scottish Area viz., replacement boilers for ex-N.B. engines and for J38 and a few J39 engines permanently resident in Scotland. By August 1950 when the B.R. scheme was introduced, the Cowlairs register had reached boiler number 2066, and 2067 to 2080 had been allocated although these fourteen received their B.R. number before they started work.

Inverurie

From the start of numbering until November 1921, it was G.N.S.R. practice to use the same boiler number as the engine's running number, and the boiler normally stayed with the same engine until the end of its usage in operating stock. At the above date there had only been eight cases (the first in June 1917) where a boiler had been transferred to another engine. Where this was done, the original boiler number received an A suffix. On 11th November 1921, Locomotive Superintendent T. E. Heywood wrote to Works Manager K. S. Robertson as follows: "I find that the new boiler which is to be put on engine No. 87, and which is now standing in the Boilershop, has a number plate on it marked 87. This is not correct, and that boiler must take the next highest number to what is at present existing. This, I believe, will be 118. The old boiler which is on engine No. 87 should have the plate marked 87 put on it, and it will retain this number until it is broken up, and then the number will disappear from the number of boilers. Kindly see that all new boilers get consecutive numbers as they are brought into service. We have a number of boilers with the letter A after them. When they are scrapped, the numbers are to disappear, and are not to be used again." These instructions were then followed until the building of the last G.N.S.R. type boiler, which started work on class D40 engine No. 6915 in April 1936 with boiler No. 183.

At the date of Heywood's letter, the G.N.S.R. had engines — and boilers — numbered consecutively from 1 to 115, together with seven engines on the duplicate list, and eight boilers to which the A suffix was applicable. The additional boiler was numbered 19A, having served with engine No. 19 from new in February 1896 to March 1919 and then having been transferred to engine No. 106 in October 1919. It will have been noted that Heywood gave 118 as the first available number. This was due to 116 and 117 having been put on the heating boilers at the Palace Hotel, Aberdeen. From 1921 until the beginning of February 1925 the boiler register included all items subject to regular boiler inspection. As mentioned by Heywood, boiler 118 went on to engine No. 87; in July 1922 boiler 119 went on to engine 92 of the same class. Nos. 120 to 127 were taken up by heating boilers at Aberdeen Station and Station Hotel, on a 3-ton travelling crane, the pumping boiler at Ballater, the boiler on the coal bank crane at Kittybrewster, that at Dyce creosote works, and the old boiler on Inverurie Works fire engine and its replacement in January 1922. Boiler numbers 128 to 139 were on the Foden and Clayton steam wagons, whilst the Inverurie grease boiler accounted for 140. Normal locomotive boilers subsequently acquired numbers 141 to 146, 149 to 163, 166/7 and 171 to 183. No. 148 was the hairdressing saloon hot water boiler at Aberdeen Station and 168 to 170 were on further Foden steam wagons. Nos. 147, 164/5 were boilers surplus to Darlington requirement (their numbers D653, D2023 and D2030) sent north in April 1923 for use in Inverurie Central Boiler House. They were accompanied by D144, but this had not been put into use by February 1925 when the Northern Scottish Area put its Stationary Boilers into a separate list, and so never took up the number 166 which had been reserved for it. All four of these Darlington boilers had put in some years' service on their class "398" 0-6-0 engines.

Twenty-two of the boilers which had started their career on Inverurie's boiler register survived to be renumbered by British Railways in 1951 to 1956.

B.R. Renumbering of ex-L.N.E.R. Boilers

Nationalisation duly brought rationalisation, but not until more than two and a half years had elapsed. Under the date of 15th August 1950 the office of the Mechanical & Electrical Engineer, Eastern & North Eastern Regions at Doncaster issued instructions for the renumbering of ex-L.N.E.R. types of locomotive boilers. Very briefly, they were as follows:—

Boilers of ex-G.N.R. classes to take numbers 21000 to 21999

Boilers of ex-G.C.R. classes to take numbers 22000 to 22999

Boilers of ex-G.E.R. classes to take numbers 23100 (sic) to 23999

Boilers of ex-N.E.R. classes to take numbers 24000 to 25910

Boilers of ex-L.N.E.R. Group Standard classes to take 27000 to 29999

Renumbering of boilers at Doncaster and Darlington began immediately, each boiler taking the next consecutive number in the group to which it belonged. There could thus be a considerable difference in age between boilers carrying consecutive numbers. For example, 21019 (ex-8461) was built in October 1931 and 21020 (ex-9322) dated from September 1942. In their instructions, Doncaster stipulated that boiler renumbering should be carried out as engines passed through the shops for any class of repair. If a boiler was taken off a frame, it was not renumbered until refitted to the same frame or taken for use on another engine. Consequently, boilers taken off and set aside for scrapping were not to be renumbered, nor did spare boilers receive new numbers until taken for use. As a result of this it was May 1956 before the renumbering was completed.

When the above renumbering scheme was formulated, the majority of ex-N.B.R. and G.N.S.R. classes were in the Scottish Region and therefore outside Doncaster's jurisdiction. Nevertheless, in the eyes of Doncaster the 26000 series was clearly intended for them. It was not until mid-January 1951 that the first ex-N.B.R. boiler was renumbered at Cowlairs. Reasons for this delay are not known, but a letter dated 13th December 1950 to the Scottish Region Locomotive Accountant stated that it had been "decided to renumber all ex-L.N.E.R. boilers as they pass through the shops." It is possible that Scottish Region did not agree with the procedure adopted by the workshops in E. & N.E. Regions, and took time in finding an alternative. When they did begin the renumbering, they allocated new numbers in date order for each diagram, and a good job was done for instance in sorting out the Diagram 77 boilers which had been in the main Cowlairs list and in the contractor-built Cowlairs series. Not only that, but whereas this latter series had originally been allotted according to the running number of the engine they were on at the time of the renumbering in 1925, the 26000 series corrected this sequence as well. Unfortunately as far as the saturated Diagram 81 boilers were concerned all this good work went for nothing because there was a subsequent renumbering to separate boilers working at different pressures.

TENDER NUMBERINGS

There was wide divergence in the way that tenders were regarded by the L.N.E.R.'s constituent companies, and this continued throughout the new company's existence. Each main works continued on exactly the same basis as it had used in pre-Grouping days, and no attempt at a Group policy was ever made. Even with numbering, nothing comprehensive was considered until 1947, and the scheme then promulgated never came to anything. Only on ex-North Eastern tenders — and then not before March 1938 — was any change made, so it is convenient to divide this account into how each main works dealt with tenders which it maintained.

Tenders at Doncaster

Until August 1901, tenders were given the same number as the engine for which they were built and to which first coupled. The number was shown on a cast brass plate of elliptical shape 6⅛in. x 3in. fixed on the centre line of the tender back, just under the curve of the coping (figs. 100 & 101). The highest number reached was 1385, which tender and plate can still be seen coupled to ex-G.N.R. small Atlantic No. 990 at the National Railway Museum. In 1901 Doncaster built a batch of ten tenders to which they gave numbers 270 to 279, but the engines to which they were first attached were the ten new 4-2-2 engines numbered 92, 100 and 261-5/8/9/70. In 1902 a further twenty similar new tenders were numbered 241 to 250 and 494 to 503, which completely broke the link between engine and tender number being the same because the engines with these numbers were all tank engines. In 1904/5, thirty more tenders were built and these took numbers 601 to 630, but a further ten of the same type completed in July and August 1906 were numbered 5001 upwards (fig. 102), starting a series which Doncaster continued to use for all subsequent tenders for which it had responsibility. On Great Northern tenders, Nos. 5211/2 were reached, these two being coupled to the first two Pacifics Nos. 1470/1 in 1922. The series continued for another twenty years, the highest number being 5740, which was coupled to new V2 class No. 3664 in March 1942. Nos. 5741 to 5750 were allotted to new tenders for a further ten class V2, and Nos. 5751 to 5760 to ten new class O2. In the event, the V2 order was transferred to Darlington and the O2's received second-hand tenders. In B.R. days, tender number 5741 did actually appear, as will be described later, but was not on a newly-built tender tend resulted from recording errors.

With his penchant for removing all possible Gresley associations, even on details, Thompson discarded the 5XXX series and initiated another one beginning at 700. On 12th June 1944 when the orders were placed for the fifteen Pacifics which became class A2/3 Nos. 500/11-24, the tenders for them were allotted Nos. 704 to 718. Tender numbers 700 to 703 were intended for four similar tenders to replace the 6-wheeled type running with intended V2's which Thompson had metamorphosed into his A2/1 class Nos. 3696-9. However, the order for these was not placed until 15th December 1945, when it was cut to three which ultimately took Nos. 700 to 702, as engine No. 3696 had acquired tender 5672 (spare from class A4 No. 4469, the engine destroyed in the air raid on York) and this was renumbered 703.

This series finally ran from 700 to 782, all of them eight-wheeled non-corridor type and attached to engines in classes A1 and A2. This numbering entirely ignored (and thus duplicated) three tenders numbered 753, 756 and 771, which Doncaster built in 1885-9, still running coupled to class J3 engines and which continued so to do until 1951-52. Even when these three Stirling tenders were scrapped, there was still duplication because B.R. Britannias had tender numbers from 759 upwards. So Thompson's departure from the well-established 5XXX series was not an entire success.

At least from 1906 onwards, Doncaster regarded tenders as independent units to be used to the best advantage. Each could be readily and positively identified from the number plate, and there was nothing to tie a tender to any particular engine as the side sheets simply displayed "G N R". Thus Doncaster could easily switch tenders and their repairs were in no way a constraint on keeping an engine out of action, so exchanges in pre-Grouping days were frequently made. The L.N.E.R.'s decision to show the engine number in 12-inch figures on each side of a tender largely stopped this as it would involve repainting, so the authorities at Doncaster were no doubt enthusiastic supporters of moving the number to the cab sides; this took effect on Pacifics from April 1928, and generally from February 1929. The disadvantage of the original system is clearly shown in fig. 118.

Because Doncaster tenders had a lifespan approaching double that of engines, the works invariably had a good surplus on hand. At Grouping there were 852 tender engines but 897 tenders. From July 1906 to December 1922, the Great Northern added 344 tender engines to its stock, but in those 16½ years only needed to build 212 new tenders. So the ready switching of tenders enabled the important engines to be upgraded to more modern tenders as these became available. For example, the 53 large

Atlantics already in service at July 1906 had by Grouping all been provided with the more modern type of tender. Further, the G.N.R. was able to provide tenders for the 2-6-0 and 2-8-0 engines it purchased from outside contractors in its final years without having to contemplate the additional expense of buying them.

The durability of G.N.R. tenders is well shown by the number of years it took for those with original engine numbers to disappear. When the last three engines of class J6 were withdrawn in June 1962, their tenders were Nos. 1066, 1171 and 1314 built in 1897, 1901 and 1898 respectively, so all had well over sixty years' active service to their credit. Compare this with the withdrawal dates of their original engines which were 1921, 1946 and 1937. After their years in running stock, many of these Stirling and Ivatt tenders were put to further use as sludge carriers, water carriers and latterly as the basic vehicle for snow ploughs. Amongst this Service Stock, there may still be an oddment bearing a pre-1906 tender number of G.N.R. origin.

On the eight-wheeled tenders built to the later design without coal rails, whether corridor or just high-sided variety, a fresh place had to be found for the tender number plate, which was then moved to the front plate. Its usual place was over the coal access door, but some had it just inside the entrance on the driver's side. The figuring was modernised, and L.N.E.R. cast plates (either new or replacements) were reduced in width to 5⅜in. but the style remained the same even for those in the 700 series (fig. 103).

Tenders at Gorton

The Great Central regarded engine and tender as an entity and plated the tender accordingly. The tender number plate was elliptical 9¾in. x 6¼in. of cast iron, and fixed in the centre of the back plate. In addition to the number, smaller characters gave builder's name and year of construction.

In 1903 water troughs were laid in at Charwelton to permit non-stop running between Marylebone and Sheffield, and in consequence, some of the main line engines built in 1901-2 then needed to have water pick-up apparatus. Instead of fitting the necessary gear to them, their existing tenders were exchanged for tenders with scoops taken from goods engines just coming into service, and so initially there was confliction between engine and tender number. However, the Running Superintendent not only exchanged the tenders, but also their number plates in order to keep engine and tender alike, and this caused absolute chaos with workshop and accountant's records. Sixteen exchanges involving thirty-two engines had been made before the cause of the bother came to light, and whilst no restriction was placed on further exchanges it was ordered that the original number plate had to be retained. With

this stipulation, tender changing was facilitated because with the sides just carrying the Company name, there was no obvious link with the engine number. Fortunately, Gorton was pretty meticulous at recording tender changes and when our research began, those made from 1920 to 1951 were available to us, thus covering the whole of the L.N.E.R. years.

From February 1924, the numbers on Great Central engines had 5000 added to them, and Gorton took this change rather further than they really need have done and renumbered the tenders as well. Fresh plates showing the increased number were cast (fig. 110), although these were slightly smaller at 9⅛in. x 5⅛in. and the fixing position was changed from the back of the tender to the centre of the front plate above the shovelling hole. On the later self-trimming tenders, described under classes B3, B7 (Part 2B) and D11 (Part 3B), there was a toolbox in the centre and the number plate was therefore affixed to the tender front plate at the usual height, but on the left-hand side.

With tender numbers running upwards from 5001, some hundreds of them duplicated numbers already in use on Doncaster tenders. Nevertheless, the system Gorton adopted in 1924 continued right through to the withdrawal of the last O4's on 17th April 1966. Indeed the preserved Director engine's tender is still plated 5501, a tender it acquired in April 1927, and tender 6202 is with the O4 being restored at Dinting.

Tenders at Stratford

Great Eastern practice was to number the tender the same as the engine to which first fitted, and their plate fixing position was also in the centre of the back plate. Rectangular cast-iron plates, as large as 10⅛in. x 6¹/₁₆in., were used with the initials G.E.R. above and STRATFORD together with the year of building underneath the number. Where new engines were turned out with second-hand tenders, e.g. in the case of certain E4's (see Part 4, p.140), J15's (Part 5, p.91) and J16's (Part 5, p.103), or an organised exchange took place as with G.E.R. Nos. 1020-9 (see Part 4, p.12), the tenders carried new number plates showing not only the number of the new engine but also the date of its construction. Stratford however had no inhibitions about exchanging tenders when it was convenient to do so, regarding a tender as having its own identity and at first there was no obvious link between engine and tender numbers, as tender sides simply carried "G.E.R." on them. The introduction of a train control system in 1920 brought with it engine numbers 19in. high painted on tender sides, and integration into the L.N.E.R. also involved display of the engine number on the tender sides until it was moved to the cab sides from February 1929. Therefore, for ten years tender changing was not to be undertaken lightly or inadvisedly, but from 1929 complete freedom to do so was regained and took place quite frequently.

As at Gorton, the L.N.E.R.'s additon of 7000 to Great Eastern engine numbers was interpreted as also being required on tender numbers, so from March 1924 as engines went through the works for repairs, fresh number plates were fitted on the same fixing position (fig. 112). They were of cast-iron, the same size as used previously, the new number and the substitution of L.N.E.R. for G.E.R. being the only changes. There were at first some exceptions in cases where a second-hand tender was involved which still carried the number of the engine to which it had originally been attached. These numbers were not infrequently left unchanged though the engine's number was altered to its new 1924 number.

Eventually surviving G.E.R. tenders were all renumbered except for one interesting exception, which perforce continued the use of a pre-Grouping engine number. When the 0-10-0 tank (the Decapod) experiment was concluded, the engine was altered to an 0-8-0 goods engine and a 1907 plate numbered 20 was put on the tender built to run with it. The engine was scrapped in June 1913, but obviously a tender only six years old could be used elsewhere. This duly happened, but when it came to changing the plate from G.E.R. to L.N.E.R. there was no tender engine numbered 7020. So the plate remained as 20 and continued in service until December 1959, mainly attached to B12 class engines. The 7000 addition resulted in there being 361 tenders numbered between 8140 and 8900, the majority of which outlasted the L.N.E.R., many of them surviving to the late 1950's and they duplicated almost that quantity of ex-North Eastern tenders from 1938 as will be described presently. This again underlines the absence of Group co-ordination in that this further duplication of tender numbering was completely ignored.

Tenders at Darlington

It was the custom at Darlington, and at Gateshead until the 1933 closure, for a tender to be regarded as belonging to the engine with which it was built, and until the early 1930's it was rare indeed for an exchange to take place. When a tender was attached to a fresh locomotive, a new plate with the appropriate number was provided. For example, when D23 class No. 274 had its own tender destroyed in a collision with class C7 No. 2205 at Darlington station early in 1929, the replacement came from D22 class No. 117 as that engine had just been withdrawn, the tender then changing its plate for one showing 274.

Prior to the Grouping, passenger engine tenders were in green livery and the majority carried "NORTH EASTERN" with the Company armorial between the two words, the others simply carrying "N.E.R.". For identification, the engine number, 3 inches high plus ½in. of shading, was painted just under the coping on the centre line of the tender back plate. When the livery was changed to that of the L.N.E.R., North Eastern engine numbers remained the same as before, but they were displayed in 12-inch shaded transfers on each side of the tender, so it was then possible to dispense with the number at the rear end. This position obtained until February 1929, after which engine numbers were moved to the cab side and the tender side (green and black) carried only "L N E R". When tenders were detached from their engines for works repairs, some means of identification was needed and the two workshops then began fitting 8⅞in. x 5¹⁄₁₆in. elliptical cast plates on the centre line at the back end about 18 inches below the top edge (fig. 106). These plates showed the engine number, the date and place of building of the tender, and they were fitted to existing and newly-built tenders until February 1938, when a tender renumbering scheme came into operation. They were also fitted to tenders which Darlington gained for maintenance from other sections, e.g. the Pacifics allocated to the N.E. Area in 1924 (fig. 108).

When the tenders began to carry only "L N E R" on their sides, this facilitated normal exchanges, and moves to take advantage of an improved tender design or to get further use from surplus tenders. A major exchange involving sixty engines and tenders was effected between March 1932 and July 1935. When built during 1911-14, the first thirty express passenger engines of what became C7 class, did not have self-trimming tenders, whereas the 0-8-0 mineral engines No. 2213 onwards (built 1917 and later) did have that type. At the instigation of a York driver (the details are given in full on pages 107/8 of Part 3A) these tenders were exchanged to give the C7's the benefit of the more modern type. Included in the required modifications was the provision of new tender number plates to maintain the coincidence of engine and tender numbers. As a result, there were some curious combinations of the tender's date and place of building compared with that of the engine whose number it bore.

From 1917, mixed traffic, goods and mineral engines began to carry the engine number between the initials "N.E.", on the tender sides of their black livery, and consequently there was no further need for the small number at the rear. The L.N.E.R. continued the tender side numbering until early 1929, and from then onwards these engines were fitted with tender number plates like the passenger engines.

So matters rested until the costing of tender repairs came under scrutiny in 1937. A Costing Committee meeting held at Doncaster in July was informed that the C.M.E. did not require separate tender costs and that these should be merged with those of the engines with which they entered

Works. The Darlington representatives were told what the practice was on Sections other than the N.E. Area. On the G.N. the cost of tender repairs was not recorded separately, being charged against the engine with which the tender came into Works. The G.E. Section had a similar procedure except that repairs were so appropriated that the cost could be ascertained. In the Scottish Area, tenders were not separately numbered. (As will be described later, this statement was only applicable to the Southern Scottish Area, and was contrary to what happened to engines shopped by Inverurie.) Tender mileage was not recorded separately in any Area or Section. Those concerned at Darlington mulled over this matter until 2nd December when the Works Manager put his tender renumbering proposals to the N.E. Area Locomotive Accountant. Current practice at Darlington of engine and tender carrying the same number was explained, as was the custom for the number on the tender to be altered when tenders were interchanged. This caused real difficulty in keeping accurate records of axles and tyres, but if the original number was left on when a tender change was made, problems then arose with charges as tenders were normally repaired against the engine number. The proposals were that all tenders should be given a distinctive number, and all repairs then charged against individual tender numbers. It was added that the Mechanical Engineer (Mr. Thompson) agreed to the suggestion in principle. Apart from altering the Code Number against which tender repairs were to be entered, the Accountant signified approval. On 15th February 1938, instructions were given to Darlington Works to renumber tenders as received, and charge all repairs to the new number. Class Q6 No. 1261 left the works after general repair on 19th February 1938 with the first renumbered tender, which was 8705. Briefly, 4200-gallon Group Standard tenders were renumbered from 7001 upwards, and those of 3500-gallon capacity from 7501 up. The older North Eastern types were given 8001 to 8584 (fig. 109), and 8585 to 8615 were for spare tenders. Numbers 8616 to 8900 were for the newer types running with classes C6, D21, Q6, C7, C9, Q7 and B16, whilst 8901 onwards were for J39 class engines which had second-hand North Eastern type tenders. Further details are given in the Appendix to this chapter. The duplication of existing Stratford tender numbers on an extensive scale was either deliberately ignored, or disregarded because it was never even mentioned in the discussion on the proposals. With one or two aberrations, Darlington implemented this renumbering, the highest number reached being 8942, and it was in use until withdrawal of the last J27 and Q6 engines in September 1967.

In the 1930's Darlington had not always practised what they preached about engines and tenders carrying the same number. On 27th November 1935 the Erecting Shop Foreman reported to the Works Manager that the tender off engine No. 2212 had been repaired and returned to traffic coupled to engine No. 2202. The plate had been changed and now read 2202 Darlington Works 1918. The following week he reported that the tender off J21 class 0-6-0 No. 1817 had been returned to traffic on 30th November coupled to sister engine No. 513, and the number plate was not changed. Clearly there was one law for the rich and another for the poor, even with tenders. Odd cases such as this, and exchanges made by running sheds, later caused some difficulties for the works in getting their 1938 renumbering completed properly. The example of a couple of D20's shows what could — and did — happen. When engine No. 2011 was sent to works in May 1938 it took tender 2021 with it, and the latter was duly renumbered 8401 which was the number correctly allocated to engine No. 2011's tender. The tender with the 2011 numberplate had been coupled previously by Neville Hill shed to engine No. 2108 and that combination went for repair in May 1940. Presumably, the wartime stresses associated with the Dunkirk evacuation proved too much for Darlington just then. Instead of 2108 returning with a tender numbered 8428 (as it should have done) it came back with another 8401, which corresponded with engine 2011, but not tender 2011. The mistake was compounded still further when this second 8401 tender was rebuilt with straight sides in June 1950. It could still have become 8428 (because that number had never been plated), but instead it was then given tender number 8941, which it retained until withdrawal in September 1957.

Darlington added one more to their list in April 1951 when a tender which had had its number plate removed during a repair at Cowlairs arrived with D49 class engine No. 62722. Cowlairs proved quite unable to help on the correct number for this ex-Great Central type tender, and so Darlington added it to their list as 8942. At that time they were unaware of the depth of research we had done, otherwise we could have informed them that 6182 should have been used. Darlington also ran into further difficulty with tenders which Cowlairs had rendered anonymous, because in December 1950 they plated one as 5854 instead of 5954. The genuine ex-G.C. tender No. 5854 was definitely cut up at Gorton in July 1931.

A tender census taken (for the first time) throughout the Eastern and North Eastern Regions in July 1952 threw up two ex-North Eastern tenders each numbered 8223, this duplication having arisen as a result of J25 class Nos. 1973 and 1991 having exchanged tenders in August 1936. When the tender with engine No. 1973 was renumbered in December 1939, it was plated 8223 whereas the correct number for it was 8210. The latter number continued to remain vacant, because to remove the duplication found in 1952, the second 8223 was renumbered 8940 in February 1953. That number was then available because the tender which had carried it was cut up in July 1949.

It has been mentioned that Darlington tender numbers 8901 onwards were for North Eastern type tenders with J39 class engines, but these only extended to 8909 in 1938, and numbers 8910 to 8916 were given to Q6 class tenders put with D49 class engines. For some reason, still unexplained, 8917/8 were never used, and when further allocations were made — from October 1940 — numbers were simply added as required, 8919 to 8940 being used between then and March 1946. Four of these (8919/31/2/40) went on to spare tenders used with J21 class engines, and when the twelve J27 class engines which had been on the G.E. Section since 1926 returned to their native territory from June 1940, their tenders became 8920/7-30/3-9 when they went for repair. When Darlington built the final batch of J39 class Nos. 3081-98 in 1941 they had to collect second-hand tenders for them, and three taken from D17 class engines were given tender numbers 8921/2/4, and the smaller capacity replacements put with the surviving D17 engines were plated 8923/5/6 instead of 1551, 2066 and 992 which they had hitherto carried.

As befitted a Company whose only Locomotive Superintendent (from 1885 to 1922) was a Stirling, and son of the famous Patrick, the Hull & Barnsley used a straightforward copy of Doncaster style for its tender numbering. Engine and tender numbers coincided, and the latter were displayed on a small brass plate at the rear just under the coping on the centre line. From April 1922, the North Eastern added 3000 to the engine number, but left the tender numbering undisturbed. In 1922 or 1923 (probably in April 1923) the tender of engine 3160 required a new plate, and one with that number was duly fitted. As its more modern style of figuring exactly matched that to which Doncaster changed, one is inclined to wonder if it was cast there. From February 1924 all surviving H. & B. engine numbers were altered to the 2405-2542 range, but again the tender numbers were unaffected, and the August 1936 "Railway Observer" carried a mention that J28 class engine No. 2414 had been noted with tender No. 22, and the latter was the engine's original number.

When the Darlington renumbering scheme was formulated early in December 1937, there were still eight tender engines of H. & B. origin (two J23 class and six J28's) still in active service, but no provision whatever was made for their renumbering.

M. & G.N. Tenders

The take-over of the M. & G.N. had no effect on their tender numbers, although some of them duplicated Doncaster tender numbers still in use. This was another line which numbered its tenders the same as the engines. The plates were mounted about the centre of the rear end of the Johnson tenders emphasising the Midland influence, as this was their style. However, the G.N.-designed engines of classes J3 and J4 followed Doncaster practice in that their tender numbers were on small plates under the top edge of the tender. For some years this resulted in three pairs of G.N. type tenders carrying numbers 86, 87 and 89 in exactly similar style.

Tenders at Cowlairs

Although it had been North British Railway practice to number their tenders the same as the engines, there was a radical alteration to the method used about the time of Grouping. Hitherto elliptical plates about 9 inches x 6 inches, carrying the number and the company name in full had been fitted on the back plate, about 18 inches below the coping. The plates were made of cast-iron, except for one. Class D25 No. (9)592 still had at Grouping the special brass tender plate which had been put on for exhibition purposes (see Part 4, page 9).

After Grouping, Cowlairs generally removed these plates and subsequently simply painted the number of the engine to which it was attached inside the leading edge of the tender. So tenders dealt with at Cowlairs completely lost their individual identity, and in a number of cases this works even removed the plates of G.N. and G.C. types from K2 and D49 class engines sent there for maintenance. This was to cause a spate of correspondence and a lot of headaches in later years, one example of which has already been quoted.

One tender number plate survived both Grouping and nationalisation. This was No. 1054, a Wheatley tender, which had presumably run with the Hurst 0-6-0 of this number at one time. It then ran behind Wheatley 0-6-0's (L.N.E.R. class J31) Nos. 1177 and 1137 before withdrawal in April 1925. Subsequently it became a service vehicle, numbered 292, and it did not go for scrapping until February 1954 (figs. 119 & 120). Instructions were then issued to Kilmarnock Works that the number plate was to be preserved as a historical relic, but so far as is known this was not done. Although withdrawn in N.B. numbering, this tender was lettered "L N E R", which was unusual with pre-Grouping number. Incidentally, an N.B.R. tender number plate of a previous pattern does survive in Selkirk Museum. This plate came off the tender attached to the Wheatley 4-4-0 No. 224 which went down with the Tay Bridge on 28th December 1879.

After British Railways was established, their recording of costs for each item of rolling stock showed how necessary it was for each tender to have its own number, as the L.N.E.R. had realised in 1947 and had drawn up an "all-line" scheme, though this was never implemented (see later). B.R. came to the same conclusion about the need for comprehensive renumbering to give logical complete coverage, but something just had to be done about these anonymous Cowlairs maintained tenders. So B.R. decided upon the limited objective of fitting a new, or restoring the former, tender number where no plate at all was fitted, and in the provision of a tender number on a new plate where the original L.N.E.R engine number was still in use as the tender number. The new numbers used began at 9000 and were applied in sequence of engine numbers according to those still in existence at the beginning of 1955 (figs. 117 & 121). Of ex-North British tender engines the only surviving classes were D30, D34, J35, J37 and J36 and the numbers were put on in that sequence; they ranged from 9000 to 9320 inclusive. Progress in January and February showed that the fitting of plates just at works would be far too protracted, so on 4th March 1955 instructions were issued to running sheds that plates would be sent to them for fitting as follows:—

(1) All plates to be placed on back plate on the true centre line.

(2) Former N.B. engines can, in the main, accept plates 2ft. 7in. up from the footplating.

(3) The majority of ex-L.N.E. tenders will accept the plate 19½in. from the top edge.

(4) Where the location point fouls a lamp bracket, the plate must in all cases be located *below* the bracket on the true centre line.

No pretension was made as to any decent finishing of the plates which were simply the cheapest iron castings carrying nothing but the number itself. On No. 64499's tender this led to the plate being fitted upside down and reading 9806 instead of the correct 9086. One of the authors was able to be of help to Carlisle Canal shed staff in pointing this out in September 1955, and noted that appropriate action had been taken when he saw this engine at Aberdeen again in November on its way to Inverurie for general repairs. On 28th September 1955, No. 64479 was noted still without a tender number plate, but otherwise fitting seemed to have been finalised.

In this 1955 tender numbering, the two ex-N.B. tenders running with class J67 tank engines on the Lauder branch were completely ignored, although they were in use until June and December 1956 (but see later).

Curiously, Cowlairs had continued to use numbering, and plates, for the lowliest items of their tender stock. Some of the small four-wheeled shunting tank engines (which became L.N.E.R. class Y9) had duties which called for greater coal capacity than was provided on the engine itself. Even by 1907, many of them ran with wood-bodied four-wheel wagons to act as tenders, more or less permanently coupled to them. From 1923 Cowlairs numbered these in the 777XXX wagon stock series, changed in 1938 to 971XXX series running consecutively from 971541 to 971566. These numbers continued in use until the last Y9's were withdrawn in 1962. It seems clear that Cowlairs regarded these vehicles — even when "permanently" coupled to the Y9's — as wagons for repair and accountancy purposes.

Tenders at Inverurie

Before they acquired L.N.E.R. livery, Great North of Scotland tenders carried the same number as the engine, in the centre of the back of the tender. These were painted and shaded in similar style and size as the company initials on each side of the tender. Group livery included the engine number on each side of the tender so the painted number on the rear plate disappeared. However, for positive identification each tender was then fitted at the front over the shovelling hole, with an elliptical cast-brass plate 3in. x 1¾in. showing the tender number. These numbers were the original series without 68XX addition. As late as 1955, plates showing 33, 45, 46, 48, 49 and 75 were still fitted despite three renumberings of their engines, but some post-1946 replacements had been made because similar plates carrying 2262 and 2278 were also recorded (figs. 113 & 114).

This style, size and position of tender number plate was also applied by Inverurie to ex-N.B. engines which passed through the works for repairs and not only to those transferred to the Northern Scottish Area. In the 1924 numbering, plates with 9176, 9652 (fig. 115) and 9768 were noted, and when J35 class 4486 (ex-9199) went for its first repairs at Inverurie, it was turned out in August 1947 with its tender plated 4486.

One of the J67 class just previously mentioned unusually went to Inverurie for repair in 1947, when its ex-N.B. tender was fitted with a small brass plate showing 8492 and this was still being carried in 1955. The other J67 had a tender with Inverurie style plate number 9784. The J36 of that number had been repaired at Inverurie in 1940 and again in 1943, but the engine was scrapped in October 1947 and the tender became available for further use.

The 1955 instructions as to numbering of ex-N.B. tenders also extended to surviving ex-G.N.S. tenders, numbers 9321 to 9335 being allotted to the fifteen still running with class D40 engines, but 9329 was not fitted due to withdrawal of engine No. 62273 in January 1955. Inverurie had one final gesture of having its own way (to which it had been accustomed throughout L.N.E.R. years) as the 9333 plate on No. 62277's tender was fitted *above* the lamp bracket. Maybe the detailed fitting instructions sent to Southern Scottish sheds never reached as far afield as Inverurie or were given scant attention there.

L.N.E.R.-Built Tenders of Pre-Group Types

Pure Great Eastern type tenders were built with the ten D16 class engines in 1923 and the ten B12/2 engines in 1928 and they carried Stratford-style plates with numbers corresponding to those of the engines. The D16 plates were duly altered from 1780-9 to 8780-9, the latter being retained until withdrawal in the 1950's as were the 8571-80 plates on the B12's. From 1938/9, these numbers were duplicated by their use in the Darlington scheme then adopted. Great Eastern type tenders were also built with the first 48 class B17 engines, and these tenders too had the same numbers (2800-47) as their engines, but in two styles. Numbers 2800 to 2842 were on Doncaster style plates 5in. x 3in. and displaying number only (fig. 105), whereas 2843-47 were on 8⅞in. x 5⅛₆in. Darlington style showing place and year of building in addition, but all 48 plates were fixed in the Stratford position about 15 inches below the coping on the back plate centre line.

Incidentally, even though the B12/2's were built by outside contractors, Beyer Peacock, their tender plates showed "Stratford 1928", as is confirmed by the plate on tender 8571 which accompanied engine 61572 to the North Norfolk Railway.

The continuation of the order for Great Central 4-6-0's which became B7 class added ten G.C. type tenders to L.N.E.R. stock, and they were numbered as the engines, ultimately becoming Nos. 5475-84. It is believed that their plates were all fitted at the front end, in the position to which Gorton changed in 1923. A further 24 G.C.-design tenders were built in 1924 to serve D11/2 class Nos. 6378 to 6401. They were numbered the same as the engines and carried their Gorton-style plates at the front end (fig. 111). Always Scottish engines, seven of them had their plates removed by Cowlairs, but in the 1955 numbering they were given tender numbers 6651 to 6674 and these were fixed on the centre line at the rear, as on the ex-N.B. engines. Despite this latter numbering, the majority continued to carry their front-end number plates, engine No. 62677 still being so fitted at withdrawal in August 1959 when plate 6384 remained undisturbed. The wholesale purchase of ex-R.O.D. 2-8-0 engines brought another 273 Great Central design tenders into L.N.E.R. stock, 6253-6377 and 6495-6642 being added to the tender numbers list and these numbers were retained until withdrawal, and never conflicted with any others elsewhere.

The years 1923 to 1925 also saw additions made to the most modern North Eastern 4125-gallon self-trimming tender design, three class A2, thirty-two class B16 and ten class Q7 engines coming out new so equipped. At that stage, plates were not needed as all carried the engine number prominently on each side of the tender. From February 1929, when the tenders began to carry only "L N E R", plates were fitted and these carried the same number as the engine, all still that of the original coupling. In June-September 1923 ten new class J27 engines came out with an earlier N.E.R. tender type of 3038 gallons water capacity. Again, plates were not needed on these until after February 1929.

Doncaster, too, added new tenders of Great Northern design to L.N.E.R. stock, the eight-wheeled type with coal rails being used for the fifty class A1 Pacifics built in 1923-25, and their 3500-gallon standard class B type was used for the fifteen class O2 mineral engines which became No. 3487-3501. On 9th April 1923, when the works order was placed for the final five to be used by engines 3497-3501, a further fifteen of the same type were ordered to improve the position on earlier engines, which had hitherto made do with second-hand tenders. These new tenders were all given numbers in Doncaster's 5XXX list, taking it up to 5292.

L.N.E.R. Group Standard Tenders

4200-Gallon Stepped Coping Type

On 18th October 1923 Darlington was authorised to build 25 express goods engines and tenders, the order stipulating that they were to be able to clear the North British gauge. The engines were based on the 1920 Doncaster 3-cylinder 2-6-0 design (L.N.E.R. class K3) with some relatively minor modifications, but there was some misunderstanding or lack of liaison between Doncaster and Darlington as to the type of tender to be fitted. The result was that the first two engines were ready before any tenders were completed, so two G.N. class B 3500-gallon tenders numbered 5157 and 5176 were loaned to the N.E. Area and engine Nos. 17 and 28 entered traffic coupled to them. The first Group Standard tender thus went out with engine No. 32, its nominal capacity being 7½ tons of coal and 4200 gallons of water, and a distinguishing feature was the stepped-out coping on either side in place of coal rails. By 1929 Darlington had built 95 and Doncaster built 28 of this type for coupling with 60 class K3, 35 class J38, and 28 class D49 engines. Although Darlington built the D49 class engines, the tenders for them were built at Doncaster who numbered them 5295 to 5322 using their small type plates (fig. 103) fixed just below the rear top edge, but Darlington did not fit any plates to those that they built, considering that the engine number on the side of the tender was sufficient identification. This caused no pain at Cowlairs when the J38's went there for repairs, even when from 1929 the tenders lost their numbering to the cab side. However, an anonymous tender was anathema at Doncaster and, as they had responsibility for shopping the 51 class K3 in the Southern Area with this type of tender, they plated them 5333 to 5383. The other nine tenders were in North Eastern Area

Fig. 63   Trial run from Newcastle to North Wylam on 6th July 1933 of diesel-electric 2-6-2 locomotive built by Armstrong Whitworth.

Fig. 64   Reid-Macleod experimental geared turbine 4-4-0+0-4-4 locomotive passing Haymarket West Junction, 3rd April 1927.

Fig. 65   Kitson-Still steam/diesel 2-6-2 tank locomotive, with indicating shelter, on trial at Beverley on a York-Hull goods train, 1933.

Fig. 66   Metro-Vick-Cammell diesel railcar at Springhead shed, Hull in 1939.

Fig. 67   L.N.E.R.-built class 8F 2-8-0 L.M.S.R. No. 8517 climbing Worsborough
Bank, August 1944.

Fig. 68   Class Y8 No. 559 at Patrington in course of transfer by road to the Spurn
Head Railway, 1940.

Fig. 69   The only known photograph of a S.R. King Arthur class 4-6-0 at work when on loan to the L.N.E.R. No. 739 *King Leodegrance* on a down class D goods train at Inveresk in 1943.

Fig. 70   S.R. class B4 4-4-0 No. 2068 being shunted at York shed by class Y8 No. 560, March 1944. On loan to the L.N.E.R. 1941-44.

Fig. 71   Class J25 No. 2073 at Malvern Road shed, Cheltenham G.W.R., April
1940.

Fig. 72   Class J25 No. 2076 on a class D goods train at Malvern Road, April 1940.

Fig. 73   U.S.A. 2-8-0 No. 2374 at Cambridge on a class C goods, September 1943.

Fig. 74   U.S.A. 2-8-0 No. 2307 on a Heaton-Niddrie class A goods waiting for signals at Monktonhall Junction, 1943.

Fig. 75   W.D. 2-10-0 No. 73788 passing Cambridge on a class C goods, July 1945.

Fig. 76   G.W.R. diesel railcar No. 6 on loan to the L.N.E.R., 1944.

Fig. 77   G.W.R. diesel railcar No. 19 at Blackhill on 25th April 1944 whilst on loan
to the L.N.E.R.

Fig. 78   Class J25 0-6-0 No. 65714 on the Derwent Valley Light Railway.

Fig. 79   Electric locomotive No. 6000 at work in Holland at Naarden-Bussum
station, September 1947.

stock and remained without plates until their numbers were moved from tender to cab side. Darlington then put their style plates on them numbered as the engine until 1938, when they became 7077 to 7085. Although engine Nos. 17 and 28 originally ran with G.N. tenders, they changed to the Group Standard type intended for them during 1927.

The tenders with the J38 class had water pick-up apparatus which was superfluous as there were no water troughs in Scotland, and their coal and water capacities proved greater than needed for their usual duties. In 1931-33 these 4200-gallon stepped sided tenders were replaced (as will be mentioned later) by 23 built at Darlington and 12 built at Doncaster, of smaller capacity and without scoop. The tenders released to Doncaster were coupled to twelve new O2 class engines Nos. 2954-61 and 2430-3, plates numbered 5542 to 5549 and 5561 to 5564 being put on them. Darlington used its 23 ex-J38 tenders for coupling to 15 new D49 class engines numbered between 201 and 298 and eight new J39 class Nos. 2977 to 2980 and 1453/69/71/80, plating them in accordance with those engine numbers. Except for 2977 to 2980, the other nineteen participated in the 1938 renumbering, but 2977-80 continued to carry those numbers as they were then on Cowlairs maintenance. However, before the 1955 Cowlairs numbering tenders 2977/8/9 had gone with their engines to sheds in the Southern Area and their subsequent maintenance was at Stratford, Derby and Gorton, in consequence of which those tender numbers were retained until withdrawal. Tender 2980, however, went with an engine to the N.E. Area, and in 1955 their J39's were on Cowlairs maintenance, so the 2980 plate was removed and 3872 superseded it.

3500-GALLON STEPPED COPING TYPE

Following the class J38 design for mineral haulage in Scotland came the very similar J39 class, which had coupled wheels 6 inches larger, but for which a smaller tender was adequate. The initial order was for 44 of which twelve were for the N.E. Area and the others for the Southern Area. Built by Darlington in 1926/7 none of their tenders was plated, but Doncaster duly added plates numbered 5384 to 5415 to the 32 maintained there and at Gorton. The other twelve in the N.E. Area received Darlington plates numbered as the engines when the tenders were left showing only "L N E R". In the 1938 renumbering, they took numbers 7506-13/4/5/27, the remaining tender having gone to the G.E. Section in 1935 with engine No. 1457, and its tender remained plated 1457 until withdrawal in September 1959.

4200-GALLON STRAIGHT SIDED TYPE

After 1928 no more tenders with stepped sides were built in either capacity. Doncaster introduced the larger type with straight sides coupled to class K3

No. 1300 in April 1929, the first of a batch of twenty built for the N.E. Area. These tenders had a chequered numbering career. When the order was placed in the works on 10th May 1928, the tender numbers reserved for them were 5333 to 5352, but before the tenders were completed these numbers had been taken for stepped-sided K3 tenders built in 1924. So the tenders for the new batch of K3's ranging between Nos. 1300 and 1398 were numbered in Doncaster style as 5456 to 5475 (fig. 104), but the plates were fixed on the *front* end of the tender. All twenty were on Darlington maintenance during the 1930's, and that works fitted them additionally with their style of plate at the rear, these plates showing the same number as the engine. In the 1938 renumbering they were given 7094, 7101/2/6/10-25 and by April 1941 all except 7112 and 7115 of these plates had been fitted. These should have gone to the tenders of engine Nos. 1365 and 1386, but from March 1939 these two were transferred to the Scottish Area, and all subsequent maintenance was at Cowlairs. They retained Doncaster numbers 5462 and 5465 at the front end until 1955 when those plates were removed. By then, engine No. 1365 had become 61876, although it still had Darlington tender plate 1365 at the back. Early in 1955, Cowlairs removed this Darlington plate, but were adrift with its replacement which was a rather rough iron casting on which appeared just 1365 surmounted by "L & N E R" (fig. 116). By March 1955 this wrong plate had been replaced by one of similar size, now showing only 7112, the number it should have received sixteen years earlier. The other K3, by now No. 61879, also received unique treatment as a Cowlairs cast-iron plate replaced the Darlington 1386 plate, but instead of the expected 7115 the number was 5465. For a short time this tender carried 5465 at both ends, on a small brass Doncaster plate at the front (fig. 104) and on a large iron plate at the rear. Then the brass plate was taken off, but the iron one remained until withdrawal in June 1959.

Apparently nobody could make up their mind as to how the above batch of tenders should be numbered. During the War, Doncaster serviced many of them, and, noticing their own number, usually removed the Darlington 1938 number plate so that (apart from 7112 already mentioned) ultimately only 7102 and 7118 remained in use, and all these three 7XXX numbers were on different plate styles. 7112 had a Cowlairs cast-iron plate, but 7118 retained its 1938 Darlington plate, whilst 7102 was a real curiosity. When Darlington put their 7102 plate on in May 1939 they took off the 5458 plate from the front of the tender. From January 1945, Doncaster did the repairs and removed the Darlington style 7102 plate, but there was then no 5458 plate simply to move from front to back (as they had done with 5456 and 5457) and so they fitted their own style of plate on the back — not in the centre but just under the top edge and that plate showed 7102!

85

Darlington commenced to turn out this type of 4200-gallon tender only a month later than Doncaster, the first batch being coupled to J39 class Nos. 2731 to 2742 built for the Scottish Area. The tenders were plated in accordance with the engine numbers and, for their 1955 numbering, Cowlairs allotted them tender Nos. 3841 to 3852. By then, six of these tenders had left the Scottish Region and never received these new numbers and on one of them a real howler occurred. Engine No. 2736 was transferred to the North Eastern Area in March 1939, and when Darlington shopped it in October 1940 they renumbered the tender to 7575 which indicated a 3500-gallon type, but this tender was definitely of the larger 4200-gallon and the mistake was never rectified. Even the July 1952 Tender Census failed in this respect; it showed the capacity correctly, but its numbering in the wrong series went unregarded right through to withdrawal in May 1962.

This design of tender became virtually the Group Standard for most new construction and although modified in some details, e.g. to a higher front plate and a division plate on the top moved forward, also to self-weighing type in 1951/2 on four of them, and two (Nos. 2859/70) which acquired streamlining, it continued to be built until April 1952. Classes to which it was coupled were A2/1(4), B1(406), B17(25), D49(33), J39(80), K1(70), K3(123), O2(4) and V2(173), giving a total of 918 built from 1929. The tender numbers put on them ranged between 5456 and 5740 in the Doncaster series; 7002 to 7296 in the Darlington series; quite a number which had, and retained, the number of the engine to which they were first attached; 3901 to 3970 for the K1 class, and 4004 to 4399 with the B1 class. In addition, some acquired numbers between 3841 and 3872 in the 1955 Cowlairs scheme, although these merely replaced plates showing their first engine number. There was also tender No. 5741 plated at Stratford in April 1953. This was J39 class 1870's original tender to which plate 5616 had been put on in error at some stage, and the 1952 Census showed up the duplication of this number so Doncaster gave instructions to Stratford to make and apply a 5741 number plate.

Darlington introduced this design in May 1928 for the J39 class it built and numbered 2691 to 2730. Further engines of this class totalling an additional 90 received this type, 60 built at Darlington and 30 by Beyer, Peacock & Co., Manchester. In 1931-33 Darlington built 23 and Doncaster another 12 which all went to Scotland to release 4200-gallon tenders from the J38 class. After the Beyer, Peacock order was completed in April 1938, only classes K4 and V4 received this smaller type. It appeared in January 1937 with No. 3441, the first of the K4's and again in July-December 1938 with the other five of that class built by Darlington. Finally, in February/March 1941 Doncaster equipped the two engines of class V4 with it, bringing the total to 173. The fourteen which Doncaster built carried (and retained) their tender numbers 5519 to 5526 and 5550 to 5553 on the J38's, with 5714 and 5725 on the V4's.

The first thirty built by Darlington, Nos. 2691 to 2720, carried the engine number on each side of the tender and, as customary, plates were not fitted. With the change of numbering to the cab sides, the remainder built at Darlington, except for the last five, were fitted with plates numbered in accordance with that of the engine. The engines numbered 2691 to 2730, 2770 to 2785 and 2962 to 2976 all went to the Southern Area where they were fitted with Doncaster style number plates showing 5416 to 5455, 5485 to 5500 and 5527 to 5541. The 23 tenders built for the J38 class were plated by Darlington with the number corresponding to the engine to which first fitted, and apart from three removed by Cowlairs, retained these plates until 1955 when they were renumbered 3818 to 3840. Likewise the tender of the first K4 was plated 3441 (fig. 107) through to 1955 when it was changed to 7576 on a Cowlairs-style plate. The other five K4's were built after the 1938 Darlington scheme was introduced and so were plated 7570 to 7574 from new. On three other J39's with this pattern of tender, Cowlairs changed the 1875 and 1894 plates to 3986 and 3988, but 1880 did not get the logical 3987. That engine had gone to the N.E. Area in August 1943 and in 1955 its tender number became 7500.

L.N.E.R. 5000 GALLON 8-WHEELED TYPE

Based on the G.N. design with coal rails, a high-sided type was developed in two versions, one with corridor and one without. The corridor type came first in April 1928, when Doncaster built a batch of ten which they numbered 5323 to 5332, and these were their first to have the number plate at the front end. One more, numbered 5484, was built in 1929 and sent to Darlington for coupling to the high-pressure 4-6-4 No. 10000. Then in 1935 the first four of the streamlined A4 class, Nos. 2509-12, came out with corridor tenders Nos. 5589 to 5592, after which only seven more were built. These were numbered 5646 to 5652 and their first couplings were to new A4 class engines Nos. 4491 to 4497. Switching of corridor tenders amongst A1, A3 and A4 class engines was carried out quite often, but engine No. 4491 was unique in keeping its original tender, which it still had at withdrawal in August 1964, and in March 1965 when they were sold for cutting up.

The high-sided non-corridor version made its appearance in February 1930 and the batch of eight were coupled to new A3 engines Nos. 2595-9 and 2795/6/7. It was May 1934 before there was any addition, and this was a single, somewhat experimental tender No. 5565 having a welded tank, and being the last one with spoked wheels. Its whole career was spent with engine No. 2001 both as class P2 and as class A2/2. In November/December 1933, nineteen more were ordered from Doncaster Works and they were numbered 5566 to 5584. Their first couplings were to the other five P2 class Nos. 2002-6, to the last batch of nine A3 class Nos. 2500-8, with the remaining five sent to Darlington for coupling to the class A2 Raven Pacifics Nos. 2400-4. Another batch of ten ordered in February 1936 was numbered 5636-45 and they were modified at the top to facilitate coupling to the streamlined engines, but the last three were never so attached, being put behind unstreamlined Pacifics. On 4th November 1936 fourteen more were ordered to run with the final series of A4 class Nos. 4462-9/99, 4500, 4900-3, but only nine numbered 5667-75 were built as the withdrawal of the five Raven Pacifics released tender numbers 5569/72/4/80/3 for use with these A4's.

Even Thompson failed to make any significant change to this Gresley design and contented himself with just breaking a forty-year old numbering system for the fifteen to go with his A2/3 class Nos. 500/11-24 built in 1946/7 by starting a new series at No. 700 for the 8-wheeled type tenders. Peppercorn continued this series with the tenders for his fifteen class A2, and also for his 49 class A1 engines, and these took the numbering up to 782 on the very last tender to L.N.E.R. design which Doncaster built. It entered traffic on 23rd December 1949 with engine No. 60162. These new engines account for 79 of the 83 numbers 700 to 782, the other four being put on three new and one renumbered tenders used with the A2/1 class (see p.161 of Part 2A).

L.N.E.R. Non-Standard Tenders

Gresley's detractors often criticised him for not going far enough or fast enough towards standardisation, and of being too much concerned with 'specials'. He gave them very little cause for such complaint on tenders. When he took over as Locomotive Engineer on 1st October 1911, Great Northern tender policy was already formulated, and the 3500-gallon Class B type was already the accepted standard for front rank engines, both passenger and goods. He built no other design until 1922, when he introduced the 8-wheeled Class G for his first two Pacifics, and this was essentially a stretched version of Class B. In the eighteen years he was in charge on the L.N.E.R., he only added two pairs of tenders which were non-standard. The first two, numbered 5293/4, were built by Doncaster in 1925 for the 2-8-2 mineral engines of class P1, and even they were the progenitors of the straight-sided design adopted as standard from 1929. Their equally divided wheelbase was a reversion to the first of the class B tenders, and their capacity of 7 tons of coal and 4700 gallons of water was not matched by any other 6-wheel tenders. After serving engine Nos. 2393 and 2394 until their withdrawal in July 1945, these tenders were used again from April and July 1946 with Thompson B2 class rebuilds Nos. 2815 and 1632. Tender 5294's finest hour was yet to come. In October 1958 its engine (then 61632) had its name changed to *Royal Sovereign,* as it then became the nominated Royal engine at Cambridge.

Darlington built the other pair in 1931 for attaching to the two booster-fitted engines which became class C9, and they were certainly a curiosity in that the tender and engine were articulated (see page 127 of Part 3A for a detailed description). Darlington plated them 727 and 2171, as the engine numbers, and the tenders hitherto with those numbers went to Q6 class 2297 and 2221, being renumbered accordingly. In the 1938 renumbering, the C9 tenders became 8684 and 8685, and they became spare in 1942/3 when their engines were withdrawn. Darlington rebuilt both in 1945 to nearer normal type, and from December 1947 tender 8685 was used by B1 class No. 1039 and in June 1949 the other one 8684 went to B1 class 61038.

1947 Proposed Renumbering of all L.N.E.R. Tenders

By early January 1947 reasonable success had been achieved in a tidy rearrangement of the engine numbering, so attention was turned to the question of the tenders which was of even greater necessity. The proposal put forward is detailed overleaf, but the time taken in discussion to obtain agreement combined with the imminence of nationalisation thwarted progress, and the comprehensive renumbering scheme was never fully implemented. However, two facets of it were already in being with the 8-wheeled non-corridor tenders being given 7XX numbers and B1 tenders receiving 4000 numbering, whilst the 1938 numbers on the former North Eastern tenders were to remain undisturbed. The only other move towards the scheme had to wait until 1955, when the N.B. and the G.N.S. tenders did get numbers in the 9000 series.

Section/ Area Types	Existing Numbering Range	Proposed Numbering Range	
L.N.E.	Odd Nos. 1800-1900 2800-2872 (B17 class) 2941-2952 5253-5800 7000-7250 7500-7575	To be re-grouped as follows:— Corridor Other 8-wheeled 6-wheeled 3500 gallons B17 class (as before) 6-wheeled 4200 gallons	1-99 500-999 1200-2399 2800-2872 3000-4599
Austerity 2-8-0	As engine numbers		4700-4899
L.M.S. 2-8-0	3100-3167		4900-4967
G.N.	Various up to 1400 (about 300 tenders); 5000-5252		5000-5999
G.C.	5000-5500; 5640-5880; 5940-6650		6000-6999
G.E.	Odd Nos. 7410-8000; 8140-8294; 8500-8579; 8780-8900		7000-7999
N.E.	8001-9000		No change
N.B.	Not numbered (except those plated at Inverurie)		9000 upwards
G.N.S.	Odd Nos. 1-112 and some with 1946 engine numbers		

Appendix
1938 Darlington Tender Renumbering

This was done on the most basic principle, i.e. starting with the lowest engine number of each class and working upwards. It entirely ignored whether the tender was stepped or straight-sided (except for one instance), took no account of year built, nor of any Doncaster number already fitted. For example, 7001 tender was a stepped tender built in 1926 for a J38 class which was later used for D49 No. 201, whereas 7002 tender was a straight-sided type which came out new in 1934 with engine No. 205. The initial allocations were:—

4200-gallon Group Standard tenders

7001-7053 D49 class in N.E. Area, engine Nos. in 201 to 377 range.

7054-7076 D49 class in Scottish Area, engine Nos. in 246 to 329 range and 2753-60.

7077-7136 K3 class in N.E. Area, engine Nos. in 17 to 3829 range.

7137-7146 V2 class in N.E. Area, engine Nos. 4772/3/6-83.

7147-7172 J39 class being built at Darlington, engine Nos. in 1804 to 1997 range.

7173-7183 V2 class 4804-14 using stepped-sided tenders from J38 and D49 engines.

7184-7211 V2 class 4815-42 built by Darlington in 1939.

7212-7236 V2 class in 4853 to 4898 range for N.E. and Scottish Areas.

7237-7251 V2 class 4899 and 3641-54 built by Darlington in 1942.

7252-7282 V2 class 3665-95 built by Darlington in 1942-44.

7283-7286 A2/1 class 3696-99 (Nos. 7283/5 were renumbered 4000/1 in November 1946).

7287-7296 B1 class 8301-10 built by Darlington in 1942-44.

3500-gallon Group Standard tenders

7501-7541 J39 class in N.E. Area, engine Nos. in 1412 to 1584 range and 2725.

7542-7557 J39 class built by Beyer, Peacock, engine Nos. in 1532-87 range.

7558-7569 J39 class being built at Darlington, engine Nos. in 1508-60 range.

7570-7574 K4 class Nos. 3442 to 3446 built at Darlington in 1938.

8001-8015   B15 class, engine Nos. in 782 to 825 range.

8016-8123   J21 class in N.E. Area, engine Nos. in 16 to 1820 range.

8124-8132   J21 class in other Areas, engine Nos. in 26 to 1806 range.

8133-8179   J24 class in N.E. Area, engine Nos. in 1821 to 1960 range.

8180-8188   J24 class in Scottish Area, engine Nos. in 1841 to 1955 range.

8189-8280   J25 class, engine Nos. in 25 to 2142 range.

8281-8370   Q5 class, engine Nos. in 83 to 2125 range.

8371-8430   D20 class, engine Nos. in 476 to 2110 range.

8431-8480   J26 class, engine Nos. in 67 to 1781 range.

8481-8580   J27 class in N.E. Area, engine Nos. in 814 to 2392 range.

8581-8583   J27 class in Scottish Area, engine Nos. 790, 839 and 1067.

8584-8602   D17 class in N.E. Area, engine Nos. in 1621 to 1929 range.

8603-8605   D17 class in Scottish Area, engine Nos. 1876, 1901/21.

8606-8615   Spare tenders from withdrawn J21 class engines.

8616-8635   C6 class, engine Nos. in 295 to 1794 range.

8636-8678   C7/1 class in N.E. Area, engine Nos. in 706 to 2211 range.

8679-8680   C7/2 class in N.E. Area, engine Nos. 732 and 2212.

8681-8683   C7/1 class in Scottish Area, engine Nos. 714, 2193/4.

8684-8685   C9 class, engine Nos. 727 and 2171.

8686-8695   D21 class, engine Nos. 1237 to 1246.

8696-8812   Q6 class in N.E. Area, engine Nos. in range 1247 to 2302.

8813-8815   Q6 class in Scottish Area, engine Nos. 2254/7/9.

8816-8830   Q7 class, engine Nos. in range 624 to 905.

8831-8900   B16 class, engine Nos. in range 840 to 2382.

8901-8905   J39 class engines 1475-9, tenders ex-Raven Pacifics.

8906-8909   J39 class engines 1453/69/71/80, tenders ex-B13 and Q6 classes.

8910-8916   D49 class engines 318/20/27/36/35/22 and 256, tenders ex-Q6 class.

8917-8918   Never used, and no obvious candidates for them.

8919-8940   Spare D17 and J21 tenders, and 12 class J27 returned from Southern Area.

NOTE: Not all these 8000 series plates were actually fitted, as twelve J21, seven J24, seven J25 and twelve D17 class were withdrawn before tender renumbering. Some went into Service Stock as fire-fighting water tanks, still plated as the engine number and could be noted as late as 1954, as was tender No. 1952 at Hull Dairycoates yard, that engine having been withdrawn in August 1933. Despite repairs at Darlington in December 1939, July 1943 and February 1945, Southern Area J21 No. 432 still had that tender number when seen in July 1945.

ENGINE ORDER NUMBERS AT DONCASTER WORKS

In the chapter on "Locomotive Works" in Part 1 of this series, reference was made to the Engine Order numbers issued at Doncaster Works. Frequent mention of these numbers has also been made in the locomotive class articles in subsequent Parts and it is felt that a complete list would be useful to the reader. For convenience the explanation of the numbering given on page 94 of Part 1 is repeated, as follows:—

In 1897 Ivatt introduced Engine Order numbers at Doncaster commencing with E.O.201 for a series of ten 4-4-0's Nos. 1071-80 (L.N.E.R. class D4). At first these order numbers applied also to Stores Orders, being used to cover orders for spare boilers as well as complete engines. Thus Stores Order 202 was for ten spare boilers whilst Engine Order 203 was for ten complete engines, 0-6-0ST's Nos. 1201-10 (L.N.E.R. class J52). This meant that there was no Engine Order 202 and this number remained a blank in the E.O. series. Thereupon it was decided to issue separate E.O.s and S.O.s for engines and boilers. This resulted in S.O. 204/5 being allocated to orders for spare boilers and S.O. 206 for the boilers associated with E.O. 204, 4-4-0's Nos. 1301-10 (L.N.E.R. class D4). To avoid further confusion caused by E.O. and S.O. series numbers being similar, all new boilers ordered after S.O. 206 were allocated order numbers in a new series commencing at S.O. 500 (these became Boiler Orders from 524 onwards, issued in May 1899), Engine Orders continuing from E.O. 205 upwards. There was a separate Tender Order series.

Engine Orders eventually terminated at E.O. 409 when the last steam engine order was completed in 1957. There were several gaps in the series, in addition to E.O. 202 already mentioned, and several cases of cancelled orders. In certain other cases of cancelled orders, the E.O. numbers were, however, reallocated. Certain outside-built engines received Doncaster E.O. numbers but not in every instance, whilst on the other hand a batch of Doncaster-built engines, 4-4-0 Nos. 1386-95 (L.N.E.R. class D2) did not receive an E.O. number but were allocated S.O.1007 in the miscellaneous Stores Order series commencing at S.O.1000.

From 1914 it became the practice with engines built at Doncaster to restrict individual Engine Orders to not more than ten engines each, and orders for more than ten engines were split up into more than one E.O.

Although the E.O. system was introduced for guidance in the works whilst the engines were under construction (fig. 99), this did not supersede the practice of fitting brass works plates bearing serial numbers which had commenced at No. 1 in 1867 and had reached 1000 by 1903 (fig. 124). By 1952, when the practice of allocating works numbers was discontinued, only ten engines had been built at Doncaster without being given serial numbers. These were the L.M.S.-type 8F 2-8-0's of class O6 Nos. 3148-57 built in 1945-46. This was deliberately done to balance ten works numbers not used in 1923, Nos. 1554-63, so that the 2,000th engine to be built at Doncaster, class A2/3 No. 500 then under construction, could be correctly given Doncaster works number 2000 of 1946.

Works plates sometimes went astray and often new ones were cast to replace them, but occasionally plates were fitted to the wrong engine and such errors were not always rectified.

L.N.E.R. Class when built		E.O. number	Works numbers	Running numbers	Date built
D4	4-4-0	201	723-32	1071-80	1897
—		202	—	—	—
J52	0-6-0T	203	735-44	1201-10	1897
D4	4-4-0	204	745-54	1301-10	1897
C12	4-4-2T	205	755-8/88-91/6/7	1009/10/3-20	1898/9
C2	4-4-2	206	769	990	1898
D4	4-4-0	207	759-68	1311-20	1898
J4	0-6-0	208	775-84	315/6/8/29/31/2/4/6/7/8	1898
D2	4-4-0	209	770-4	1321-5	1898
—	4-2-2	210	787	266	1898
D2	4-4-0	211	785/6/92-5/8-801	1326-35	1898
C12	4-4-2T	212	812-21	1501-10	1899

L.N.E.R. Class when built		E.O. number	Works numbers	Running numbers	Date built
D4	4-4-0	213	802-11	1341-50	1898
C12	4-4-2T	214	832-41	1511-20	1899
—	4-2-2	215	902	267	1900
D2	4-4-0	216	852-61	1336-40/61-5	1899
J4	0-6-0	217	822-31/42-51	343/4/5/8-53/9-64/7/8/71/5/81	1899
C2	4-4-2	218	872-81	949/50/82-9	1900
D4	4-4-0	219	862-71	1351-60	1899
J4	0-6-0	220	882-901	165/77/9/80/92, 302/3/4/6/8/ 84/6/7/8/90/2/4/6/8/9	1900
D2	4-4-0	221	903-22	1366-73/80/74/82/3/4/75-9/81/5	1900/1
—	4-2-2	222	934-43	92, 100, 261-5/8/9/70	1901
C12	4-4-2T	223	924-33	1521-30	1901
C2	4-4-2	224	974	271	1902
J53	0-6-0T	225	—	Fitting of condensing gear (5)	1900
Q1	0-8-0	226	923	401	1901
J52	0-6-0T	227	944-63	1251-70	1901/2
J53	0-6-0T	228	—	Fitting of condensing gear (4)	1900
Q1	0-8-0	229	964-73	402/5/6/7/3/8/9/10/04/11	1902
C2	4-4-2	230	996-1003/5/6	252/3/6/5/4/7/9/0/60/58	1903
D2	4-4-0	(S.O. 1007)	975/7/9-81/90/2-5	1386/8/91/89/7/90/4/5/2/3	1903
Q1	0-8-0	231	976/8/82-9	412/4/3/5/7/6/8-21	1902/3
C1	4-4-2	232	991	251	1902
Q1	0-8-0	233	1007-16/27/8/9/50-5	423/2/5/4/6/7/9/30/28/31-40	1903/4
C12	4-4-2T	234	1017-26	1531-40	1903/4
R1	0-8-2T	235	1004	116	1903
C1	4-4-2	236	1030 49	272-81/3/5/2/6/4/7/9/8/90/1	1904
Q1	0-8-0	237	—	Cancelled — re-issued as E.O. 247 & 259A	—
R1	0-8-2T	238	1056-65	117-26	1904
C1	4-4-2	239	1066	292	1905
C1	4-4-2	240	1067-76	293/6/7/4/5/8/9, 301, 300, 1400	1905
C1	4-4-2	241	1077-86	1401/2/3/5/4/6-10	1905
J52	0-6-0T	242	1087-96	1271-80	1905
R1	0-8-2T	243	1097-1106	127-36	1905
Railmotor		244	1107/8	2, 1	1905
C1	4-4-2	245	1109-18	1411-20	1906
R1	0-8-2T	246	1119-38	137-56	1906
Q1	0-8-0	247	1139-43	441-5	1906/7
C1	4-4-2	248	1166	1421	1907
C1	4-4-2	249	1144/6-54	1422-5/7/8/6/9/30/1	1907
C12	4-4-2T	250	1155-64	1541-50	1907
N1	0-6-2T	251	1145	190	1907
D2	4-4-0	252	1165/7-70	1396-9, 1180	1907

L.N.E.R. Class when built		E.O. number	Works numbers	Running numbers	Date built
C1	4-4-2	253	1171-5/86-90	1432-41	1907/8
N1	0-6-2T	254	1176-85	1551-60	1907/8
C1	4-4-2	255	1191-7/9, 1200/1	1443/4/2/5-8/50/49/51	1908
J1	0-6-0	256	1198, 1202-15	1-15	1908
J52	0-6-0T	257	1216-25	1281-90	1908/9
D2	4-4-0	258	1226-35	41-50	1909
Q1	0-8-0	259A	1236-40	446-50 (saturated)	1909
Q2	0-8-0	259B	1241/4/5/8/50	451-5 (superheated)	1909
J5	0-6-0	260	1242/3/6/7/9/51-5	31-5/7/6/8/9, 40	1909/10
N1	0-6-2T	261	1256-65	1561-70	1910
J5	0-6-0	262	1266-75	21-30	1910
C1	4-4-2	263	1276-85	1452-61	1910
N1	0-6-2T	264	1286-95	1571-80	1910/1
D1	4-4-0	265	1296-1310	51-65	1911
J6	0-6-0	266	1311-25	521-35	1911
N1	0-6-2T	267	1326-40	1581-91/3/2/4/5	1911/2
N1	0-6-2T	268	1341-50	1596-1605	1912
J2	0-6-0	269	1351/2/3/5-61	71-80	1912
K1	2-6-0	270	1354	1630	1912
J6	0-6-0	271	1362-71	536-45	1912
K1	2-6-0	272	1372-80	1631-9	1913
J6	0-6-0	273	1381-1400	546-65	1913
O1	2-8-0	274	1411/2/3/5/8	456-60	1913/4
J6	0-6-0	275	1401-10	566-75	1913
J51	0-6-0T	276	1414/6/7/9-24/7	157/8/9/61/0/2/3/6/4/7	1913/4
K2	2-6-0	277	1425/6/8-35	1640-9	1914
J6	0-6-0	278	1436-45	576-85	1914
J6	0-6-0	279	1446-55	586-95	1914
J51	0-6-0T	280	1456-65	168-76/8	1914/5
K2	2-6-0	281	1466-75	1650-9	1916
J6	0-6-0	282	1476/7/8	596/7/8	1917
O2	2-8-0	283	1481	461	1918
J6	0-6-0	284	1479/80	599, 600	1918
J6	0-6-0	285	1482-91	601-10	1918/9
O1	2-8-0	286	—	Order transferred to N.B.L. Co. (462-71)	—
O1	2-8-0	286A	—	Order transferred to N.B.L. Co. (472-6)	—
J6	0-6-0	287	1502-8/10/1/2	621-30	1919/20
O2	2-8-0	288	—	Order transferred to N.B.L. Co. (477-86)	—
J51	0-6-0T	289	1492-1501	211-20	1919
K3	2-6-0	290	1509/13-7/20/2/6/9	1000-3/6/4/5/7/8/9	1920/1
J6	0-6-0	291	1532-5/7/8/40-3	631-40	1921/2

L.N.E.R. Class when built		E.O. number	Works numbers	Running numbers	Date built
N2	0-6-2T	292	1518/9/21/3/4/5/7/8/30/1	1606-15	1920/1
A1	4-6-2	293	1536/9	1470/1	1922
N2	0-6-2T	294	—	Constructed by N.B.L. Co. (1721-70)	—
K2	2-6-0	295	—	Constructed by Kitson & Co. (1680-1705)	—
J50	0-6-0T	296	1544-53	221-30	1922
—	—	—	1554-63	Not used	—
A1	4-6-2	297	1564-73	4472-81	1923
O2	2-8-0	298	1574-82/4	3487-96	1923/4
O2	2-8-0	299	1587/9/92/4/5	3497-3501	1924
J50	0-6-0T	300	1583/5/6/8/90/1/3/6/7/9	3231/3/2/4-40	1924
A1	4-6-2	301	1598, 1600-8	2543-52	1924
A1	4-6-2	302	1609-18	2553-62	1924/5
P1	2-8-2	303	1619/20	2393/4	1925
J72	0-6-0T	304	1621/4/6/7/30/1/3-6	500/12/6/24/42/66/71/4/6/81	1925
N2	0-6-2T	305	1622/3/5/8/9/32	892-7	1925
J50	0-6-0T	306	1637-46	583/6/8/9/91/3/4/6, 601/3	1926
J50	0-6-0T	307	1647-55	609/10/6/7/8/21/2/35/6	1926
J50	0-6-0T	308	1656-65	1037/41/5/58/63/8/9/70/4/9	1926/7
J50	0-6-0T	309	1666/7/8	1081/2/6	1927
N7	0-6-2T	310	1669-78	2600-9	1927
N7	0-6-2T	311	1679-87	2610-8 (one more cancelled)	1927/8
N7	0-6-2T	312	1688-92/6-9, 1701	2619-28	1928
N7	0-6-2T	313	1702/4/6	2629-31	1928
A3	4-6-2	314	1693/4/5, 1700/3/5/7-10	2743-52	1928/9
K3	2-6-0	315	1711-20	1300/12/8/31/45/64/5/7/8/86	1929
K3	2-6-0	316	1721-30	1387/8/9/91/2/4-8	1929
A3	4-6-2	317	1731/3/6/8/41-4	2595/6/7, 2795/6/7, 2598/9	1930
J50	0-6-0T	318	1732/4/5/7/9/40	2789-94	1930
V1	2-6-2T	319	1745-54	2900-9	1930/1
V1	2-6-2T	320	1755-64	2910-9	1931
V1	2-6-2T	321	1765-72	2920-7	1931
V1	2-6-2T	322	—	Cancelled (2928-37)	—
V1	2-6-2T	323	—	Cancelled (2938-47)	—
V1	2-6-2T	324	1799, 1801-5	2928-33 (to have been 2948-53)	1934/5
S1	0-8-4T	325	—	Order transferred to Gorton (2798/9)	—
O2	2-8-0	326	1773-80	2954-61 (2962-8 cancelled)	1932
A3	4-6-2	327	—	Five engines cancelled	—
O2	2-8-0	328	1781-8	2430-7	1933/4
P10	2-8-2T	329	—	Ten engines cancelled	—
P2	2-8-2	330	1789	2001	1934
A3	4-6-2	331	1790-5/7/8, 1800	2500-8	1934/5

L.N.E.R. Class when built		E.O. number	Works numbers	Running numbers	Date built
P2	2-8-2	332	1796	2002	1934
V1	2-6-2T	333	1806-15	417/46/77/9/81/4/6/7/97/8	1935
P2	2-8-2	334	1836/9/40/2	2003-6	1936
V1	2-6-2T	335	1816/7/20/2/4-9	402/14/5/6/8, 2897, 419/22/3/8	1935/6
V1	2-6-2T	336	—	Ten engines cancelled	—
V1	2-6-2T	337	1830-5/8/44	440, 2898, 454/5/61/5/6, 2899	1936
A4	4-6-2	338	1818/9/21/3	2509-12	1935
V2	2-6-2	339	1837/41/3/5/6	4771-5	1936
A4	4-6-2	340	1847-56	4482-91	1936/7
A4	4-6-2	341	1857-63	4492-8	1937
A4	4-6-2	341A	1864/5/6	4462/3/4	1937
A4	4-6-2	342	1867-76	4465-9/99, 4500, 4900/1/2	1937/8
A4	4-6-2	343	1877	4903	1938
V1	2-6-2T	344	1878-87	404/7/20/4/5/47/8/51/67/9	1938
V1	2-6-2T	345	1888-97	472/8/80/3/5/8-91/6	1938/9
V2	2-6-2	346	1898-1901/12/3/5-8	4843-52	1939/40
V3	2-6-2T	347	1902-11	390-3/5-9, 401	1939/40
EM1	Electric	348	1914	6701 (a further nine cancelled)	1940
EM1	Electric	349-54	—	Six orders of ten each cancelled	—
V4	2-6-2	355	1919/20	3401/2	1941
V2	2-6-2	356	1921-30	3655-64	1941/2
V2	2-6-2	357	—	Transferred to Darlington (3665-74)	—
V3	2-6-2T	358	—	Five engines cancelled	—
O2	2-8-0	359	1931-40	3833-42	1942
J50	0-6-0T	360	—	Ten engines. Order transferred from Gorton but cancelled	—
V2	2-6-2	361	—	Transferred to Darlington (3675-84)	—
V2	2-6-2	362	—	,, ,, (3685-94)	—
V2	2-6-2	363	—	,, ,, (3695-9)	—
O2	2-8-0	364	1941-50	3843-52	1942
O2	2-8-0	365	1951-5	3853-7	1942/3
V3	2-6-2T	366	—	Ten engines cancelled	—
V3	2-6-2T	367	—	Ten engines cancelled	—
J50	0-6-0T	368	—	Ten engines cancelled	—
J50	0-6-0T	369	—	Five engines cancelled	—
Diesel	0-6-0	370	1960/3/73/8	8000-3	1944/5
8F	2-8-0	371	1956-9/61/2/4-7	L.M.S. 8510-9	1943/4
O6	2-8-0	372	—	Order ex-Gorton, transferred to Darlington (3158-67)	—
8F	2-8-0	373	1968-72/4-7/9	L.M.S. 8520-9	1944/5
8F	2-8-0	374	1980-3/5-90	L.M.S. 8530-7/9/8	1945
O6	2-8-0	375	Not allotted	3148-57 (transferred from Darlington)	1945/6

L.N.E.R. Class when built		E.O. number	Works numbers	Running numbers	Date built
O6	2-8-0	376	1991-9, 2001	3158-67 (transferred from Darlington)	1946
L1	2-6-4T	377	1984	9000	1945
A2	4-6-2	378	2000/2-10	500/11-9	1946/7
A2	4-6-2	379	2011-5	520-4	1947
A2	4-6-2	380	2016-25	525-31, 60532/3/4	1947/8
A2	4-6-2	381	2026-30	60535-9	1948
A1	4-6-2	382	2031-40	60114-23	1948/9
A1	4-6-2	383	2041-6	60124/6/5/7/8/9	1949
Diesel	0-6-0	384	—	Constructed by Brush (15004)	1949
A2	4-6-2	385	—	Ten engines cancelled	—
A2	4-6-2	386	—	Three engines cancelled	—
A2	4-6-2	387	—	Seven engines cancelled	—
A1	4-6-2	388	2047-56	60153-62	1949

Engine order numbers in this series continued to be allotted during B.R. days until the final steam locomotives were built at Doncaster in 1957. E.O. 389-94 covered L.M.S.-type Class 4 2-6-0's; E.O. 395/6/7/9, 400/1/5/8/9 covered B.R. Class 4 2-6-0's; E.O. 398 B.R. Class 4 2-6-4T's; and E.O. 402/3/4/6/7 B.R. Class 5 4-6-0's. Works numbers ceased at 2111 (E.O. 395 No. 76024).

B.R. E PREFIX TO LOCOMOTIVE NUMBERS

After nationalisation of the railways on 1st January 1948, the first visible evidence of new ownership of L.N.E.R. locomotive stock appeared on Thursday 15th January when three engines, class A3 No. 112, C12 No. 7369 and J50 No. 8929, were ex Doncaster Plant. Although their previous livery was unchanged, the letters "L N E R" had been replaced by "BRITISH RAILWAYS" in yellow painted and unshaded Gill Sans characters, and a small letter E prefixed the running number. It had been realised that confusion was possible between like numbered locomotives from the four main line companies and it was decided that former L.N.E.R. stock should have an E prefix applied to the number, whilst L.M.S. engines would use M, G.W.R. W and Southern S.

By Saturday 17th January Gorton Works had applied the E prefix to class L3 No. 9053 and O4 No. 3600, whilst Stratford had done the same to class N7 No. 9717. Darlington followed suit on Friday 23rd with class B1 No. 1068. All these works, together with Doncaster, continued to apply the prefix to engines that were out-shopped during the ensuing eight weeks (figs.125&126).

For some reason the two ex-L.N.E.R. works in the Scottish Area, Cowlairs and Inverurie, chose to largely ignore the instruction to apply the E prefix, even though the former L.M.S. works at St. Rollox was busy applying M to the engines that it overhauled. Cowlairs turned out only one engine with an E prefix — class B1 No. 1072 on 6th March, whilst Inverurie's sole contribution never entered traffic as such. Class J35 No. 4461 had the E put above the number but before it returned to traffic on 20th March, the E was painted over and the engine was renumbered 64461. About two years later the E on one side only was beginning to show through and the engine ran for some time thus (see fig. 86, Part 1).

During the period concerned, Armstrong Whitworth's Scotswood Works were carrying out general repairs on many of the 200 "Austerity" 2-8-0 engines which the L.N.E.R had bought at the end of 1946 and to which the numbers 3000 to 3199 had been given. Beginning with No. E3027, ex-works 3rd February 1948, that works also applied the prefix.

By mid-March 1948 British Railways had decided to implement a complete renumbering scheme in place of the letter prefixes for its locomotive stock. As already mentioned, former L.N.E.R. steam engines were to have their numbers increased by 60000 (except for class W1 No. 10000 which was allotted the number 60700). Between 18th and 25th March all six L.N.E.R. workshops turned out their first engine with five-figure number, these being:—

Doncaster 18/3/48: J6 64173
Cowlairs 19/3/48: J36 65228
Inverurie 19/3/48: B12 61513
Gorton 20/3/48: J11 64407/52
Stratford 23/3/48: J67 68529
Darlington 25/3/48: D49 62758, J25 65718, J72 68692

On 31st March, six days after Darlington had commenced its share of the renumbering scheme, class G5 No. E7335 and Q6 No. E3405 were ex-works. They had been repainted earlier, but were not altered before being returned to traffic. These were the last engines to receive the E prefix. In all, 508 engines received it, including newly built class A2 Nos. 527-31, B1 1288-1303 and L1 9001/4-12, and they are listed below.

A2	527-31
A2/1	508
A2/2	504
A2/3	500/22
A3	50, 62/4, 72, 99, 103/12
A4	4, 21/2/7
A5	9803/8/13/6/35/8
A7	9775/9/80
A8	9856/67/79
B1	1045/6/51/6/64/6/8/9/72/3/94, 1100, 1288-1303
B2	1639
B7	1370/84/7/91
B12	1510/30/55/9/67
B16/1	1412/23/31/47/58
B16/3	1467
B17	1610/21/31/61/2/4/7
C1	2877/85
C7	2982
C12	7369/87/97
C13	7400/3/14/6/22/32
D2	2188
D3	2140
D9	2302/30
D10	2652/9
D16	2524/6/9/93, 2606/10/8/9/20
D20	2354/61/9/72/9/82/6
D49	2713/8/36/70/3
E4	2793/4
F2	7109/11
F5	7195, 7216
F6	7226
G5	7243/66/74/6/80/6/96, 7304/34/5/43
J2	5022
J3	4117/9/27/48
J6	4191, 4216/31/48/70

J10	5134/49/58/9/80/6
J11	4282/8, 4328/46/8/51/8/68/79, 4394/6/9, 4404/6/11/5/41
J15	5391, 5452/69/75
J17	5522/48/65/73/4
J19	4664
J20	4687
J21	5030/62/77/91/8
J24	5644
J25	5645/6/51/8/63/91/6, 5716/25/6
J26	5730/8/69/78
J27	5805/8/49/78/90
J39	4702/14/7/8/23/31/50/2/6/62/7/73, 4802/3/ 83/6/92, 4901/52/5
J50	8909/14/21/6/7/9/38/74
J52	8764/88/91/5, 8819/23/9/55
J62	8200
J66	8376/82
J67	8512/31/40/7/86
J69	8495, 8528/48/79, 8619
J71	8230/44/7/9/58/72/3/7/80, 8303/4/8/10/1
J72	8672/82/7/93, 8723/7/9/30/48
J77	8402/4/33
J94	8013
K2	1753/66/73
K3	1812/39/43/4/5/59/61/7/77/8/97, 1914/7/20/ 5/20/5/30/52/7/66/72/86
L1	9001/4-12
L3	9053/6/65/8
N1	9431/46/8/51/2/4/8/69/82
N2	9498, 9504/57/9/91/4
N4	9233/40
N5	9262/72/83/8/9, 9300/10/8/9/22/8/43/9/53/70
N7	9600/10/40/52/4/7/8/68/84/97, 9717
N8	9376/9
N9	9422
N10	9097
N13	9117/8
O1	3579, 3646/76, 3752/77/84, 3865
O2	3946/70/8/9
O3	3479
O4	3570/5/86/99, 3600/7/11/6/48/80/8, 3710/ 3/24/41/6/72/88, 3824/42/3/52/6/8, 3870/ 88/9/93, 3904/6/13
O7	3006/14/24/7/31/9/40/9/51/4/9/84/6/8/90/ 1/5/8, 3100/12/3/5/9/24/30/1/2/6/7/54/60/ 1/7/81/9/96/8/9
Q1	9928
Q4	3221/5/35/43
Q5	3260/81, 3311/4/26
Q6	3342/53/70/3/5/84/96, 3404/5/21/43
V1	7604/24/41/3/56
V2	804/10/5/9/23/51/60/2/5/7/72/3/5/87/9/ 91/3, 903/12/24/37/57/8/64/83
Y1	8143/9/51
Y3	8165/84

There is a possibility that class O4 No. 3864 should be included in the above list but conflicting reports regarding it were received. It did not visit works between November 1946 and March 1949 so is an unlikely candidate.

The prefix was usually applied only at workshops where, if only a light repair was concerned, the engine was not repainted. In consequence, many had the E combined with the letters "L N E R". Such a case was class O4 No. 3752 which was turned out to traffic on 30th January 1948 after a full general overhaul by Gorton, with L.N.E.R. style shaded transfers on engine and tender (presumably the tender had been repainted before instructions were issued to put "BRITISH RAILWAYS" on it). The E prefix was put above the engine number on the cab sides. The O4 re-entered Gorton for a light repair, which took place 11-13th November 1948, and the opportunity was taken to renumber the engine 63752, in Gill Sans numerals. However, somebody missed blacking out the E on the right-hand side so that the engine ran for sometime as E63752, lettered "L N E R".

There was one application later which is inexplicable. Class E4 No. E2794 entered Stratford Works on 17th February 1950 for a general repair. When it emerged on 1st April 1950 its tender had the B.R. emblem in place of "BRITISH RAILWAYS", but on the cab side E62794 appeared. Possibly in the date ex-works lies the clue to the explanation (fig. 127).

LOCOMOTIVE SHEDS

Introduction

From the earliest days of railways it was customary to provide buildings in which locomotives were stabled and where facilities were provided for coaling, watering, turning, repairs, cleaning and preparation for the road (kindling or lighting-up, raising steam, oiling and filling sandboxes). These premises were traditionally known as engine sheds (sometimes engine-houses in early days) and they varied considerably in size, architectural design and track layout. Sheds could be constructed of stone, brick, wood, corrugated iron or concrete. The simplest arrangement was what was called a straight shed, sometimes known as a long shed, in which the engines stood in line on one or more dead-end roads. In Scotland a shed road was commonly called a "lye", a more specific term defined in Chambers and other dictionaries as a "short side-branch of a railway", the same term being applied to lines in stations and yards. The word "road" was applicable to both main lines and sidings. Obviously the long shed had severe disadvantages as it hampered the free movement of engines, and the "through" shed was developed. This was a long shed, open at both ends, requiring plenty of space to allow for convergence of the roads at both ends to facilitate shunting and movement of engines into their proper sequence for leaving the shed. This type of shed tended to be somewhat draughty and doors were often provided, but in practice these were seldom closed as they were what might be termed "accident-prone"! An alternative arrangement to the long type of shed was the roundhouse which existed in three forms. There was the semi-circular, or crescent, formation where the engine stalls radiated from the turntable. The other two types provided a complete circle of stalls, but the building itself could be square or circular. The circular roundhouse could be completely roofed or left open over the turntable. In the case of large depots there might be two or more "roundhouses" arranged in a row within one large building. Then there were examples of mixed sheds where the long type and the roundhouse appeared together.

On the L.N.E.R., only the North Eastern employed the roundhouse type of shed to any great extent and even so it still had long sheds also. The North British, which mainly favoured the long type of shed, had a crescent-shaped roundhouse at Berwick (demolished by the L.N.E.R.), a complete circular roundhouse at Burntisland (also demolished by the L.N.E.R.) whilst at St. Margaret's a circular roundhouse and a square roundhouse co-existed with a straight shed. However, one of the roundhouses (the one originally built to accommodate N.E. engines) was demolished by the L.N.E.R. to make way for a longer turntable and new disposal sidings, whilst the other roundhouse, severely damaged by fire, remained in use in derelict condition for many years. There was a square roundhouse at Canal shed, Carlisle and in L.N.E.R. days this was supplemented by the conversion of the adjacent wagon shop to a long engine shed. Similar conversion of premises had taken place at other L.N.E.R. sheds before Grouping, including King's Cross, which also had a roundhouse (originally occupied by Midland engines but latterly by suburban tank engines and demolished by the L.N.E.R.). The G.N.S. shed at Kittybrewster was a crescent-shaped roundhouse, but all other sheds on this section were of the long type.

In normal practice only a proportion of a shed's allocation of engines could be found on the premises at any given time, except on Sundays when it was usually difficult, often impossible, to cram all the engines into the shed and many engines had to stand in the open. Sometimes adjacent or nearby lines or sidings had to be used, and at St. Margaret's the expedient was even adopted latterly of preparing engines on Sunday and sending them to Portobello where they stood on a running loop from Craigentinny ready for work on Monday morning.

Stratford shed on the Great Eastern Section was noteworthy as having by far the largest allocation of engines in this country, no less than 557 at Grouping, reduced to 426 at Nationalisation. These were exceptionally large totals, even allowing for the considerable number of engines actually out-stationed at sub-sheds.

The facilities provided at sheds varied widely — at one end of the scale were large depots where provision was made for all kinds of repairs, even extending in some cases to complete overhauls and repainting (e.g. Norwich and Burntisland), whilst at the other extreme were locations without even a shed building, where the engine(s) stood in the open with only primitive facilities (possibly a pit, water column and an old carriage or van body to house stores and documents). A very simple coal stage might be provided, or coal would be shovelled from a wagon, but in some cases coal was taken elsewhere during the day. Many sub-sheds would perhaps have been more accurately described as stabling points.

The roundhouse had the advantage that an engine could be moved at any time independently of the others in the shed, so there was no need to arrange the engines in order of their expected departure. The roundhouse, however, had the serious disadvantage that in the event of the turntable being out of use (sometimes due to an engine falling into the well!), all the engines were immobilised. At many depots of the straight type, men were detailed specially for the duty of placing the engines in the shed according to the time they would next be required. Even so, it was still necessary to carry out the ritual known as "shunting the shed". For example, at Doncaster a J52 would appear pulling a line of dead engines, possibly up to ten in number, and including Pacifics and 2-8-0's, and then propel them back into the various roads.

Perhaps it ought to be mentioned that published lists of depots, including those issued officially, were sometimes erroneous and company records were often ambiguous and even contradictory. The accompanying lists have been compiled from various sources and every effort has been made to ensure accuracy, although it will be found that certain details are at variance with previously published material. The term "depot", particularly in staff records, referred to the establishment — engines, men and administration — and so it was possible to have a depot without an actual shed building. The closure date of a depot is when it ceased to function completely as an establishment for engines and men with appropriate management and facilities. It should be noted that a shed could exist many years after closure, when the building and yard were used to service visiting engines (e.g. London Road, Carlisle). Redundant sheds also stood empty for long periods, or were used for other purposes. As an example of the complexity of the subject of locomotive depots, Queen Street, York, shed was owned by the L.N.E.R., but was used exclusively by the L.M.S. for some years after Grouping. After the L.M.S. engines moved to York South shed, Queen Street was used by the L.N.E.R., but only for engines from other depots, and so does not appear in the accompanying list at all!

SHEDS AT GROUPING

(Total allocation, including sub-sheds, shown in brackets after each main shed)

	Closed by L.N.E.R.
G.N. SECTION	
DONCASTER DISTRICT (NO. 1)	
Doncaster (Carr) (190)	—
Retford (30): Became sub-shed of Retford (G.C.)	—
York (South) (14): (N.E. shed used): G.N. engines to Leeman Road -/25? (shed remained in use for N.E. section engines)	—
PETERBOROUGH DISTRICT (NO. 2)	
New England (Peterborough) (178)	—
Spalding (M. & G.N. shed used)	—
Stamford	—
Boston (62)	—
Spilsby	-/31?
Wainfleet	—
Lincoln (Holmes) (32)	—
Horncastle	6/24
Louth (7)	—
Mablethorpe	6/24
Grimsby (G.C. shed used): Ceased to be used by G.N. Section 6/25	—
LONDON DISTRICT (NO. 3)	
King's Cross (London) (156)	—
Hornsey (75)	—
Hatfield (30)	—
Hitchin (29)	—
Cambridge (6)	-/24

Nottingham District (No. 4)

    Colwick (235) — —

        Pinxton — -/24

        Derby (Friargate) — —

        Burton (Midland shed used) — —

        Stafford (L.N.W. shed used) — —

West Riding District (No. 5)

    Ardsley (95) — —

    Copley Hill (Leeds) (45) — —

    Bradford (Bowling Junction) (89) — —
    (later known as Hammerton Street)

        Ingrow — c. -/36

        Holmfield — c. -/33

Grantham District (No. 6)

    Grantham (71) — —

        Newark: Became sub-shed of Retford 7/47 — —

        Sleaford — —

        Leicester (Belgrave Road): Became sub-shed of Leicester (G.C.), but
                         engines supplied by Colwick — —

Manchester District (No. 7)

    Trafford Park (15) (C.L.C. shed used) — —

G.C. SECTION

    Neasden (London) (62) — —

        Aylesbury — —

    Woodford (48) — —

    Annesley (Nottingham) (87) — —

        Arkwright Street (Nottingham) — ?

    Leicester (Central) (26) — —

    Langwith (60) — —

    Tuxford (16) — —

    Mexborough (182) — —

        Doncaster (Hexthorpe): Became Signing-on Point under Doncaster (Carr) — -/23

        Wakefield (Balne Lane) — c. -/36

    Sheffield (Neepsend) (108): Replaced by new shed at Darnall 4/43 — —

    Barnsley (43) — —

    Retford (44) — —

        Worksop — —

    Staveley (47) — —

    Immingham (105) — —

        Grimsby — —

        New Holland: Closed 4/41, but later reopened — —

Fig. 80   The original *Locomotion* No. 1 passing through Stockton station, 2nd July 1925, hauling a replica of the train that ran on the occasion of the opening of the Stockton & Darlington Railway on 27th September 1825.

Fig. 81   Class U1 Garratt locomotive No. 2395 brand new in works grey livery in the S. & D. Centenary procession, 2nd July 1925.

Fig. 82   Class A2 No. 2400 *City of Newcastle* heading a train of new stock in the procession.

Fig. 83   General view of exhibition of locomotives held at Faverdale in July 1925.

Fig. 84   Stockton & Darlington Railway *Locomotion* No. 1 on display at Bank
Top station, Darlington, in March 1957.

Fig. 85   S. & D. *Derwent* No. 25 at Bank Top station, August 1975, prior to
removal to the museum at North Road station.

Fig. 86   N.E.R. Class "1001" 0-6-0 No. 1275 and Tennant 2-4-0 No. 1463 on display in the original railway museum at York. Blenkinsop wheels and rack railway in foreground.

Fig. 87   N.E.R. class M1 4-4-0 No. 1621 and L.B.S.C.R. 0-4-2 *Gladstone* in the old museum at York.

Fig. 88   Stirling 8-foot single G.N.R. No. 1 heading the first rail tour run by the R.C.T.S. from King's Cross to Peterborough, 11th September 1938.

Fig. 89   No. 1 after arrival back at King's Cross at the end of the R.C.T.S. tour.

Fig. 90   Class J15 No. 7564 preserved on the North Norfolk Railway, at Weybourne, September 1981, whilst temporarily painted in L.N.E.R. livery.

Fig. 91   Class J17 No. 1217ᴇ after restoration, Hellifield shed, February 1965.

Fig. 92   Class J21 N.E.R. No. 876 preserved at Beamish, August 1977.

Fig. 93   Class J27 N.E.R. No. 2392 at Grosmont on the North Yorkshire
Moors Railway, May 1973.

Fig. 94   Class J94 No. 68077 at Oxenhope, Keighley
& Worth Valley Railway, April 1978.

Fig. 95   Class J36 N.B.R. No. 673 *Maude* at Falkirk, May 1984.

Fig. 96   Class J72 N.E.R. *Joem* (ex-B.R. 69023) at York Layerthorpe (D.V.L.R.) in August 1977.

Fig. 97   Class J72 69023 and another under construction in Darlington Works, April 1951. This class was first introduced in 1898 by the N.E.R. and added to by both the L.N.E.R and B.R.

Fig. 98   L.N.E.R. boiler plate between water gauge cocks on class D34 No. 9291,
October 1934.

Fig. 99   Class V4 No. 3401 under construction in Doncaster Works, December
1940 showing Engine Order plate on frame (''V4 Class 1st E.O. 355'').

Fig. 100

Fig. 101

Fig. 102

Fig. 103

Fig. 104

Fig. 105

TENDER NUMBER PLATES

Doncaster plates. 1026 and 1080 were from the pre-1901 series of tenders which carried the numbers of the engine to which they were first attached. 5029 from the new series of numbers commenced in 1906. 5322 was a G.S. tender built at Doncaster for attachment to a D49 constructed at Darlington. 5465 was carried until 1955 by K3 61879 despite being maintained by Darlington, then Cowlairs. 2807 was a Doncaster style plate on class B17 built by N.B. Loco Co.

Keadby (13): Replaced by new shed at Frodingham	6/32
Frodingham: Replaced by new shed at Frodingham 6/32	—
Lincoln (37): Engines and men to Lincoln (Holmes)	5/39
Gorton (Manchester) (178)	—
Dinting	—
Macclesfield: L.N.E. shed closed; engine then stabled in L.M.S. shed	c.-/33
Hayfield	—
Trafford Park (Manchester) (79)*	—
Altrincham (G.C. & L.N.W. Joint)	2/31
Wigan (Lower Ince)	—
St. Helens	-/29
Liverpool (Brunswick) (54)*	—
Warrington (Central)*	—
Warrington (Padgate)*	c.-/29
Widnes (Tanhouse Lane) (G.C. & Midland Joint shed used)	—
Southport (Lord Street)*	—
Walton-on-the-Hill (Liverpool) (32)*	—
Stockport (Heaton Mersey) (47)*	—
Northwich (35)*	—
Helsby*	-/29
Winsford*	7/29
Wrexham (55)	—
Bidston	—
Chester (Northgate)	—
Birkenhead (Shore Road)*	—

*C.L.C. shed used

G.E. SECTION

STRATFORD DISTRICT (No. 1)

Stratford (London) (557)	—
Bethnal Green (Spitalfields)	—
Millwall	5/26
Enfield Town	—
Wood Street (Walthamstow)	—
Palace Gates	—
Epping	—
Ongar	—
Hertford	—
Buntingford	—
Southminster	—
Wickford	—
Brentwood	—
Southend (Victoria)	—
Ilford	5/39

G.E. SECTION (STRATFORD DISTRICT) (Continued)

Romford	§
Canning Town	§
Silvertown	§
Devonshire Street	§
Ware	—

§ Later demoted to the status of signing-on point

PETERBOROUGH DISTRICT (No. 2)

Peterborough East (85)	5/39
March (96)	—
Doncaster (5) (L.N.W.R. shed used — not used by owners): Engines and men to Doncaster (Carr)	-/25
Lincoln (Pyewipe) (12): Engines and men to Lincoln (G.C.)	8/25

NORWICH DISTRICT (No. 3)

Norwich (Thorpe) (122)	—
Cromer (High)	—
Dereham	—
Swaffham	—
Wells	—
Lowestoft (21)	—
Beccles	c. -/44
Yarmouth (Vauxhall) (20)	—
Yarmouth (South Town)	—

IPSWICH DISTRICT (No. 4)

Ipswich (131)	—
Felixstowe	—
Aldeburgh	—
Hadleigh	2/32
Framlingham	—
Eye	2/31
Bury St. Edmunds: Became sub-shed of Cambridge 6/38	—
Ipswich Dock	—
Stowmarket	—
Colchester (47)	—
Kelvedon	—
Clacton	—
Walton-on-Naze	—
Brightlingsea	c. 6/39
Braintree	—
Maldon	—
Sudbury	—
Chelmsford: Became sub-shed of Stratford	—
Parkeston (20)	—

CAMBRIDGE DISTRICT (No. 5)

Cambridge (176)	—
Ely	—
Huntingdon	—
Saffron Walden	—
Ramsey	9/30
Thaxted	—
Bishop's Stortford: Became sub-shed of Stratford 6/38	—
King's Lynn (44)	—
Hunstanton	—
Wisbech	—
Stoke Ferry	9/30

N.E. SECTION

SOUTHERN DIVISION

York (North) (also known as Clifton or Leeman Road) (133)	—
York (South)	—
Normanton: Joint shed with Midland; still used by L.N.E.R. after being taken over by L.M.S. 10/38	—
Scarborough (27)	—
Malton (18)	—
Whitby (21)	—
Pickering	—
Dairycoates (Hull) (146)	—
Doncaster (Carr) (G.N. shed used): Engine and men integrated with G.N. 1/23	—
Botanic Gardens (Hull) (47)	—
Bridlington (7)	—
Springhead (Hull) (144)	—
Alexandra Dock (Hull)	—
Cudworth (36)	—
Bullcroft	12/31
Denaby	5/27
Neville Hill (Leeds) (82)	—
Ilkley	—
Starbeck (Harrogate) (67)	—
Thirsk	11/30
Bradford (Manningham) (Midland shed used; closed to L.N.E.R. 10/38)	—
Masham	1/31
Pateley Bridge	—
Selby (57)	—
Darlington (Bank Top) (104)	—
Darlington (North Road)	—
Richmond	12/33
Northallerton	—
Barnard Castle	5/37
Middleton-in-Teesdale	—
Hawes Junction (Garsdale) (Midland shed used; closed to L.N.E.R. 5/39)	—

Ferryhill (28)	11/38
Middlesbrough (66)	—
Guisborough	—
Rosedale	1/29
Newport (89)	—
Stockton (47)	—
Saltburn (16)	—
Haverton Hill (13)	—

NORTHERN DIVISION

Tyne Dock (94)	—
Sunderland (South Dock) (88)	—
Durham	—
Shildon (59)	7/35
West Auckland (29): Closed 4/31; re-opened 7/35	—
Wearhead	—
Wear Valley Junction	7/35
Stanhope	5/30
Gateshead (High) (also known as Greensfield) (108)	—
Bowes Bridge	—
Heaton (Newcastle) (130)	—
Blaydon (Newcastle) (73)	—
Hexham	—
Tweedmouth (60)	—
Alnmouth	—
Haymarket (Edinburgh) (N.B. shed used): Integrated with N.B. 1/23	—
London Road (Carlisle) (48): Administered jointly with Canal (and taken into the Scottish Area) from 6/25	-/33
Alston	—
Percy Main (33)	—
Borough Gardens (also known as Park Lane) (Gateshead) (65)	—
North Blyth (28)	—
South Blyth (29)	—
Kirkby Stephen (15)	—
Penrith (C.K. & P. shed used; closed to L.N.E.R. 5/39)	—
West Hartlepool (77)	—
East Hartlepool (36)	4/39
Waskerley (11)	9/40
Consett: Became main shed 9/40	—
Annfield Plain (10)	9/40
Pelton Level	—

N.B. SECTION

Southern District

St. Margaret's (Edinburgh) (213)	—
Dunbar	—
North Berwick	—
Roslin	5/33
Penicuik	—
Polton	—
Longniddry	—
Dolphinton	4/33
Gullane	9/32
Lauder	9/32
Gifford	4/33
Musselburgh	c. -/30
Galashiels	—
Peebles	—
Selkirk	c. -/31
Haymarket (50)	—
Hawick (30)	—
Kelso	—
St. Boswells	—
Jedburgh	—
Riccarton	—
Hexham (N.E. shed used): Integrated with N.E. 8/24	—
Reedsmouth: To N.E. Area 8/24	—
Rothbury: To N.E. Area 8/24	—
Blaydon (N.E. shed used): Integrated with N.E. 6/25	—
Carlisle (Canal) (39)	
Longtown	c. -/24
Port Carlisle	7/28
Langholm	5/32
Silloth	—
Berwick (28): Engines and men to Tweedmouth (N.E. Area)	8/24
Duns: Became sub-shed of Tweedmouth (N.E. Area) 8/24	—

Northern District

Dunfermline (51)	—
Loch Leven	—
Burntisland (30): Became sub-shed of Thornton 7/33	—
Thornton (75)	—
Anstruther	—
Methil	—
Leslie	1/32
Ladybank	—
Perth (23)	—

Keith (14)	—
Banff	—
Boat of Garten	—
Elgin (14): Became sub-shed of Keith -/46	—

Shed Closures by the L.N.E.R.

Soon after Grouping, some rationalisation was put into effect insofar as where two constituent companies had sheds in close proximity, one was closed and the engines transferred to the other. An example of this was at Cambridge where the G.N. shed was closed and the engines and men moved over to the G.E. shed. (Nevertheless, the G.N. turntable and ashpits remained in use until October 1931, when a larger turntable was installed at the G.E. shed.) In other cases the accommodation at the other shed was inadequate for the combined stock of the two sheds and the latter continued to operate separately. However, in certain instances two sheds were considered to be one for administrative purposes (such as Canal N.B. and London Road N.E. at Carlisle), or one was considered to be a sub-shed of the other. An example of this second alternative was at Leicester, where the G.N. shed at Belgrave Road became a sub-shed of the G.C. depot at Leicester Central, even though there was no direct physical connection, nor was the allocation of engines made from the G.C. shed.

Another early development in L.N.E.R. days was the rearrangement of engine diagrams to facilitate closure of a number of very small sub-sheds, particularly on the G.N. Section (e.g. Horncastle).

From the late 1920's until the mid-thirties many sub-sheds became victims of the retrenchment of that period due to falling-off in mineral traffic and the closing of branch lines to passenger traffic. The G.E., N.E. and N.B. Sections were particularly affected in this connection, typical examples being Eye, Bullcroft and Gullane respectively.

Other closures during the L.N.E.R. era affected main sheds which had been replaced by more modern buildings in the same vicinity, as at Sheffield where an up-to-date installation at Darnall entailed the closure of the outmoded premises at Neepsend.

New Sheds Opened by the L.N.E.R.

Three entirely new locomotive depots were built by the L.N.E.R., two on the G.C. Section and one on the N.B. Section. To expedite the handling of the heavy mineral traffic in connection with the large steel plants at Scunthorpe, a shed was opened at Frodingham in 1932. There had previously been a small out-station here, under Keadby shed, and the latter ceased to function when the new Frodingham shed was brought into use.

The G.C. shed at Neepsend had a very cramped layout and a new replacement depot was constructed in Sheffield, but situated at Darnall (opened April 1943). In view of the projected electrification scheme for the Wath-Sheffield-Manchester lines, the new shed was designed with a view to dealing with steam and electric locomotives.

By 1931 the N.B. shed at Thornton was inadequate for the number of engines using it and furthermore there was serious trouble due to mining subsidence. The replacement shed was built on a new site further west on the Thornton-Dunfermline line. It was opened in July 1933 by Miss Whitelaw, daughter of the Company Chairman, and as part of the official ceremony the first engine to enter the new depot (class D30 No. 9501 *Simon Glover*) was driven by W. Crawford, the senior footplateman at Thornton. The opportunity was taken to move some of the engines from Burntisland to the new shed at Thornton, the former then being reduced to the status of a sub-shed.

A new depot for multiple-unit electric stock was opened at South Gosforth in September 1923, being shown as a sub-depot to Heaton for staff purposes.

Closed Sheds Re-opened by the L.N.E.R.

Two sheds which had been closed before Grouping were brought back into use by the L.N.E.R. — one in the N.E. Area and one in the Scottish Area.

The old North Eastern shed at Leyburn, which had been closed in 1915, was re-opened in February 1939 to suit revised train working when the service was cut back and the Garsdale engine moved to Leyburn.

On the N.B. Section, to relieve pressure on St. Margaret's when traffic was very heavy during the 1939-45 War, Seafield (Edinburgh) was reopened as a sub-shed in May 1945. This shed had previously been used by the N.B.R. for several years during and after the 1914-18 War, but the premises actually belonged to the L.M.S. (formerly the Caledonian), by whom they were not used.

There was also one instance of a shed closed completely by the L.N.E.R. being re-opened by the Company. This was West Auckland, closed April 1931 and re-opened in July 1935.

Sheds Taken Over After Grouping

During 1923/24, three small companies with locomotives were absorbed, of which the East & West Yorkshire Union had one shed, the Colne Valley & Halstead had two sheds, whilst the Mid-Suffolk had one. These acquisitions were all consequent upon the Grouping under the Railways Act of 1921, and very few locomotives were involved.

Much more significant were two later developments, when the L.N.E.R. assumed responsibility for locomotive working on the Midland & Great Northern Joint line in 1936, and the operation of the Metropolitan steam service from Rickmansworth to Aylesbury in the following year. In the latter case, however, only one small sub-shed (Chesham) was actually taken over as the engines at the main depot were merely transferred from Neasden L.P.T.B. to Neasden L.N.E.R. It should be noted that Chesham did not appear in an official L.N.E.R. shed list dated July 1939.

SHEDS AT DATE OF ABSORPTION BY L.N.E.R.

E. & W.Y.U.R. (July 1923)

Robin Hood	Sub-shed to Ardsley: Closed 7/26

C.V. & H.R. (July 1923)

Halstead	Sub-shed to Colchester: Closed c. 1934
Haverhill	Sub. Colchester, later sub. Bury St. Edmunds: Closed by 1947

M.S.L.R. (July 1924)

Laxfield	Sub-shed to Ipswich

M. & G.N.J.R. (Locomotives taken over 1/10/36; official date of absorption 1/1/37)

Peterborough (Spital Bridge)	L.M.S. shed used, but engines transferred to New England and Peterborough East immediately on takeover
Spalding	Sub-shed to New England
Bourne	,, ,, ,,
South Lynn	Taken into Southern Area (Eastern Section), Cambridge District
Melton Constable	Taken into Southern Area (Eastern Section), Norwich District
Norwich City	
Cromer Beach	

L.P.T.B. (Locomotives taken over 1/11/37)

Neasden (L.P.T.B.)	Engines transferred to Neasden (L.N.E.R.) immediately on takeover
Chesham	Sub-shed to Neasden

Sub-Sheds

In addition to the main sheds, there was another category of locomotive depot known as a sub-shed. Like the principal sheds, these varied considerably in size and equipment, but the essential difference between a sub-shed and a main shed lay in its administration. Except for certain large sub-sheds, which had a foreman, the man responsible was a driver-in-charge or a fitter-in-charge and the engines usually proceeded to the main depot for boiler washout and minor repairs. The sub-sheds normally housed only enough engines to cover normal working and changes of engine had to be arranged by the main shed in the event of breakdown, shopping, boiler washout and other routine attention. Sub-sheds were provided at places where engines were required for local working in insufficient numbers to justify the establishment of a main shed. They were also to be found at or near branch termini, where an engine was required to start work early in the morning and/or finish late in the evening; much light engine mileage was thus obviated and shorter opening hours for signal boxes were possible. Normally sub-sheds were looked after by the nearest main shed, but for administrative or operational reasons it occasionally happened that a sub-shed was transferred from the responsibility of one main shed to another. It should also be noted that a main shed could be reduced to the status of a sub-shed and vice versa to suit changes in traffic patterns, or provision of new and better facilities in a particular locality. Unfortunately the distinction between a main shed and a sub-shed was not always clearly defined, and thus lists and articles are often very confusing in this respect. Generally speaking, sub-sheds were not quoted as having a definite allocation of particular engines (even though some individual engines remained at the same sub-shed for many years) but there were exceptions to this rule; in fact, the North Eastern Area always gave allocations of individual engines to all its sub-sheds, no matter how small these depots were. Thus, in N.E. Area shed lists, a clear distinction was not always made between main sheds and sub-sheds.

Signing-on Points

In addition to sub-sheds, there was another variety of out-station from the main depots, usually known as a "signing-on point". At signing-on points there was an establishment of men only, and this happened at places where the engines were continuously employed (treble-shifted) from early Monday morning until the following Sunday morning at some distance from the main shed. In this way the payment of enginemen's travelling time (at overtime rates) was reduced to a minimum. A classical example of the signing-on point was Portobello, Edinburgh, where there were five shunting pilot engines and three transfer goods train engines, requiring altogether twenty-four sets of men. If these men had signed on and off at the main shed (St. Margaret's), each would have had to be paid one hour overtime per day, so transfer to the out-station at Portobello effected a significant saving. Travelling time was incurred only at the weekend, when the engines were taken into the main shed, and the men were paid the walking time back to the signing-on point.

List of Signing-on Points

Southern Area

Annesley:
Kirkby Bentinck

Doncaster:
Hexthorpe (Doncaster)
Marshgate (Doncaster)

Mexborough:
Aldam Junction

Sheffield:
Broughton Lane (Sheffield)
Rotherham

Tuxford:
Attercliffe Goods (Sheffield)

Barnsley:
Birdwell
Stairfoot
Barnsley Junction (Penistone)
Wentworth

Retford:
Kirton Lindsey
Gainsborough

Staveley:
Woodhouse
Beighton

Immingham:
Barnetby

Keadby:
Stainforth

Gorton:
Guide Bridge
Ardwick (Manchester)

North Eastern Area

Dairycoates:
Drypool (Hull)

Neville Hill:
Wellington Street (Leeds)

Tyne Dock:
Washington

Scottish Area

Haymarket:
Waverley West

St. Margaret's:
Hardengreen
Portobello
Niddrie
Granton
Waverley East
North Leith
South Leith
Duddingston
Craigentinny*
Heriothill
Leith Walk
(All in Edinburgh except Hardengreen)

Eastfield:
Singer (Glasgow)
Rothesay Dock (Glasgow)

Dunfermline:
Inverkeithing
Kelty

This list of signing-on points was applicable in 1925, but certain locations later fell into abeyance.

* The signing-on point at Craigentinny applied only to the men on the Carriage Siding Pilots, and had no connection with train engines staged in Craigentinny Up Loop on Sundays.

Modernisation of Depots by the L.N.E.R.

Many of the sheds taken over by the L.N.E.R. were very old (e.g. York South, built by the Great North of England Railway in 1841) and their track plans and equipment were no longer adequate. This was especially true of the main line sheds which had to deal with much larger engines than formerly. So the L.N.E.R. had to provide new and larger turntables at many depots, and from 1933 onwards a further improvement

109

was the conversion of turntables to vacuum operation. This system was patented by Cowans, Sheldon, the first example being installed at King's Cross shed. Attached to the turntable there was a small vacuum engine with two double-acting oscillating cylinders geared to a tractor. The vacuum brake pipe of the engine to be turned was connected with the corresponding pipe on the tractor and the vacuum ejector handle placed in the "brake off" position. The suction through the brake pipe caused the tractor to work. To enable an engine without an ejector to be turned using the vacuum-operated machinery, a large vacuum storage cylinder was fixed beneath the table. Provision was also made for turning by hand if necessary. One Mundt turntable (made by Ransomes and Rapier to a Dutch design), which did not require a pit or balancing and which could be worked by electricity or manually, was installed at York. No further examples of this type of turntable were put into service on the L.N.E.R., but the York one did remain in use and appeared to be satisfactory. There were four other sheds on the L.N.E.R. where electrical power was used for turning, Gateshead, Stratford, Mexborough and Southend, the last-mentioned involving the use of a winch. At Doncaster, however, where there was space available a triangular layout (known as "The Angle") was installed instead of a turntable. The triangle had the disadvantage that two engines in steam were required to turn a dead engine (as the siding at each end of the two "corners" only held one engine) and, as all engines entering Doncaster works had to be turned the same way (facing south), this was a common occurrence. Two other sheds had a specially made turning triangle (New England and Woodford), whilst Grantham boasted a turntable and an arrangement of lines, which although not strictly a triangle, enabled engines to be turned within the shed limits.

Mechanical coaling plants existed at a few pre-Grouping sheds (notably Stratford and Dairycoates), but from 1930 a new type of tall concrete coaling plant was provided at most of the larger sheds and a number of smaller ones. There were two different varieties of these 1930's mechanical coaling plants, supplied by contractors Lees and Mitchell, whilst the latter firm also produced a small steel type which handled coal tubs. The old manual coaling stages were often left in situ for use in case of mechanical failure. Apart from breakdowns of this nature, mechanical coaling plants were also susceptible to other minor troubles, such as the mischance of tipping a wagon-load of sand or perhaps engine brake-blocks into the coal hopper! A notable exception to the general provision of mechanical coaling was the extremely busy shed at St. Margaret's, where coaling continued by hand until the shed closed, even though an extensive modernisation scheme had been carried out in 1942.

Other features to facilitate repairs and speed up the turnround of engines were wheel-drops (already in use at a few sheds before Grouping), and wet ash pits, and two Sentinel steam ash cranes were put to work at Scottish Area sheds (see page 19). Keystone sand-driers replaced the old-fashioned sand kilns at a number of sheds from 1928 onwards. A late, but very welcome, innovation was the light tunnel of 1944, which was designed to allow thorough examination of locomotives during the wartime "blackout" examples of which were to be found at Doncaster, New England, March and Thornton.

Various experiments were tried by the L.N.E.R. to improve efficiency, such as cleaning engines by high-pressure steam, but these were not generally adopted and were allowed to fall into abeyance or to remain in use at individual sheds. Additional hot water washout plants were installed by the L.N.E.R.

Shed Indication on Engines

The G.N.R. and G.E.R. both employed a similar system whereby each District was given a number. A small plate bearing this number was fixed to the cab roof, or rear spectacle plate on tank engines. It will be noted that these plates did not show the actual shed, all engines from sheds in the same District carrying the same number. These plates remained in position after Grouping on many engines, even though they had been superseded by L.N.E.R. type shed plates and/or painted names on the bufferbeam. Indeed, some pre-Grouping shed plates even survived nationalisation in 1948 and the introduction of yet another shed indication system (the L.M.S. pattern smokebox door plate).

It is said that the G.C.R. engines had the name of the shed painted in abbreviated form inside the cab.

As far as is known the N.E.R. and N.B.R. gave no indication whatever of an engine's home shed, but it was sometimes possible to deduce an engine's shed from the headlamps which bore the name of the shed, or in the case of engines working goods trains from the name of the home station painted on the brake van.

As in so many other instances, the different Areas of the L.N.E.R. tended to go their own way in the matter of shed display. In the North Eastern Area, from November 1924, the shed name (usually in abbreviated form) was painted on the left-hand side of the cab interior under the eaves. Shortly afterwards, the Southern Area began to fix white enamelled plates with black lettering in a similar position, but on the right-hand side of the cab, and the name was usually rendered in full (fig. 148). During 1938 the subject of shedplates was brought to Gresley's notice, and he expressed a desire that a uniform practice should be adopted in all areas. The North Eastern Area then fell into line with the Southern Area as from December 1938. However, the Scottish Area did not introduce the plates until May 1940, when presumably wartime conditions influenced the decision as engines had tended to become "common-user" and were often to be found far away from home. Prior to this date, the Scottish Area also ignored any shed indication borne by engines from other areas, a notable example being the B12's working between Aberdeen and Elgin with shedplates such as Ipswich!

When the North Eastern and Scottish Areas eventually adopted the plates, they used shortened forms of the names in many instances, such as D'GTON (Darlington) and D'F'LINE for Dunfermline. The plates were not always readily legible from ground level and so on 14th April 1943 the instruction was issued to paint the name of the shed on the front bufferbeam. Nevertheless the shedplates were left inside the cab, but were no longer changed when the engines were moved and they were often painted over.

After Nationalisation, a new shed code system was drawn up, based on the L.M.S. model, and appropriate shedplates displayed on the smokebox door. However, many L.N.E.R. engines retained the enamelled plates inside the cab, and Cowlairs Works in particular continued to paint the name of the shed on the bufferbeam. It then became possible to find engines with three different shed indications showing simultaneously!

It is most important to note that the well-known L.N.E.R. shedcodes used for many years in the *Railway Observer* were entirely unofficial and were devised by the *R.O.* editors for private use within the R.C.T.S.

Area Organisation

In April 1923, W. G. P. Maclure (previously Locomotive Running Superintendent of the G.C.R.) was appointed Locomotive Running Superintendent of the Southern Area of the L.N.E.R., with an office in Hamilton House adjacent to Liverpool Street Station. He was therefore responsible for the combined systems of the former G.N., G.C., and G.E. Railways. When Maclure retired at the end of March 1931, he was succeeded by I. S. W. Groom (who had been Maclure's assistant from 1923 until 1926) and he occupied the post until his resignation due to ill-health in July 1937. The position was then held by A. H. Peppercorn for one year after which he became Mechanical Engineer of the North Eastern Area. For certain purposes, the Southern Area had already been divided into an Eastern Section (the former G.E. lines) and a Western Section (the former G.N. and G.C. lines), and this division was now applied to the Locomotive Running Department. C. H. Elwell and G. A. Musgrave thus took charge of the Eastern and Western Sections respectively in August 1938. The Eastern and Western Section headquarters remained at Hamilton House,

temporarily evacuated during the 1939-45 War to Shenfield and Gerrards Cross respectively. When C. H. Elwell became Assistant Mechanical Engineer (Outdoor), with special responsibility for maintenance and repair of locomotives, in December 1941, he was succeeded as head of the Eastern Section by L. P. Parker.

In the North Eastern Area the N.E.R. Locomotive Running Superintendent (J. H. Smeddle) remained in charge, but he moved his office from Darlington to York in May 1923. After his retirement in June 1931, C. M. Stedman took charge and he remained in this post until Nationalisation.

The N.B. Section became known as the Southern Scottish Area, with J. P. Grassick continuing in office as Locomotive Running Superintendent, whilst T. E. Heywood was in charge in the Northern Scottish Area, remaining in his former post on the G.N.S.R. but now known as Mechanical Engineer and Locomotive Running Superintendent, Inverurie. When Heywood went to Gorton as Mechanical Engineer in July 1924, Grassick's jurisdiction was extended to include the Northern Scottish Area but his office remained at Queen Street, Glasgow. After the death of Grassick in March 1926, I. S. W. Groom was appointed to succeed him. When Groom went to the Southern Area in April 1931, G. A. Musgrave took over. Musgrave likewise went to the Southern Area in April 1938, but he had charge of the Western Section only. The last L.N.E.R. Locomotive Running Superintendent in Scotland was E. D. Trask (appointed September 1938), but the office was transferred to Edinburgh (Waverley) in July 1939. Happily at the time of writing, Mr. Trask is still alive, aged 93.

District Organisation

In the Southern Area, the G.N. and G.E. Sections carried on with the Districts shown in the 1923 list of sheds, whilst the G.C. Section had Districts represented by the main centres at London, Nottingham, Immingham, Sheffield and Manchester. However, with the combination of the G.N. and G.C. Sections to form the Western part of the Southern Area, there was some reorganisation whereby certain Districts included sheds from both of the former constituent companies. For example, Mexborough came under Doncaster, and Annesley under Colwick.

By 1936 the Southern Area was divided into fourteen Districts with principal sheds as follows:

Western — Ardsley, Colwick, Doncaster, Gorton, Immingham, King's Cross, Neasden, New England and Sheffield.

Eastern — Cambridge, March, Ipswich, Norwich and Stratford.

In the last ten years of the L.N.E.R. the number of Districts shown in the Southern Area was ten, as under:

Western — Ardsley, Colwick, Doncaster, Gorton, King's Cross, Lincoln and New England.

Eastern — Cambridge, Norwich and Stratford.

In this last arrangement, the largest depot was not necessarily the principal shed of a District (for example, Immingham came under Lincoln, and March under Cambridge). At the same time, a number of subordinate sheds were placed in a different District.

By 1936, the North Eastern Area was divided into seven Districts, namely Heaton, Gateshead, Darlington, Middlesbrough, York, Hull and Leeds, but latterly the number of Districts was reduced to five (Darlington, Gateshead, Hull, Sunderland and York). In the later arrangement, Hull remained unaltered, but York and Leeds were combined, as were Darlington and Middlesbrough. Heaton became subordinate to Gateshead, and the new district of Sunderland included a number of sheds formerly in the Gateshead District. In addition to the sheds of the former North Eastern Railway, the N.E. Area of the L.N.E.R. acquired a few former sub-sheds owned by the N.B.R. in Northumberland and Berwickshire. However, it lost the important depot at London Road (Carlisle) which was taken into the Southern Scottish Area. The N.E. Area absorbed the engines and men from the N.B. shed at Berwick, but the shed itself was closed and very soon demolished. The N.E. shed at Tweedmouth was able to assimilate all the Berwick engines and men.

The District organisation of the Scottish Area remained essentially the same as at Grouping, except that the Districts were eventually renamed Edinburgh (ex-Southern), Burntisland (ex-Northern), and Glasgow (ex-Western) for the N.B. sheds, and Aberdeen for the G.N.S. sheds with the addition of Ferryhill.

Promotional Arrangements for Enginemen

Under the terms of the National Agreement signed in 1919, and applicable to all main line railway companies in Great Britain, very strict rules governed the promotion of footplatemen. The only recognised "line of promotion" was Cleaner, Fireman (or Assistant Motorman) and Driver (or Motorman). Promotion was by seniority, from the date of entry into the grade of Cleaner — irrespective of whether or not the individual had previously been employed by the Company in some other capacity. In the event of two or more men having the same seniority date, seniority was then determined by age.

On the L.N.E.R., the network was divided into eleven "Promotional Areas", of which Nos. 1 to 4 covered the Southern Area, Nos. 5, 6 and 7 the North Eastern Area, whilst Nos. 8 to 11 were in the Scottish Area. In 1927 the Southern and North Eastern Areas became Promotional Areas by the merger of Areas 1-4, and 5, 6 and 7 respectively, but the Scottish Area did not follow suit in this respect until 1943.

Initially men were given the opportunity of moving from one Promotional Area to another if they so wished, but thereafter promotion could only be within the particular area in which a man was situated. Provision was also made to allow redundant men to move to another depot in the same Promotional Area in order to retain their grade, if there was a junior man in the grade at the other depot. Furthermore, men of the same grade, of equal or unequal seniority, were allowed a mutual exchange of depots within the same Promotional Area, subject to whatever conditions had been agreed by the Local Departmental Committees at the sheds concerned.

Link Working

It was customary to arrange footplatemen's rosters according to type of duty in groups (known as "links" or sometimes as "gangs") so that a rotation of the different signing-on times could be obtained. The rules appertaining to Link Working were also laid down in the 1919 National Agreement, but these took years to implement and it was not until after Grouping that all the men were in their rightful place. There were slight variations in the link working pattern depending on the range of duties at each particular shed, but the basic procedure was a graduation from Shed Duties to Main Line Passenger work as follows:

Disposal and Preparation
Shunting Pilots
Assisting or Trip Pilots
Local Goods Trains
Long Distance Goods Trains
Suburban and Branch Passenger Trains
Long Distance Passenger Trains

At a large depot there could be several links in one or more of the above categories, and many sheds had a link, or links, of "Spare" men who covered for absence of the men in other links and undertook special workings. Normally no deviation was allowed from the recognised sequence of promotion through the links except for health reasons, compassionate grounds, goodwill to allow performance of Trade Union or Civic duties, or as punishment in disciplinary cases. Provision was usually made however to allow men over the age of 60 to relinquish main line duties if they so desired, and they were then allocated to certain "scheduled" transfer goods trains, pilots, or shed duties. The normal retiring age at Grouping was 70, later reduced to 68, and then to 65. During the 1939-45 War, men were given the option of remaining in service beyond the age of 65.

Fig. 106

Fig. 107

Fig. 108

Fig. 109

Fig. 110

Fig. 111

TENDER NUMBER PLATES

Figs. 106-8: Darlington plates (the same size and style as used on locomotives). 2731 was the first straight-sided 4,200-gal. tender built at Darlington. 3441 was for the first K4. 2569 was attached to class A3 *Gladiateur* when on Darlington maintenance up to 1930.

Fig. 109: 8420 — Gateshead-built tender renumbered by Darlington in 1938. Fig. 110: 5242 — Gorton plate. Fig. 111: 6401 — Gorton style on class D11 built for use in Scottish Area.

Fig. 112

Fig. 114

Fig. 116

Fig. 113

Fig. 115

Fig. 117

TENDER NUMBER PLATES

Fig. 112: 7477 — Stratford plate, differing in size, shape and style from all other L.N.E.R. plates. Figs. 113/4: Inverurie plates — 49 original G.N.S.R. number (not removed until 1955) and 2262 L.N.E.R. 1946 number.

Fig. 115: 9652 — Inverurie plate attached to ex-N.B.R. tender repaired there. Fig. 116: 1365 — plate attached briefly by Cowlairs to the tender of K3 61879 in 1955. Fig. 117: 9231 — B.R. plate of the type introduced by Cowlairs in 1955 on unnumbered tenders.

Fig. 118   Class D11 No. 6395 coupled to tender numbered 6396 at Aberdeen, June 1927. Showing disadvantage of putting the engine number on the tender.

Fig. 119   Service vehicle No. 292, an ex-N.B.R. Wheatley tender showing Cowlairs number plate 1054, St. Margaret's 1946. Normally all such plates had been removed at the time of the Grouping.

Fig. 120   Service vehicle No. 292 showing N.B.R. engine number 1177 and also L.N.E.R lettering, Kilmarnock Works, February 1954.

Fig. 121   Scottish Region tender number plate 9296 attached to previously un-numbered tender in 1955.

Fig. 122   Post-withdrawal use of tender from class C11 as A.R.P. water tank,
Cowlairs, May 1948.

Fig. 123   Tender from class C11 9869 in use as a sludge carrier at Bawtry,
August 1958.

LOCOMOTIVE WORKS PLATES

Fig. 124   A selection of Doncaster works plates, 1923-48. Nos. 1567 (class A1 4475), 1620 (class P1 2394), 1796 (class P2 2002, rebuilt to A2), 1810 (class V1 481), 1936 (class O2 3838), 2030 (class A2 60539).

Fig. 125   Class A3 No. 103 *Flying Scotsman* at Finsbury Park,
March 1948.
B.R. "E" prefix above number.

Fig. 126   Class N5 No. 9343 at Trafford Park shed, March 1948.
"E" prefix in front of number.

Fig. 127   Class E4 No. 62794 at Stratford, May 1953.
Still carrying "E" prefix wrongly applied in 1950.

Fig. 128   King's Cross (ex-G.N.R.) engine sheds, 1932.

Fig. 129   View of shed yard at Doncaster, April 1932.

Fig. 130   Neasden (ex-G.C.R.) shed, just after Grouping.

Fig. 131   Annesley (ex-G.C.R.), July 1937.

Fig. 132   Heaton Mersey, Stockport (C.L.C.), 1937.

Fig. 133   Parkeston shed (ex-G.E.R.), 1935.

Fig. 134   Bishops Stortford (ex-G.E.R.), c.1936. Although termed an engine shed, there was no actual covered accommodation.

Fig. 135   King's Lynn shed (ex-G.E.R.), September 1936.

Fig. 136   Middlesbrough roundhouse (ex-N.E.R.), October 1937. Class J25 Nos.
2140, 1987, 2068, 463, 2042 and 2046.

Fig. 137   Dairycoates, Hull (ex-N.E.R.), 1936. Class Q6 No. 1362, L.M.S. Class 5 No.
5206, J39 (unidentified), B16 No. 930.

There were slight deviations from the standard procedure at individual sheds, and in general latterly there was a move towards a more egalitarian system, with enlargement of the links and mixing of different types of duty. At some depots it even became obligatory for senior men to come off the long distance passenger trains and go on to local trains or pilots as they approached retirement, where such an arrangement had been agreed by the appropriate Local Departmental Committee.

British Railways

Initially after Nationalisation, the L.N.E.R. locomotive depots continued to operate under the same District organisations, but fell into different B.R. Regions. Southern Area sheds came into the Eastern Region, the N.E. Area practically reverted to its pre-Grouping status in becoming the North Eastern Region, whilst the Scottish Area sheds joined the L.M.S. Northern Division depots in the Scottish Region.

As had happened after Grouping, there was some rationalisation whereby sheds were closed where different companies had sheds in close proximity. The next important development was the transfer of depots from one District to another according to geographic considerations, mainly where "penetrating lines" from one Region to another existed. Further reorganisation took place when sheds from Districts were united under new District management.

B.R. adopted the L.M.S. system of shed codes in which each Motive Power District was given a number, followed by a letter for each shed, with A indicating the principal shed in the District. The codes were introduced in 1949, at first for internal correspondence and later evidenced by the well-known elliptical cast metal plates affixed to the smokebox of locomotives. District numbers for the Regions were:—

1 to 28	London Midland
30 to 33	Eastern (Eastern Section)
40 to 46	Eastern (Western Section)
50 to 54	North Eastern
60 to 68	Scottish
70 to 75	Southern
81 to 89	Western

Within a few months the series 40 to 46 allotted to the Western Section of E.R. was changed to 34 to 40. It is the latter series which has been used in the accompanying list.

The E.R. Districts were as follows:— Stratford 30, Cambridge 31, Norwich 32, Plaistow (ex-L.M.S.) 33, London (King's Cross) 34, Peterborough (New England) 35, Doncaster 36, West Riding (Ardsley) 37, Nottingham (Colwick) 38, Manchester (Gorton) 39, Lincoln 40. These corresponded closely with the position at the end of the existence of the L.N.E.R. except that Immingham had been the main depot in the

Lincoln District. Boston was transferred from Peterborough to Lincoln District, Sheffield from Doncaster to Gorton District, and Retford from Lincoln to Doncaster District. Trafford Park, together with Heaton Mersey, Northwich, Brunswick, Walton and Wigan, had been transferred to L.M.R. in November 1948 and formed District 13 (previously the Plaistow District). At the same time, Chester (Northgate), Wrexham and Bidston had joined L.M.R. Chester District 6.

In the N.E.R. the Districts were:— York 50, Darlington 51, Newcastle (Gateshead) 52, Hull (Dairycoates) 53, Sunderland 54. The only loss was Normanton which was coded in the L.M.R. 20 Leeds District (Holbeck). As the L.N.E.R. engines used the L.M.S. shed there, this was logical. In June 1948, prior to the formulation of the shed codes, the N.E. Area lost Duns (an ex-N.B.R. shed) which became a sub-shed of Hawick in Scottish Region.

A full reorganisation of Motive Power Districts took place in the Scottish Region due to the assimilation of former L.M.S. and L.N.E.R. lines, which required an early introduction of the new scheme and the codes were brought into operation on 1st January 1949. The Districts were:— Inverness 60, Aberdeen (Kittybrewster) 61, Burntisland (Thornton) 62, Perth 63, Edinburgh (St. Margaret's) 64, Glasgow (Eastfield) 65, Glasgow (Polmadie) 66, Glasgow (Corkerhill) 67, Carlisle (Kingmoor) 68. Of former L.N.E.R. depots, Kittybrewster was the main shed for the Aberdeen District, unchanged except for the loss of Boat of Garten to the Inverness District as a sub of Aviemore. The Burntisland District (with its main shed at Thornton) was also little different save for Perth (N B.) and Stirling (Shore Road and Forth & Clyde) going to the Perth South District. Edinburgh (St. Margaret's) was enlarged by the acquisition of Polmont and Bathgate from the former L.N.E.R. Glasgow District. The ex-L.M.S. sheds at Dalry Road and Carstairs were also taken into the Edinburgh District, but Carlisle Canal went to the Upperby District of L.M.R. Eastfield (Glasgow) gained the L.M.S. sheds at St. Rollox, Dawsholm, Grangemouth and Yoker. In addition to losing Polmont and Bathgate to the Edinburgh District, Eastfield rather strangely had Fort William and Mallaig taken from it and placed in the Perth District. This seeming aberration was rectified in 1955, only to be changed back again in 1960.

Principal changes, with appropriate recodings, to the original overall scheme affecting former L.N.E.R. sheds were as follows:—

(i) May 1950. The L.M.R. Trafford Park District, set up in November 1948, lost its separate identity and the sheds were distributed among adjacent Districts:—

Liverpool (Edge Hill) 8 — Brunswick, together with its sub-shed at Widnes (Tanhouse Lane) which was then attached to the nearby ex-L.M.S. shed.

Manchester (Longsight) 9 — Trafford Park, Heaton Mersey, Northwich.

Wigan (Springs Branch) 10 — Wigan (Lower Ince).

Liverpool (Bank Hall) 27 — Walton-on-the-Hill with Brunswick's former sub shed at Southport.

(ii)   October 1951. Carlisle Canal was returned by L.M.R. to Scottish Region, to Kingmoor District 68.

(iii) April 1955. Fort William and Mallaig were transferred from the Perth to Glasgow (Eastfield) District.

(iv)   November 1955. Sheffield (Darnall) became a separate E.R. District, 41.

(v)   October 1956. Consequent upon the transfer of former L.M.S. and L.N.E.R. lines in the West Riding from L.M.R. and E.R. to N.E.R. control, two new Districts were acquired by N.E.R. — Leeds (Holbeck) 55 and Wakefield 56. E.R.'s West Riding District ceased to exist and Ardsley, Copley Hill and Bradford became part of the Wakefield District: this was effective from July 1956. Normanton, where several N.E.R. engines stabled, came under Holbeck, the inter Regional transfer from L.M.R. taking place on 1st January 1957.

(vi)   January 1957. In L.M.R., Trafford Park and Heaton Mersey were transferred from Manchester District 9 to Derby 17.

(vii) February 1958. As from 1st February 1958 a major transfer took place of lines, and depots, from one Region to another. The main upheaval in E.R. was the loss to L.M.R. of the entire former G.C.R. route from Manchester to Marylebone except for the Sheffield area. Former G.C. sheds were absorbed into nearby L.M.R. Districts as follows:—

Rugby 2 — Woodford.
Manchester (Longsight) 9 — Gorton.
London (Cricklewood) 14 — Neasden.
Wellingborough 15 — Leicester (Central).
Nottingham 16 — Annesley.

Other changes affected the E.R. shed at Wrexham in Wales which went to the W.R. Wolverhampton District 84, whilst Kirkby Stephen (N.E.R.) and Carlisle Canal (Sc.R.) went to L.M.R. Carlisle District 12. British Railways obviously found it hard to make its mind up about Canal!

Simultaneously, reorganisation within E.R. resulted in the abolition of the Peterborough and Colwick Districts coupled with a considerable expansion of the Sheffield District. Gains by this and other Districts were:—

King's Cross 34 — New England, Grantham.
Lincoln 40 — Colwick.
Sheffield 41 — Mexborough, Barnsley (from Doncaster), Staveley (from Colwick), Langwith, Tuxford (from Lincoln).

(viii) April 1958. Two months after the above-mentioned inter-Regional transfers, L.M.R. suffered an internal reorganisation. Former L.N.E.R. sheds at Carlisle, Kirkby Stephen, Gorton and Woodford were re-coded within their existing Districts, whilst Liverpool (Brunswick) and Northwich were moved from District 8 and 9 to 27 (Bank Hall) and 8 (Edge Hill) respectively. Trafford Park and Heaton Mersey reverted from the Derby District 17 to Manchester (Longsight) District 9, and in fact regained the shed codes that they had had sixteen months previously.

(ix)   September 1958. The Sunderland District in N.E.R. was disbanded and its sheds incorporated in the Newcastle (Gateshead) District 52, Sunderland, Borough Gardens, Tyne Dock and Consett being involved in this change.

(x)   January 1960. In the N.E. Region, the Hull District 53 was abolished and Dairycoates (the only depot then still open to steam) came under the jurisdiction of York 50, which at the same time lost Neville Hill to the Holbeck District 55.

(xi)   May 1960. The Scottish Region sheds at Fort William and Mallaig once more returned to the Perth District 63 from Glasgow (Eastfield) 65, whilst Polmont was transferred from being under St. Margaret's to Eastfield.

(xii) September 1963. A L.M.R. reorganisation resulted in Woodford being moved from the Rugby to Willesden District 1, and Walton-on-the-Hill from the Bank Hall 27 to Edge Hill 8 Districts in Liverpool. Reddish electric depot gained a shed code (9C) in the Longsight District.

(xiii) January 1966. Colwick was transferred from E.R. to L.M.R. Nottingham District 16.

Sub-sheds followed the same coding as their parent depots unless otherwise shown.

With the rundown of steam stock, and the widespread use of diesel propulsion, many steam sheds were closed, but others survived after conversion to diesel depots. However, before this phase was complete, one entirely new steam shed was opened at Thornaby (code 51L) in the North Eastern Region (opened June 1958, closed to steam December 1964). There were also two new electric depots in connection with the

Manchester-Sheffield-Wath scheme, at Wath (opened February 1952) and Reddish (opened July 1953). Where a shed continued in use for diesel purposes, the closure date is followed by the sign * in the list of depots. Any re-codings that occurred after closure to steam have not been given in the accompanying list.

SHEDS AT NATIONALISATION
SOUTHERN AREA (EASTERN)

STRATFORD DISTRICT	*Closed to steam*
30A Stratford (426)	10/62*
Brentwood	9/56(b)
Chelmsford	c.-/60
Epping	11/57
Ongar	11/49
Bethnal Green (Spitalfields)	c. -/59
Wood Street (Walthamstow)	11/60
Palace Gates	6/54
Enfield Town	11/60
30B Hertford East (a)	11/60
Ware	11/56(b)
Buntingford	6/59
30C Bishop's Stortford (a)	11/60
(Recoded Sub 31A 2/59)	
30D Southend (Victoria) (a)	c.2/59
(Recoded Sub 30A 12/56)	
Southminster	9/56
Wickford	9/56
30E Colchester (46)	11/59*
Clacton	4/59*
Walton-on-Naze	4/59*
Kelvedon	5/51
Maldon	c.12/59
(Recoded Sub 30F 11/59)	
Braintree	12/59
(Recoded Sub 30F 11/59)	
30F Parkeston (29)	1/61*

(a) The codes 30B, 30C and 30D were new identities introduced in February 1950, separate allocations not being recorded by the L.N.E.R. Previously Colchester was provisionally 30B and Parkeston 30C. The total of 426 locomotives at Stratford at 1/1/48 includes the allocations at Hertford, Bishop's Stortford and Southend.

(b) Closure date is that of withdrawal of class Y11 petrol shunter allocated there.

CAMBRIDGE DISTRICT	
31A Cambridge (127)	6/62
Ely	c.-/62
Huntingdon East	6/59
Saffron Walden	7/58
Thaxted	9/52
31B March (157)	11/63*
31C King's Lynn (52)	4/59*
Hunstanton	11/58
Wisbech	3/53*
(Recoded Sub 31B 7/52)	
31D South Lynn (36)	11/60
(Recoded Sub 31C 4/59)	
31E Bury St. Edmunds (15)	1/59
Sudbury	10/59
(Recoded Sub 31A 1/58)	

NORWICH DISTRICT	
32A Norwich (Thorpe) (122)	3/62
Cromer (High)	9/54
Dereham	9/55*
Wells	9/55*
Swaffham	6/56
32B Ipswich (85)	10/59
Aldeburgh	6/56
Felixstowe	1/59
Framlingham	11/52
Ipswich Dock	12/54
Laxfield	7/52
Stowmarket	6/56*
32C Lowestoft (25)	12/60*
32D Yarmouth (South Town) } (22)	11/59*
32E Yarmouth (Vauxhall) }	1/59*
32F Yarmouth (Beach) (23)	2/59
32G Melton Constable (28)	2/59
Norwich (City)	2/59
Cromer (Beach)	1/59*
(Recoded Sub 32A 9/54)	

SOUTHERN AREA (WESTERN)

KING'S CROSS DISTRICT	
34A King's Cross (London) (172)	6/63
34B Hornsey (London) (70)	7/61*
34C Hatfield (27)	1/61*
34D Hitchin (30)	6/61*
34E Neasden (London) (75)	6/62
(Recoded 14D 2/58)	
Aylesbury	6/62
Chesham	9/60

PETERBOROUGH DISTRICT	
35A New England (Peterborough) (206)	1/65*
(Recoded 34E 2/58)	
Spalding	3/60
(Recoded Sub 40F 12/57)	
Bourne	6/53
Stamford	6/59
35B Grantham (56)	9/63
(Recoded 34F 2/58)	
40F Boston (48)	1/64
Sleaford	10/58*
Wainfleet	c.-/52

DONCASTER DISTRICT

36A Doncaster (Carr) (194)	4/66*
36B Mexborough (83)	3/64
(Recoded 41F 2/58)	
39B Sheffield (Darnall) (97)	6/63*
(Recoded 41A 11/57)	
36C Frodingham (69)	2/66
36D Barnsley (39)	1/60
(Recoded 41G 2/58)	

WEST RIDING DISTRICT

37A Ardsley (91)	11/65
(Recoded 56B 10/56)	
37C Bradford (Hammerton Street) (49)	1/58*
(Recoded 56G 10/56)	
37B Copley Hill (Leeds) (32)	9/64
(Recoded 56C 10/56)	

NOTTINGHAM DISTRICT

38A Colwick (194)	12/66*
(Recoded 40E 2/58; 16B 1/66)	
Derby (Friargate)	2/55
Burton (L.M.S. shed used). Duties	
transferred to L.M.R. 5/49	—
Stafford (L.M.S. shed used). Duties	
transferred to L.M.R. c.-/49	—
38B Annesley (Nottingham) (78)	1/66
(Recoded 16D 2/58; 16B 9/63)	
38C Leicester (Central) (23)	7/64
(Recoded 15E 2/58; 15D 9/63)	
Leicester (Belgrave Road)	6/55
38D Staveley (33)	6/65
(Recoded 41H 2/58)	
38E Woodford (52)	6/65
(Recoded 2G 2/58; 2F 4/58; 1G 9/63)	

LINCOLN DISTRICT

40A Lincoln (Holmes) (55)	1/64
40B Immingham (98)	2/66
Grimsby	c.-/57
New Holland	2/57*
40C Louth (10)	12/56
36E Retford (G.C. & G.N.) (69)	G.C. 1/65
	G.N. 6/65
Newark	1/59
40D Tuxford (16)	2/59
(Recoded 41K 2/58)	
40E Langwith (62)	2/66
(Recoded 41J 2/58)	

MANCHESTER DISTRICT

39A Gorton (Manchester) (157)	6/65
(Recoded 9H 2/58; 9G 4/58)	
Dinting	2/58
Hayfield	6/56
Macclesfield: L.M.S. shed used by	
E.R. until 9/50	—

13A Trafford Park (Manchester) (37)	3/68
(Recoded 9E 5/50; 17F 1/57; 9E 4/58)	
13G Wigan (Lower Ince) (13)	3/52
(Recoded 10F 5/50)	
13E Liverpool (Brunswick) (41)	9/61
(Recoded 8E 5/50; 27F 4/58)	
Widnes (Tanhouse Lane)	4/56
(Recoded Sub 8D Widnes L.M.S. 5/50)	
Southport (Lord Street)	1/52
(Recoded Sub 27E 5/50)	
Warrington (Central)	c.-/67
(Recoded Sub 8E 5/50; Sub 27F 4/58; Sub 9E 9/61)	
13F Walton-on-the-Hill (Liverpool) (14)	12/63
(Recoded 27E 5/50; 8R 9/63)	
13C Stockport (Heaton Mersey) (32)	5/68*
(Recoded 9F 5/50; 17E 1/57; 9F 4/58)	
13D Northwich (29)	3/68
(Recoded 9G 5/50; 8E 4/58)	
6D Chester (Northgate) (11)	1/60*
6E Wrexham (Rhosddu) (26): Engines and men to Croes Newydd (ex-G.W.R.)	1/60
(Recoded 84K 2/58)	
6F Bidston (7)	2/63
Birkenhead (Shore Road)	6/61

NORTH EASTERN AREA

YORK DISTRICT

50A York (Leeman Road) (173)	6/67*
York (South)	5/61
20D Normanton (L.M.S. shed used)	1/68
(Recoded 55E 1/57)	
50C Selby (61)	9/59
50E Scarborough (11)	5/63*
50F Malton (15)	4/63
Pickering	4/59
50B Neville Hill (Leeds) (59)	6/66*
(Recoded 55H 1/60)	
Ilkley: Shed shared with	
L.M.R. Ceased to be used	
by N.E.R. 4/54	—
50D Starbeck (Harrogate) (45)	9/59
Pateley Bridge	4/51
50G Whitby (17)	4/59

DARLINGTON DISTRICT

51A Darlington (Bank Top) (122)	3/66
North Road (Darlington Works)	c. 11/55
Middleton-in-Teesdale	9/57
51J Northallerton (13)	3/63
Leyburn	5/54
51H Kirkby Stephen (11)	11/61
(Recoded 12E 2/58; 12D 4/58)	
51F West Auckland (38)	2/64
Wearhead	5/54

51B Newport (120)	6/58
51C West Hartlepool (80)	9/67*
51D Middlesbrough (61)	6/58
Guisborough	9/54
51E Stockton (37)	6/59
51G Haverton Hill (17)	6/59
51K Saltburn (11)	1/58

NEWCASTLE DISTRICT

52A Gateshead (Greensfield) (121)	3/65*
52B Heaton (Newcastle) (132)	8/64*
(Recoded Sub 52A 6/63)	
52C Blaydon (Newcastle) (102)	6/63*
(Recoded Sub 52A 3/63)	
Hexham	1/59*
Alston	9/59
Reedsmouth	9/52
Sub 52F Rothbury	9/52
52E Percy Main (21)	2/65*
52F North Blyth (22)	9/67*
South Blyth (18)	5/67*
52D Tweedmouth (38)	6/66*
Alnmouth	6/66
Duns	9/51
(Sub Hawick 64G 6/48)	

SUNDERLAND DISTRICT

54A Sunderland (58)	9/67
(Recoded 52G 9/58)	
Durham	12/58
Sub 52A Bowes Bridge	9/62
54C Borough Gardens (Gateshead) (50)	6/59
(Recoded 52J 9/58)	
54B Tyne Dock (59)	9/67
(Recoded 52H 9/58)	
Pelton Level	c. 11/63
54D Consett (16)	5/65*
(Recoded 52K 9/58)	

HULL DISTRICT

53A Dairycoates (Hull) (113)	6/67*
(Recoded 50B 1/60)	
53C Springhead (Hull) (35)	12/58*
Alexandra Dock (Hull)	2/58*
53B Botanic Gardens (Hull) (58)	6/59*
53E Cudworth (8)	7/51
53D Bridlington (5)	6/58*

SCOTTISH AREA

ABERDEEN DISTRICT

61B Ferryhill (Aberdeen) (21) (L.M.S.	
shed used) Engines and men	
integrated with ex-L.M.S. 9/50	2/67*

117

61A Kittybrewster (Aberdeen) (69)	6/61*
Ballater	4/58*
Peterhead	6/61*
Fraserburgh	6/61*
Alford	1/50
Inverurie	3/59*
Macduff	9/51
61C Keith (23)	6/61*
Banff	7/64
(Recoded Sub 61B 6/61)	
Boat of Garten	11/58
(Sub Aviemore L.M.S. 60B 1/49)	
Elgin	6/61*

BURNTISLAND DISTRICT

62B Dundee (Tay Bridge) (75)	5/67
Arbroath	1/59
Montrose	5/66
St. Andrews	9/60
Tayport	9/51
62C Dunfermline (61)	5/67*
Loch Leven	1/51
Sub 63A Perth (17): Engines and men to	
63A Perth South ex-L.M.S.	12/49
Sub Stirling L.M.S. 63B Stirling (Shore Road	
and Forth & Clyde) (25)	9/57
Alloa	1/67
(Recoded Sub 62C 2/49)	
62A Thornton (103)	11/66*
Anstruther	11/60
Burntisland	c. -/58*
Ladybank	c. -/58*
Methil	c. -/58*

EDINBURGH DISTRICT

64A St. Margaret's (Edinburgh) (199)	4/67
Seafield (Edinburgh)	10/62
Dunbar	6/64
Penicuik	9/51
North Berwick	2/58
Galashiels	c. 4/62
Peebles	10/55
Longniddry	6/59
Polton	10/51
64B Haymarket (Edinburgh) (86)	9/63
12B Carlisle (Canal) (57)	6/63
(Recoded 68E 10/51; 12D 2/58; 12C 4/58)	
Silloth	7/53
64G Hawick (26)	1/66
St. Boswells	11/59
Jedburgh	8/48
Kelso	7/55
Riccarton	10/58

GLASGOW DISTRICT

65A Eastfield (Glasgow) (154)	5/67*
Aberfoyle	9/51
Kilsyth	8/51
Lennoxtown	9/51
Sub Dawsholm L.M.S. 65D Stobcross	
(Glasgow) (c)	10/50

65C Parkhead (Glasgow) (66)		10/65
(Recoded Sub 65A 7/62)		
65H Helensburgh (c)		11/60
Arrochar (c)		10/59*
65I Balloch (c)		11/60
65E Kipps (Coatbridge) (53)		4/62*
64F Bathgate (42)		8/66*
Morningside		11/54
(Recoded Sub Motherwell L.M.S. 66B 10/50)		
64E Polmont (42)		5/64
(Recoded 65K 5/60)		
Kinneil (Bo'ness)		9/52

63D Fort William (12)		6/62*
(Recoded 65J 4/55; 63B 5/60)		
Mallaig		7/61

(c) Separate allocations normally were not recorded for 65H Helensburgh and 65I Balloch, whose engines were supplied by Parkhead and Eastfield respectively. Stobcross continued to be supplied with engines from Eastfield. The totals of engines shown against Eastfield and Parkhead reflect this situation.

NUMERICAL INDEX OF LOCOMOTIVES

This index is intended to assist readers in the identification of locomotive classes which bore the numbers listed. The first column of classifications relates to the period up to 1946, at which time the general renumbering of L.N.E.R. locomotive stock took place. The second column shows the position thereafter. B.R. numbers can, with few exceptions, be deduced by adding 60,000 to the listed numbers, the applicable classifications of course being those indicated in the second column.

Where more than one class is shown against a given number in either column, it is an indication that the original locomotive of that number had been withdrawn or renumbered and a new locomotive was built to take its place, or that there had been rebuilding resulting in reclassification. A class in parenthesis indicates reclassification without rebuilding.

The numbering of L.N.E.R. locomotives from 1923 is set out in detail in Part 1 of this series (page 28 et seq) but it will be convenient to summarise here the general scheme adopted. From February 1924 onwards N.E.R. locomotives retained their original numbers, whilst those of the G.N.R., G.C.R., G.N.S.R., G.E.R. and N.B.R. were increased by 3,000, 5,000, 6,800, 7,000 and 9,000 respectively. The H. & B.R. locomotives, which had their numbers increased by 3,000 when that company was absorbed by the N.E.R. in 1922, were renumbered between 2405 and 2542, following on the highest number in the N.E.R. series (Appendix A). G.C.R. duplicate list engines, which had previously been designated by a "C" after their original numbers, were allotted a new series between 6402 and 6494 (Appendix B). A few N.B.R. duplicate list locomotives, which carried four-figure numbers, were given numbers in the 9,000 range, but this idea was soon discarded and the locomotives received their correct numbers above 10,000.

Appendix C lists the remaining locomotives, all of which were not allotted numbers in the L.N.E.R. series mainly due to their having been withdrawn from service before the 1924 renumbering scheme was drawn up.

It will be seen that the first column of classifications of the main index, taken together with Appendices A, B and C, lists all locomotives taken into L.N.E.R. stock at Grouping. An asterisk against an entry indicates that the engine concerned failed to receive its intended L.N.E.R. number, due either to withdrawal or rebuilding to another class beforehand. Clearly, this information cannot be given for ex-N.E.R. locomotives, all of which retained their existing numbers.

Locomotives of pre-Grouping classes built or purchased by the L.N.E.R. were in some cases given numbers in the series of the originating company. In other cases, in common with new L.N.E.R. types, they were numbered in the gap between the H. & B. and G.N.R. series, or in blanks in the N.E. series. In the latter case, however, more attempt was made to keep the numbers of the locomotives of any one class within a small range than had been the practice on the N.E.R. By 1936 all the long gaps below 3,000 had been filled, and from then onwards new construction was numbered in the G.N.R. series.

There were a number of acquisitions of stock from smaller companies by the L.N.E.R. after Grouping. These were dealt with in one or other of two ways. Some, such as the engines from the East & West Yorkshire Union, the Colne Valley & Halstead and the Mid-Suffolk Light Railways in 1923-24 took vacant numbers in the appropriate series on a geographical basis, i.e. in the G.N. and G.E. groups at 3112-5 and 8312-7. This, too, occurred again in 1937 when eighteen engines from the London Passenger Transport Board received numbers 6154-63 and 6415-22 in the G.C.R. series. However, when the Midland & Great Northern Joint Railway's stock of 86 locomotives were taken over in 1936 they were all allotted (and 64 received) an "0" prefix to their existing numbers, reviving the G.E.R. system of designation of their Duplicate List stock. These M. & G.N. engines are shown in Appendix D.

In 1942 Thompson instituted a partial renumbering scheme to clear the G.E. series numbers from 8301 upwards to make way for his new class B1 4-6-0 engines. Classes involved were B12, D15, D16, F7, Y1 and Y11 and they were to be given numbers in the 7,000 series, which were then vacant except for those occupied by surviving members of class E4 which were moved to 7791-7808.

The above scheme was aborted after 37 engines had been renumbered, the reason being that a more ambitious scheme was drawn up in mid-1943 in which the whole of the locomotive stock would be renumbered on a systematic basis. This was not begun until January 1946 and was completed by January 1947. Certain local renumberings were carried out beforehand. The general layout of the scheme was as follows:—

1- 999 Largest passenger and mixed-traffic tender locos. (4-6-2 and 2-6-2).

1000-1999 Medium-sized six-coupled passenger and mixed-traffic tender locos. (4-6-0, 2-6-0 and 2-6-2).

2000-2999	Four-coupled passenger tender locos.
3000-3999	Eight-coupled tender locos.
4000-5999	0-6-0 tender locos
6000-6999	Electric locos.
7000-7999	Four-coupled and 2-6-2 passenger tank locos.
8000-8999	Diesel, 0-4-0T and 0-6-0T shunting locos.
9000-9999	Large tank locomotives (apart from 2-6-2T).
10000	The class W1 4-6-4 already bearing that number.

Only the locomotives *actually* renumbered under the 1946 scheme are shown in the second column of classifications in the main table.

During the first months after Nationalisation, L.N.E.R. locomotives came out of shops with an E prefix to their numbers. These are listed herein at page 96. Then from mid-March 1948 onwards renumbering took place by the addition of 60,000 to the numbers then carried. These B.R. numbers can be calculated from the Index by adding this figure to the numbers shown, but it must be stressed that not all locomotives shown in the second column of classification survived to take up B.R. numbers. Those that did can be found by reference to the summary table at the end of each class article in previous Parts of this series. Classes in the index marked with a dagger symbol carried only B.R. 60,000 series numbers and never ran with L.N.E.R. numbers — these were either new constructions or renumberings by B.R. Exceptions to the addition of 60,000 to the L.N.E.R. number were class W1 No. 10000, which became 60700, and the diesel and electric locomotives which received new numbers in the 15,000 and 26,000 ranges respectively. Second thoughts by B.R. put the petrol driven locomotives of class Y11 into the 15,000 series and the class O7 Austerity 2-8-0's into the 90,000 range. These exceptions are shown in Appendix E. Later, there was a separate group of numbers allocated to the Departmental locomotives operating in the Eastern and North Eastern Regions and these are listed on pages 24-27.

Key

* L.N.E.R. 1924 number allotted but not carried.

† B.R. 60,000 series number only (i.e. L.N.E.R. number not carried).

A class in parentheses denotes reclassification without rebuilding.

No.	Class Pre-1946	Class Post-1946
1	Electric (ES1). D3	A4
2	Electric (ES1)	A4
3-10	Electric (EF1)	A4
11	Electric (EB1)	A4
12	Electric (EF1)	A4
13	Electric (EE1)	A4
14	N8	A4
15	J77	A4
16	J21	A4
17	"398" (0-6-0). K3	A4
18	D22. Y3	A4
19	"901" (2-4-0). Y1	A4
20	J74	A4
21	F8. Y3	A4
22	J21	A4
23	D23. Y3	A4
24	Y7	A4
25	J25	A4
26	J21	A4
27	J71	A4
28	K3	A4
29	J25	A4
30/1	J21	A4
32	"398" (0-6-0). K3	A4
33	K3	A4
34	J21	A4
35	F8. Y3	A3
36	K3	A3
37	J77	A3
38/9	K3	A3
40/1	F8	A3
42	D22. Y3	A3
43	J77	A3
44	"44" (0-6-0T). Y1	A10. A3
45	"398" (0-6-0). Y1	A3
46	K3	A3
47	J77	A10. A3
48	J21	A3
49	"44" (0-6-0T). Y3	A3
50	J71	A3
51	J21	A3
52	K3	A3
53	"901" (2-4-0). K3	A3
54	J71	A3
55	F8. Y3	A3
56	J21	A3
57	J77	A10. A3
58	K3	A3
59	J22. Y1	A3
60	G6. Y3	A3
61	"398" (0-6-0). Y3	A3
62/3	G6. Y3	A3
64	J74. Y3	A3
65	G6. Y3	A10. A3
66	X1	A3
67	J26	A3
68	J21	A10. A3†
69	K3	A3
70	J71	A10. A3
71	J77	A3
72	F8	A3
73	K3	A3
74	N8	A3
75	K3	A3
76	N8	A3
77	J71	A3
78	J22. Y3	A3
79	"398" (0-6-0). Y1	A3
80	K3	A3
81	"398" (0-6-0). Y3	A3
82	J74	A3
83	Q5	A3
84	J71	A3
85	D22	A3
86	J21. Y3	A3
87	G6. Y3	A3
88	J74	A3
89	N10	A3
90	"398" (0-6-0). Y3	A3
91/2	G6. K3	A3
93	J21	A3
94	"44" (0-6-0T). Y3	A3

No.	Class Pre-1946	Class Post-1946
95	J21	A3
96	D22. Y3	A3
97	J21	A3
98	"44" (0-6-0T). Y3	A3
99	J21	A3
100	"398" (0-6-0). Y1	A3
101/2	J21	A3
103	J71	A10. A3
104	J21	A3
105	J77	A3
106	"44" (0-6-0T). Y1	A10. A3
107	J21	A3
108	G6. Y1	A3
109	K3	A3
110	J21	A3
111	K3	A3
112	K3	A10. A3
113	K3	A1
114	K3	A1†
115	D22	A1†
116	"398" (0-6-0). K3	A1†
117	D22. Y3	A1†
118	K3	A1†
119	"398" (0-6-0). Y1	A1†
120/1	K3	A1†
122/3	J21	A1†
124	J76. Y1	A1†
125/6/7	K3	A1†
128	F8	A1†
129	Y7	A1†
130	Q5	A1†
131	J22	A1†
132	J26	A1†
133	J21	A1†
134/5	K3	A1†
136	N8	A1†
137	J71	A1†
138	J77	A1†
139	J21	A1†
140/1	K3	A1†
142	J22. Y1	A1†
143	K3	A1†
144	J71	A1†
145	J77	A1†
146	"398" (0-6-0). K3	A1†
147	J21	A1†
148	J21. Y3	A1†
149	G5	A1†
150	"1440" (2-4-0). Y1	A1†
151	J77	A1†
152	J21	A1†
153	K3	A1†
154	D22. Y3	A1†
155	F8. Y3	A1†
156	K3	A1†
157	J21	A1†
158/9	K3	A1†
160	J21	A1†
161	J71	A1†
162	Q5	A1†
163	K3	—
164	J77	—
165	J71	—
166	J77	—
167	K3	—
168	J71	—
169	F8	—
170	K3	—
171	J76. Y1	—
172	F8. Y3	—
173	J77	—
174/5	"398" (0-6-0). Y1	—
176/7	J71	—
178	K3	—
179	J71	—
180	K3	—
181	J71	—
182	J21	—
183	"398" (0-6-0). Y1	—
184	K3	—
185	N8	—
186	K3	—

No.	Class Pre-1946	Class Post-1946
187	F8. Y1	—
188	K3	—
189	G6. Y3	—
190	X3	—
191	K3	—
192	J22. Y3	—
193	J76. Y3	—
194	D22	—
195	K3	—
196	"398" (0-6-0). Y3	—
197/8	J76. Y3	—
199	J77	—
200	K3	—
201	F8. D49	—
202	"398" (0-6-0). K3	—
203	K3	—
204	"398" (0-6-0). K3	—
205	F8. D49	—
206	"398" (0-6-0). K3. K5	—
207	K3	—
208	J22. K3	—
209	J21	—
210	N8	—
211	J76. D49	—
212/3	N8	—
214	D23. D49	—
215/6	N8	—
217	D23. D49	—
218/9	N8	—
220	"1440" (2-4-0). D49	—
221	J71	—
222	D23. D49	—
223	D23	—
224/5	J71	—
226	G6. D49	—
227	"398" (0-6-0). K3	—
228/9	K3	—
230	D22. D49	—
231	K3	—
232	J22. D49	—
233	J26	—
234	D49	—
235	J22. D49	—
236	D49	—
237	J71	—
238	N8. D49	—
239-42	J71	—
243	J26	—
244	J71	—
245/6	D49	—
247	G6. D49	—
248	J71	—
249/50	D49	—
251	"398" (0-6-0). D49	—
252	J71	—
253	"398" (0-6-0). D49	—
254	J71	—
255/6	G6. D49	—
257	J25	—
258	D23. D49	—
259	J21	—
260/1	J71	—
262	F8	—
263	J71	—
264/5/6	D49	—
267	N8	—
268	J71	—
269	"901" (2-4-0). D49	—
270	D49	—
271	N8	—
272	J71	—
273	G6. D49	—
274	D23. D49	—
275	J71	—
276	J77	—
277	D49	—
278	J71	—
279	F8. D49	—
280	J71	—
281	"38" (4-4-0). D49	—
282	"398" (0-6-0). D49	—
283	D49	—

No.	Class Pre-1946	Post-1946
284	N8	—
285/6	J71	—
287	N8	—
288	G6. D49	—
289	J21	—
290	J77	—
291	J21	—
292	"398" (0-6-0). D49	—
293	N8	—
294	J21	—
295	C6	—
296	J71	—
297	G6. D49	—
298	D49	—
299	J71	—
300	J21	—
301	J71	—
302/3	"398" (0-6-0)	—
304	J71	—
305	J77	—
306/7	D49	—
308	"398" (0-6-0)	—
309	"398" (0-6-0). D49	—
310	D49	—
311	"398" (0-6-0). D49	—
312-6	J21	—
317	J71	—
318	D49	—
319	J77	—
320	D49	—
321	G6	—
322	G6. D49	—
323	G6	—
324	J77	—
325	"398" (0-6-0)	—
326	J71	—
327	"398" (0-6-0). D49	—
328	D23	—
329	D49	—
330	"398" (0-6-0)	—
331	J21	—
332	"398" (0-6-0)	—
333	J77	—
334	G6	—
335/6	D49	—
337	D23	—
338	J71	—
339	"398" (0-6-0)	—
340	D22	—
341	G6	—
342	J26	—
343	G6	—
344	J77	—
345/6	N8	—
347	J71	—
348-51	N8	—
352	D49	—
353	G6. D49	—
354	J77	—
355/6	D22	—
357	D49	—
358	G6	—
359	D49	—
360	J21	—
361/2	D49	—
363	"901" (2-4-0). D49	—
364	D49	—
365	D49. D	—
366	"901" (2-4-0). D49	—
367	"901" (2-4-0)	—
368	D49	—
369	J22	—
370	"901" (2-4-0). D49	—
371	N8	—
372	D23	—
373	N8	—
374	D49	—
375	"398" (0-6-0). D49	—
376/7	D49	—
378	—	—
379	J26	—
380/1	G5	—

No.	Class Pre-1946	Post-1946
382	—	—
383	N9	—
384	G5	—
385/6	—	—
387	G5	—
388	J22	—
389	"398" (0-6-0)	—
390	V3	—
391/2	"398" (0-6-0). V3	—
393	V3	—
394	G5	—
395	V3	—
396/7/8	"398" (0-6-0). V3	—
399	J71. V3	—
400	J71	—
401	J71. V3	—
402	J71. V1	—
403	J71	—
404	F8. V1	—
405	G5	—
406	J26	—
407	J79. V1	—
408	G5	—
409	N7	—
410/1	Q5	—
412	J26	—
413	G5	—
414/5	F8. V1	—
416	G6. V1	—
417	"398" (0-6-0). V1. V3	—
418/9/20	F8. V1	—
421	"398" (0-6-0). N7	—
422	J22. V1	—
423	F8. V1	—
424	J21. V1	—
425	F8. V1	—
426	N7	—
427	G5	—
428	N8. V1	—
429	N10	—
430	Q5	—
431/2	J21	—
433	G5	—
434	J26	—
435/6/7	G5	—
438	J26	—
439	G5	—
440	J22. V1	—
441	G5	—
442	J26	—
443/4	Q5	—
445	N8	—
446	J22. V1	—
447/8	J71. V1	—
449/50	J71	—
451	J71. V1. V3	—
452/3	J71	—
454	F8. V1	—
455	J22. V1	—
456/7	N7	—
458	J21	—
459	J25	—
460	N7	—
461	J74. V1	—
462	J72	—
463	J25	—
464	"901" (2-4-0). N7	—
465/6	G6. V1	—
467	J74. V1	—
468	G5	—
469	F8. V1	—
470	J21	—
471	N7	—
472	D23. V1. V3	—
473	N7	—
474	Q5	—
475	N7	—
476	D20	—
477	V1	—
478	J71. V1	—
479	V1	—
480	J21. V1	—

No.	Class Pre-1946	Post-1946
481	V1	—
482	J71	—
483	F8. V1. V3	—
484	V1	—
485	F8. V1	—
486	"1440" (2-4-0). V1	—
487	V1	—
488	"398" (0-6-0). V1	—
489	J74. V1	—
490	F8. V1	—
491	J22. V1	—
492-5	J71	—
496	J71. V1	—
497/8	J22. V1	—
499	J71	—
500	J72	A2
501	J71	A2
502	J22	A10. A2
503/4	N8	A2
505	G5	A2
506	J22	A2
507	F8	A3. A2
508	J22	A3. A2
509	N8	A2
510	J21	A2
511	J21	A10. A2
512	J72	A2
513	J21	A2
514	D22	A2
515	N8	A2
516	J72	A2
517	J26	A3. A2
518	Y7	A3. A2
519	Y7	A2
520	J21	A3. A2
521	D23	A3. A2
522	J22	A3. A2
523	N8	A2
524	J72	A2
525	J26	A2
526	G5	A2
527	Q5	A2
528	N8	A3. A2
529	G5	A2
530	J21	A2
531	N8	A3. A2
532	C6	A2†
533	J71	A2†
534	J21	A2†
535	N8	A2†
536	J25	A2†
537	F8	A3. A2†
538	J21	A10. A2†
539	J21	A2†
540	G5	—
541	J71	—
542	J72	A3
543	J26	—
544	J73	—
545	J73	A3
546-53	J73	—
554/5	J26	—
556	J21	—
557	D23	—
558	J21	A3
559/60	Y8	—
561	Y8	A3
562/3	Y8	—
564	J21	—
565	J22	A3
566	J72	—
567	J22	—
568/9	J21	—
570	J21	A3
571	J22. J72	—
572	J71	—
573	N8	—
574	J72	—
575	F8	A3
576	J72	—
577	J71	—
578	Q5	—

No.	Pre-1946	Post-1946	No.	Pre-1946	Post-1946	No.	Pre-1946	Post-1946
579	J21	—	718-22	C7	V2	881	J26	V2
580	G5	—	723/4/5	D20	—	882	—	V2
581	J72	—	726	B13	—	883	J27	V2
582	J21	—	727	C7. C9	—	884-7	—	V2
583	J50	—	728	C7	—	888	J27	V2
584	J71. J50	—	729	C7	V2	889/90	—	V2
585	G6. J50	A4	730/1	C8	—	891	J27	V2
586	J50	—	732	C7	—	892-5	N2	V2
587	Y7. J50	A4	733	C7	V2	896	"398" (0-6-0). N2	V2
588	G6. J50	A4	734-7	C7	—	897	N2	V2
589	J50	—	738-41	B13	—	898	Y7	V2
590	J78. J50	—	742	C6	—	899	J21	V2
591	J50	—	743-9	B13	—	900	Y7	V2
592	D20	—	750	B13	V2	901-5	Q7	V2
593/4	J50	—	751-61	B13	—	906	B16	V2
595	G6. J50	—	762	B13	V2	907	N7	V2
596	J50	—	763	B13	—	908/9	B16	V2
597	J77	—	764	Q5	—	910	"901" (2-4-0)	V2
598/9	J76. J50	—	765	J26	—	911	B16	V2
600	"398" (0-6-0). J50	—	766	B13	—	912	N7	V2
601	J50	—	767	Q5	—	913	"398" (0-6-0). N7	V2
602	J76. J50	—	768	B13	—	914/5	B16	V2
603	J50	—	769/70	Q5	—	916	"398" (0-6-0). N7	V2
604	J77	—	771	Q5	V2	917	J27	V2
605	G6. J50	A4	772/3/4	Q5	—	918/9	N7	V2
606	J22. J50	—	775	B13	—	920-34	B16	V2
607	J77	—	776	J21	—	935	N7	V2
608	"398" (0-6-0). J50	—	777	D22	—	936/7	B16	V2
609/10	J50	—	778	J21	—	938	J27	V2
611	J21. J50	—	779	D22	—	939	Q5	V2
612	J77	—	780	N8	—	940/1	N7	V2
613	J21	—	781	Q5	—	942/3	B16	V2
614	J77	—	782	B15	—	944	J21	V2
615	G6. J50	—	783	Q5	—	945/6	Y7	V2
616/7/8	J50	—	784	C6	—	947	G6. N7	V2
619	J21	—	785	Q5	—	948	J77	V2
620	J22	—	786/7/8	B15	—	949	G6	V2
621/2	J50	—	789	Q5	—	950	G6. N7	V2
623	J77	—	790	J27	—	951	G6	V2
624	G6. Q7	—	791	B15	—	952	G6. N7	V2
625	Q7	—	792/3/4	Q5	—	953/4	J77	V2
626	"398" (0-6-0). Q7	—	795	B15	V2	955	G6	V2
627	"398" (0-6-0)	—	796/7/8	B15	—	956	J77	V2
628-34	Q7	—	799	B15	V2	957	X2	V2
635	J50	—	800	J21	V2	958	J77	V2
636	"398" (0-6-0). J50	—	801	F8	V2	959	N8	V2
637	—	—	802	J71	V2	960	J21	V2
638	G6	—	803	D22	V2	961	N8	V2
639/40	—	—	804	F8	V2	962/3	J21	V2
641	"398" (0-6-0)	—	805	"398" (0-6-0)	V2	964	N/	V2
642-8	Q5	—	806/7	J21	V2	965	J21	V2
649	C6	—	808	D22	V2	966/7/8	N7	V2
650-61	Q5	—	809	N8	V2	969	J71	V2
662	J74	—	810	J21	V2	970/1	N7	V2
663	D22	—	811	J71	V2	972	J71	V2
664	—	—	812	J22	V2	973-6	J21	V2
665-8	J21	—	813	B15	V2	977/8	J71	V2
669	Q5	—	814	J27	V2	979	J21	V2
670	"398" (0-6-0)	—	815	B15	V2	980	J71	V2
671	F8	—	816	J26	V2	981	J21	V2
672	G6	—	817	B15	V2	982/3	Y7	V2
673	D22	—	818	J26	V2	984/5/6	Y7	—
674	F8	—	819-25	B15	V2	987/8	N7	—
675-9	D23	—	826-30	N7	V2	989	—	—
680	J21	—	831	J26	V2	990/1	"398" (0-6-0)	—
681/2	J22	—	832/3/4	N7	V2	992/3	J21	—
683	N8	—	835	J26	V2	994	J21	A2
684	D22	—	836	J27	V2	995	J78	—
685	F8	—	837/8	N7	V2	996/7	J21	—
686-95	A6	—	839	J27	V2	998/9	J77	—
696-9	C6	—	840-9	B16	V2	1000	J77	B1
700	C6	W1†	850-3	N7	V2	1001	J27	B1
701	C6	V2	854	F8	V2	1002	Q5	B1
702-5	C6	—	855-64	N8	V2	1003-8	J27	B1
706	C7	—	865-8	N7	V2	1009	Q5	B1
707/8	D20	—	869	J21	V2	1010-8	J27	B1
709/10	C7	V2	870	N7	V2	1019/20	G6	B1
711	D20	V2	871/2	J21	V2	1021	J77	B1
712/3	D20	—	873	N7	V2	1022-5	J27	B1
714	C7	V2	874-8	J21	V2	1026	D20	B1
715	Q5	—	879	—	V2	1027-30	J27	B1
716/7	C7	—	880	J27	V2	1031/2	Q5	B1

No.	Class Pre-1946	Class Post-1946
1033	J77	B1
1034/5/6	J27	B1
1037	J50	B1
1038	"398" (0-6-0)	B1
1039/40	J27	B1
1041	"398" (0-6-0). J50	B1
1042	D20	B1
1043	J26	B1
1044	J27	B1
1045	J50	B1
1046-50	J27	B1
1051	D20	B1
1052/3	J27	B1
1054	Q5	B1
1055	G6	B1
1056	J27	B1
1057	J26	B1
1058	J50	B1
1059	J76	B1
1060/1	J27	B1
1062	Q5	B1
1063	J50	B1
1064-7	J27	B1
1068/9/70	J50	B1
1071	J21	B1
1072	N8	B1
1073	J21	B1
1074	J50	B1
1075	J21	B1
1076	"398" (0-6-0)	B1
1077	B13	B1
1078	D20	B1
1079	J50	B1
1080	"398" (0-6-0)	B1
1081	J50	B1
1082	"398" (0-6-0). J50	B1
1083/4/5	J71	B1
1086	J50	B1
1087	"398" (0-6-0)	B1
1088/9	—	B1
1090	"398" (0-6-0)	B1
1091	N8	B1
1092	"398" (0-6-0)	B1
1093/4	—	B1
1095	J71	B1
1096	G5	B1
1097	"398" (0-6-0)	B1
1098	J26	B1
1099	—	B1
1100/1	K3	B1
1102	J22. K3	B1
1103	J71	B1
1104/5	N8	B1
1106	J22. K3	B1
1107	D23	B1
1108	K3	B1
1109	N10	B1
1110/1	Q5	B1
1112	N10	B1
1113/4	A7	B1
1115/6	J77	B1
1117	"398" (0-6-0). K3	B1
1118	K3	B1
1119	"398" (0-6-0). K3	B1
1120	D23	B1
1121	K3	B1
1122	J21	B1
1123	J71	B1
1124	N8	B1
1125	K3	B1
1126	A7	B1
1127	N8	B1
1128	Q5	B1
1129	A7	B1
1130/1	J26	B1
1132	N10	B1
1133	"398" (0-6-0). K3	B1
1134	J71	B1
1135	"398" (0-6-0). K3	B1
1136	A7	B1
1137	D22. K3	B1
1138	N10	B1

No.	Class Pre-1946	Class Post-1946
1139	J26	B1
1140	J71	B1
1141	J22. K3	B1
1142/3/4	J71	B1
1145	N8	B1
1146	J26	B1
1147	D20	B1
1148	N10	B1
1149/50	Q5	B1
1151	J71	B1
1152	N8	B1
1153	J71	B1
1154	"398" (0-6-0). K3	B1
1155	J71	B1
1156	K3	B1
1157	J71	B1
1158	"398" (0-6-0). K3	B1
1159	J26	B1
1160	F8	B1
1161	J21	B1
1162	K3	B1
1163	J71	B1
1164	"398" (0-6-0). K3	B1
1165	N8	B1
1166	K3	B1
1167	J71	B1
1168	N8	B1
1169	G5	B1
1170	A7	B1
1171	F8	B1
1172	J26	B1
1173	Q5	B1
1174/5/6	A7	B1
1177/8	Q5	B1
1179-83	A7	B1
1184	D20	B1
1185	A7	B1
1186	Q5	B1
1187/8	J21	B1
1189	J27	B1
1190-3	A7	B1
1194	J26	B1
1195	A7	B1
1196-9	J71	B1
1200	J26	B1
1201	J27	B1
1202	J26	B1
1203/4/5	J27	B1
1206/7	D20	B1
1208	J26	B1
1209/10	D20	B1
1211-4	J27	B1
1215	Q5	B1
1216	J27	B1
1217	D20	B1
1218	Q5	B1
1219-22	J27	B1
1223	D20	B1
1224-31	J27	B1
1232	D20	B1
1233	J39	B1
1234/5/6	D20	B1
1237-46	D21	B1
1247-54	Q6	B1
1255	J39	B1
1256	J27	B1
1257	Q6	B1
1258	D20	B1
1259	J39	B1
1260	D20	B1
1261/2	Q6	B1
1263	J39	B1
1264	Q6	B1
1265-70	J39	B1
1271	Q6	B1
1272/3/4	J39	B1
1275	"1001" (0-6-0). J39	B1
1276	Q6	B1
1277	J39	B1
1278/9/80	Q6	B1
1281/2	J39	B1
1283/4/5	Q6	B1

No.	Class Pre-1946	Class Post-1946
1286/7	J39	B1
1288	Q6	B1
1289/90	J39	B1
1291-4	Q6	B1
1295/6	J39	B1
1297	"398" (0-6-0)	B1
1298	J39	B1
1299	"398" (0-6-0)	B1
1300	K3	B1
1301	J21	B1
1302	Y7. K3	B1
1303	Y7	B1
1304	Y7. K3	B1†
1305	J21	B1†
1306/7/8	Y7. K3	B1†
1309	J21	B1†
1310	Y7. K3	B1†
1311	Q6	B5. B1†
1312	G6. K3	B5. B1†
1313	J77	B1†
1314	J71	B1†
1315	J21	B1†
1316	G5	B1†
1317	N10	B1†
1318	K3	B1†
1319	G5	B1†
1320	Q5	B1†
1321	N10	B1†
1322	F8. K3	B1†
1323	J21	B1†
1324	D22. K3	B1†
1325	"901" (2-4-0). K3	B1†
1326-30	H1. A8	B1†
1331	K3	B1†
1332	J21. K3	B1†
1333	"398" (0-6-0). K3	B1†
1334	G5	B1†
1335	Q6	B1†
1336/7/8	J21	B1†
1339	J21. K3	B1†
1340-4	J77	B1†
1345	K3	B1†
1346/7/8	J77	B6. B1†
1349	J77	B8. B1†
1350-9	T1	B8. B1†
1360	J26	B7. B1†
1361/2/3	Q6	B7. B1†
1364/5	K3	B7. B1†
1366	J26	B7. B1†
1367/8	K3	B7. B1†
1369/70	J26	B7. B1†
1371-85	B16	B7. B1†
1386-9	K3	B7. B1†
1390	J26	B7. B1†
1391/2	K3	B7. B1†
1393	J27	B7. B1†
1394-7	K3	B7. B1†
1398/9	K3	B1†
1400/1	J38	B16. B1†
1402	J27	B16. B1†
1403-9	J38	B16. B1†
1410/1	J38	B16
1412	"398" (0-6-0). J39	B16
1413	"398" (0-6-0). J38	B16
1414-7	J38	B16
1418	"398" (0-6-0). J39	B16
1419	"398" (0-6-0). J38	B16
1420	J38	B16
1421	"398" (0-6-0). J38	B16
1422/3/4	J38	B16
1425	"398" (0-6-0). J39	B16
1426/7/8	J38	B16
1429	"398" (0-6-0). J39	B16
1430-3	J77	B16
1434	J38	B16
1435	J77	B16
1436	G6. J39	B16
1437	J38	B16
1438/9	J77	B16
1440	J38	B16
1441/2/3	"1440" (2-4-0). J38	B16
1444/5	J38	B16

Fig. 138   Kirkby Stephen (ex-N.E.R.), 1939. Class E4 No. 7496 and Q5 No. 715.

Fig. 139   Barnard Castle (ex-N.E.R.), June 1930.

Fig. 140   Cudworth (ex-H. & B.R.) on a Sunday, c.1924.

Fig. 141   Denaby (ex-H. & B.R.), c.1925. Class N12 No. 2487.

Fig. 142   Eastfield, Glasgow (ex-N.B.R.), June 1946.

Fig. 143   Fort William (ex-N.B.R.), June 1936. Class K2 Nos. 4685 and 4674, D34
Nos. 9035 and 9496.

Fig. 144   Haymarket, Edinburgh (ex-N.B.R.) showing the mechanical coaling plant.

Fig. 145   Burntisland (ex-N.B.R.) circular roundhouse.

Fig. 146   Kittybrewster, Aberdeen (ex-G.N.S.R.), 26th August 1928, crescent-shaped roundhouse with class D31 No. 9211 completely blocking operation.

Fig. 147   Keith (ex-G.N.S.R.), 1937.

Fig. 148   Shed allocation plates as fitted inside the cab of L.N.E.R. engines.

Fig. 149   Ro-railer KE6001 built in 1934 by Karrier Motors Ltd. for use on permanent
way maintenance on the West Highland line.

No.	Pre-1946	Post-1946
1446	"1440" (2-4-0). J38	B16
1447	J38	B16
1448/9	"1440" (2-4-0). J39	B16
1450/1	"398" (0-6-0). J39	B16
1452	J39	B16
1453	"398" (0-6-0). J39	B16
1454/5	J39	B16
1456	"398" (0-6-0). J39	B16
1457/8/9	J39	B16
1460	J77. J39	B16
1461/2	J77	B16
1463-8	E5. J39	B16
1469-78	E5. J39	B9. B16†
1479	E5. J39	B18
1480	J22. J39	B18
1481-9	J22. J39	B4
1490/1	J22. J39	B19
1492/3	J39	B19
1494-8	J39	B3
1499	H1. A8	—
1500-3	H1. A8	B12
1504/5	E5. J39	B12
1506	E5. J39	—
1507	J21	B12
1508/9	J21. J39	B12
1510-6	J21	B12
1517-31	H1. A8	B12
1532/3	D22. J39	B12
1534	D22. J39	—
1535-46	D22. J39	B12
1547/8	J21. J39	B12
1549/50	J21	B12
1551	J21. J39	B12
1552-7	J21	B12
1558	J21. J39	B12
1559	J21	B12
1560	J21. J39	B12
1561/2	J21	B12
1563	J21. J39	B12
1564-76	J21	B12
1577	F8. J39	B12
1578/9	F8	B12
1580	F8. J39	B12
1581/2/3	F8	—
1584/5/6	F8. J39	—
1587	J21. J39	—
1588-96	J21	—
1597/8/9	F8	—
1600/1/2	F8	B17
1603	F8	B2
1604/5/6	F8	B17
1607	J21	B17. B2
1608-13	J21	B17
1614/5/6	J21	B2
1617	N9	B17. B2
1618	N9	B17
1619	D19	B17
1620-31	D17	B17
1632	D17	B2
1633-8	D17	B17
1639	D17	B2
1640-3	N9	B17
1644	N9	B17. B2†
1645-55	N9	B17
1656-60	T1	B17
1661	—	B17
1662	J79	B17
1663/4	—	B17
1665	D20	B17
1666	J71	B17
1667	N10	B17
1668	—	B17
1669	Q5	B17
1670	J26	B17
1671	J26	B2
1672	D20	B17
1673/4	J26	—
1675	—	—
1676	J26	—
1677	—	—
1678	J26	B5
1679	X3	B5
1680	C6	B5
1681	—	B5
1682	Q5	B5
1683	N10	B5
1684/5	Q5	B5
1686	J27	B5
1687	G5	B5
1688/9/90	J71	B5
1691/2	G5	—
1693	G5	B15
1694	Q5	—
1695	G5	B15
1696	Q5	B15
1697	N10	B15
1698	J26	—
1699	N10	B13
1700	Q5	V4
1701	G5	V4
1702/3	G5	B7†
1704	Q5	B7†
1705	N9	B7†
1706/7	N10	B7†
1708	Q5	—
1709	Q5	B7†
1710/1	N10	B7†
1712	A5	B7†
1713	G5	B7†
1714	J25	—
1715	J72	—
1716	N10	—
1717	Q5	—
1718	J72	—
1719	A5	—
1720/1/2	J72	K2
1723-7	J25	K2
1728	J72	K2
1729	Q5	K2
1730	G5	K2
1731	Q5	K2
1732/3/4	J72	K2
1735	J71	K2
1736	J72	K2
1737	G5	K2
1738	A5	K2
1739/40	G5	K2
1741/2	J72	K2
1743	J25	K2
1744	J72	K2
1745	G5	K2
1746/7	J72	K2
1748	G5	K2
1749	J72	K2
1750	A5	K2
1751/2	G5	K2
1753	C6	K2
1754/5	G5	K2
1756	A5	K2
1757	Q5	K2
1758	J71	K2
1759	G5	K2
1760	A5	K2
1761	J72	K2
1762	G5	K2
1763	J72	K2
1764/5	G5	K2
1766/7/8	A5	K2
1769	G5	K2
1770	J72	K2
1771	A5	K2
1772	G5	K2
1773	J26	K2
1774	N10	K2
1775	G5	K2
1776	C6	K2
1777	J26	K2
1778/9/80	G5	K2
1781	J26	K2
1782	A5	K2
1783	G5	K2
1784	A5	K2
1785	N10	K2
1786	G5	K2
1787	J79	K2
1788	G5	K2
1789	J71	K2
1790	A5	K2
1791	G5	K2
1792	C6	K2
1793	G5	K2
1794	C6	K2
1795	G5	—
1796/7	J71	—
1798/9	Y7	—
1800	Y7	K3
1801/2	J21	K3
1803/4	J21. J39	K3
1805/6/7	J21	K3
1808	J21. J39	K3
1809-12	J21	K3
1813	J21. J39	K3
1814-20	J21	K3
1821/2/3	J24	K3
1824	J24. J39	K3
1825/6/7	J24	K3
1828	J24. J39	K3
1829/30	J24	K3
1831-4	J71	K3
1835	J71. J39	K3
1836	J71	K3
1837-40	G5	K3
1841-53	J24	K3
1854	J24. J39	K3
1855	J24	K3
1856/7	J24. J39	K3
1858/9/60	J24	K3
1861	J71	K3
1862	J71. J39	K3
1863	J71. J39	K5
1864	J71	K3
1865-8	G5	K3
1869/70	D18. J39	K3
1871-4	D17	K3
1875	D17. J39	K3
1876-9	D17	K3
1880	D17. J39	K3
1881-90	G5	K3
1891/2/3	J24	K3
1894	J24. J39	K3
1895	J24	K3
1896	J24. J39	K3
1897	J24	K3
1898	J24. J39	K3
1899	J24	K3
1900	J24	K3
1901/2	D17	K3
1903	D17. J39	K3
1904-10	D17	K3
1911-20	G5	K3
1921	D17	K3
1922	D17. J39	K3
1923/4/5	D17	K3
1926/7/8	D17. J39	K3
1929	D17	K3
1930	D17. J39	K3
1931/2	J24	K3
1933	J24. J39	K3
1934-9	J24	K3
1940	J24. J39	K3
1941	J24	K3
1942/3	J24. J39	K3
1944-51	J24	K3
1952	J24. J39	K3
1953-60	J24	K3
1961-4	J25	K3
1965	J25. J39	K3
1966-70	J25	K3
1971	J25. J39	K3
1972/3	J25	K3
1974	J25. J39	K3
1975/6	J25	K3
1977	J25. J39	K3
1978/9	J25	K3
1980	J25. J39	K3
1981/2/3	J25	K3

No.	Pre-1946	Post-1946	No.	Pre-1946	Post-1946	No.	Pre-1946	Post-1946
1984	J25. J39	K3	2311-5	J72	D9	2528	J75	D15
1985-92	J25	K3	2316	J72	—	2529-32	J75	D16
1993/4/5	J25	K4	2317/8/9	J72	D9	2533-6	N13	D16
1996	J25. J39	K4	2320	J72	—	2537	N13	—
1997	J25. J39	K1	2321/2	J72	D9	2538	J28	D15
1998	J25	K4	2323	J72	—	2539-42	J28	D16
1999	J25	—	2324/5	J72	D9	2543	A1(A10)	D16
2000	J25. D3	D3	2326/7	J72	—	2544/5	A1. A3	D16
2001-6	B13. P2. A2	K1†	2328-33	J72	D9	2546/7	A1 (A10)	D16
2007-10	B13	K1†	2334-7	J72	—	2548	A1 (A10). A3	D16
2011-30	D20	K1†	2338/9	J27	D20	2549	A1. A3	D16
2031-58	J25	K1†	2340-5	J27	D20	2550	A1 (A10). A3	D16
2059/60	J25	D31. K1†	2346	J27	—	2551-5	A1. A3	D16
2061	J25	K1†	2347-55	J27	D20	2556	A1 (A10)	D16
2062	J25	D31. K1†	2356	J27	—	2557	A1 (A10). A3	D16
2063	J25	K1†	2357-62	J27	D20	2558-61	A1. A3	D16
2064-9	J25	D31. K1†	2363-7	B16	D20	2562	A1 (A10). A3	D16
2070	J25	K1†	2368	B16	—	2563	A1. A3	D16
2071-4	J25	D31	2369-82	B16	D20	2564	A1 (A10)	D16
2075-80	J25	—	2383/4	J27	D20	2565	A1 (A10). A3	D16
2081-99	G5	—	2385	J27	—	2566	A1. A3	D16
2100	G5	—	2386-92	J27	D20	2567	A1 (A10)	D16
2101	D20	D6	2393/4	P1	D20	2568	A1. A3	D16
2102/3	D20	—	2395	U1	D20	2569	A1 (A10)	D16
2104	D20	D6	2396/7	—	D20	2570/1	A1. A3	D16
2105	D20	—	2398/9	—	—	2572	A1 (A10). A3	D16
2106	D20	D6	2400-4	A2	D29	2573-82	A1. A3	D16
2107-10	D20	—	2405	N13	D29	2583-94	N2	D16
2111/2	B14	D17	2406	J28	D29	2595-9	A3	D16
2113/4	B14	—	2407	N13	D29	2600-20	N7	D16
2115	B14	D3	2408/9	J28	D29	2621-49	N7	—
2116	Q5	D3	2410	N13	D29	2650-9	N7	D10
2117	Q5	—	2411/2/3	J28	D29	2660/1	N7	D11
2118	Q5	D3	2414	J28	—	2662-90	N2	D11
2119	Q5	—	2415	N13	D29	2691-4	J39	D11
2120-5	Q5	D3	2416	J28	—	2695-9	J39	—
2126-8	J25	D3	2417	J28. K3	D30	2700-42	J39	D49
2129	J25	—	2418	J28	D30	2743-52	A3	D49
2130-42	J25	D3	2419	N13	D30	2753-60	D49	D49
2143/4/5	H1. A8	D3	2420-4	J28	D30	2761-7	K3	D49
2146	H1. A8	—	2425-9	D24. K3	D30	2768	K3	D
2147/8	H1. A8	D3	2430-7	J23. O2	D30	2769	K3	D49
2149	H1. A8	—	2438/9/40	J23. K3	D30	2770-5	J39	D49
2150-7	H1. A8	D2	2441	J23	D30	2776-9	J39	—
2158	H1. A8	—	2442	J23. K3	D30	2780-8	J39	E4
2159-62	H1. A8	D2	2443	J23. K3	D32	2789-94	J50	E4
2163	C7	D2	2444	J23	D32	2795/6/7	A3	E4
2164	C7	—	2445/6/7	J23. K3	D32	2798/9	S1	—
2165-70	C7	D2	2448/9/50	J80. K3	D32	2800/1/2	B17	C1
2171	C7. C9	D2	2451	J23. K3	D32	2803-7	B17	—
2172	C7	D2	2452	J23	D32	2808	B17	C1
2173-81	J72	D2	2453	J23. K3	D32	2809	B17	—
2182	J72	—	2454	J23	D32	2810/1/2	B17	C1
2183-91	J72	D2	2455	J23. K3	D33	2813	B17	—
2192	J72	—	2456/7	J23	D33	2814	B17. B2	—
2193-9	C7	D2	2458/9	J23. K3	D33	2815	B17. B2	C1
2200/1	C7	D2	2460	J23	D33	2816	B17. B2	—
2202	C7	—	2461	J23. K3	D33	2817	B17	C1
2203	C7	D1	2462	J23	D33	2818/9/20	B17	—
2204	C7	—	2463	J23. K3	D33	2821/2/3	B17	C1
2205	C7	D1	2464	J23	D33	2824	B17	—
2206	C7	—	2465/6	J23. K3	D33	2825	B17	C1
2207-10	C7	D1	2467/8	J23. K3	D34	2826/7	B17	—
2211	C7	—	2469	J23	D34	2828-35	B17	C1
2212	C7	D1	2470-3	J23. K3	D34	2836/7/8	B17	—
2213	Q6	—	2474-7	J23	D34	2839	B17. B2	C1
2214/5/6	Q6	D1	2478-82	N11	D34	2840/1/2	B17	C1
2217-24	Q6	—	2483/4/5	N12	D34	2843/4	B17	—
2225	Q6	D41	2486	N12	—	2845	B17	C1
2226	Q6	—	2487-91	N12	D34	2846/7/8	B17	—
2227-32	Q6	D41	2492-7	J75	D34	2849/50/1	B17	C1
2233	Q6	—	2498	Q10. K3	D34	2852	B17	—
2234-56	Q6	D41	2499	Q10. K3	—	2853/4/5	B17	C1
2257/8/9	Q6	—	2500	Q10. A3	D16	2856/7/8	B17	—
2260/1/2	Q6	D40	2501-8	Q10. A3	D15	2859	B17	C1
2263	Q6	—	2509	Q10. A4	D15	2860-5	B17	—
2264-80	Q6	D40	2510/1	Q10. A4	D16	2866	B17	C1
2281/2/3	Q6	D31†	2512	Q10. A4	D15	2867	B17	—
2284-99	Q6	—	2513-9	J23	D16	2868/9/70	B17	C1
2300/1/2	Q6	D9	2520	J23	D15	2871	B17. B2	C1
2303-9	J72	D9	2521/2	J23	D16	2872	B17	C1
2310	J72	—	2523-7	J75	D16	2873	—	C1

No.	Class Pre-1946	Class Post-1946
2874	—	—
2875/6/7	—	C1
2878	—	—
2879	—	C1
2880	—	—
2881	—	C1
2882	—	—
2883-6	—	C1
2887	—	—
2888	—	C1
2889-94	—	—
2895/6	—	C5
2897/8	V1	C5
2899	V1	—
2900-4	V1	C4
2905	V1	—
2906-10	V1	C4
2911	V1	—
2912-25	V1	C4
2926-30	V1	—
2931	V1	C6
2932	V1	—
2933	V1	C6
2934	K3	C6
2935/6	K3	—
2937	K3	C6
2938	K3	—
2939	K3	C6
2940	K3	—
2941	J39	C6
2942-6	J39	—
2947	J39	C6
2948-53	J39	—
2954	O2	C7
2955	O2	—
2956	O2	C7
2957	O2	—
2958	O2	C7
2959	O2	—
2960	O2	C7
2961	O2	—
2962	J39	—
2963	J39	C7
2964-9	J39	—
2970-5	J39	C7
2976/7	J39	—
2978	J39	C7
2979	J39	—
2980-3	J39	C7
2984/5	J39	—
2986	J39	C7
2987	J39	—
2988/9	J39	C7
2990	J39	—
2991/2/3	J39	C7
2994	J39	—
2995/6	J39	C7
2997/8/9	J39	—
3000	J39	O7
3001-15	J1	O7
3016-20	—	O7
3021-40	J5	O7
3041-50	D2	O7
3051-65	D1	O7
3066-70	—	O7
3071-80	J2	O7
3081-98	J39	O7
3099	—	O7
3100	—	O6. O7
3101	J4	O6. O7
3102	J4. J3	O6. O7
3103-10	—	O6. O7
3111	J53*. J52	O6. O7
3112/3	J84	O6. O7
3114	J85	O6. O7
3115	N19	O6. O7
3116-24	R1	O6. O7
3125-34	R1. O6	O6. O7
3134A	J57	—
3135	R1	O6. O7
3135A	J4	—
3136-9	R1	O6. O7

No.	Class Pre-1946	Class Post-1946
3139A	J54*. J55	—
3140	R1	O6. O7
3140A	J57	—
3141-4	R1	O6. O7
3144A	J57	—
3145-7	R1	O6. O7
3147A	J4*	—
3148/9	R1. O6	O6. O7
3149A	J57	—
3150	R1. O6	O6. O7
3150A	J4	—
3151-3	R1. O6	O6. O7
3153A	J54. J55	—
3154/5	R1. O6	O6. O7
3155A	J53. J52	—
3156	R1	O6. O7
3156A	J7	—
3157-64	J51. J50	O6. O7
3165	J4. J3	O6. O7
3166/7	J51. J50	O6. O7
3168-70	J51. J50	O7
3170A	J4*	—
3171-5	J51. J50	O7
3175A	J4	—
3176	J51. J50	O7
3177	J3	O7
3178	J51. J50	O7
3179	J4. J3	O7
3180	J4. J3. J50	O7
3181/2	J4. J50	O7
3183-6	J50	O7
3187	J4. J50	O7
3188	J7. J50	O7
3189	J50	O7
3190	N1	O7
3191	J4*	O7
3192	J4*. J3	O7
3193	J4	O7
3194	—	O7
3195/6	J4	O7
3197	—	O7
3198/9	J4	O7
3200-7	—	Q4
3208/9	—	—
3210	—	Q4
3211	J51. J50	—
3212/3/4	J51. J50	Q4
3215	J51. J50	—
3216/7	J51. J50	Q4
3218	J51. J50	—
3219/20	J51. J50	Q4
3221	J50	Q4
3222	J50	—
3223-9	J50	Q4
3230	J50	—
3231-6	J50	Q4
3237	J50	—
3238	J50	Q4
3239	J50	—
3240	J50	Q4
3241	—	Q4
3242	—	—
3243	—	Q4
3244-9	—	—
3250	C2	Q5
3251	C1	Q5
3252-60	C2	Q5
3261-70	—	Q5
3271	C2	Q5
3272-99	C1	Q5
3300/1	C1	Q5
3302	J4. J3	Q5
3303	J3	Q5
3304	J4	Q5
3305	—	Q5
3306	J3	Q5
3307	J4	Q5
3308	J3	Q5
3309/10/1	—	Q5
3312	J4	Q5
3313	J4*. J3	Q5
3314	J4	Q5

No.	Class Pre-1946	Class Post-1946
3315	J4*. J3	Q5
3316	J3	Q5
3317	J4	Q5
3318	J4*. J3	Q5
3319-22	—	Q5
3323	J4	Q5
3324-8	—	Q5
3329	J4*. J3	—
3330	—	Q5
3331/2	J4*. J3	Q5
3333	—	Q5
3334	J4. J3	Q5
3335	—	Q5
3336	J4*. J3	Q5
3337	J4. J3	Q5
3338	J4*. J3	Q5
3339	J4	Q5
3340/1	—	Q6
3342/3/4	J3	Q6
3345	J4*. J3	Q6
3346/7	—	Q6
3348	J4	Q6
3349	J4*. J3	Q6
3350/1	J3	Q6
3352	J4*. J3	Q6
3353	J3	Q6
3354	J4	Q6
3355-8	—	Q6
3359	J4*. J3	Q6
3360	—	Q6
3361	J4*. J3	Q6
3362	J3	Q6
3363/4	—	Q6
3365	J4*	Q6
3366/7	—	Q6
3368	J4*. J3	Q6
3369/70	—	Q6
3371	J4*. J3	Q6
3272/3	J4	Q6
3374	J7	Q6
3375	J3	Q6
3376/7	—	Q6
3378	J4*. J3	Q6
3379	J3	Q6
3380	—	Q6
3381	J3	Q6
3382	—	Q6
3383	J4*	Q6
3384	J3	Q6
3385	J4	Q6
3386/7/8	J3	Q6
3389	—	Q6
3390	J3	Q6
3391	—	Q6
3392	J4	Q6
3393	—	Q6
3394	J4	Q6
3395	—	Q6
3396	J4. J3	Q6
3397	J55	Q6
3398	J4*. J3	Q6
3399	J3	Q6
3400	D3	Q6
3401	Q1. V4	Q6
3402	Q2. V4	Q6
3403/4	Q1	Q6
3405/6/7	Q2	Q6
3408/9	Q1	Q6
3410	Q2	Q6
3411-5	Q1	Q6
3416/7	Q2	Q6
3418/9	Q1	Q6
3420	Q3	Q6
3421	Q2	Q6
3422-40	Q1	Q6
3441-4	Q1. K4	Q6
3445	Q1. K4. K1	Q6
3446	Q1. K4	Q6
3447/8/9	Q1	Q6
3450-5	Q2	Q6
3456-9	O1 (O3)	Q6
3460	O1 (O3)	Q7

No.	Class Pre-1946	Post-1946
3461	O2	Q7
3462-70	O1 (O3)	Q7
3470A	(G.N. 0-6-0T)	—
3471/2/3	O1 (O3)	Q7
3473A	J55	—
3474	O1 (O3)	Q7
3475/6	O1 (O3)	O3
3477-93	O2	O3
3494	J54*. J55*. O2	O3
3494A	J55	—
3495	O2	—
3496	J55*. O2	—
3496A	J55	—
3497/8/9	O2	—
3500/1	O2	O4. O6
3502-20	—	O4. O6
3521-8	J6	O4. O6
3529	J6	O1. O6
3530-41	J6	O4. O6
3542	J6	O1. O6
3543-59	J6	O4. O6
3560/1	J6	O1. O6
3562	J6	O4. O6
3563	J6	O1. O6
3564/5/6	J6	O4. O6
3567	J6	O1. O6
3568/9/70	J6	O4
3571	J6	O4. O1†
3572-7	J6	O4
3578	J6	O1
3579	J6	O4. O1†
3580-8	J6	O4
3589	J6	O4. O1†
3590/1/2	J6	O1
3593	J6	O4
3594	J6	O4. O1
3595	J6	O4
3596	J6	O4. O1†
3597/8/9	J6	O4
3600-8	J6	O4
3608A	J56	—
3609	J6	O4
3610	J6	O1
3610A	J55	—
3611/2	J56	O4
3613	J56*	O4
3614	—	O4
3615	J56	O4
3616	—	O4
3617	J54*	O4
3618	—	O4
3619	J54. J55	O1
3620	J55*	O4
3621-9	J6	O4
3630	J6	O1
3631/2/3	J6	O4
3633A	J54*. J55*	—
3634/5	J6	O4
3634/5A	J54	—
3636	J6	O4
3636A	J55	—
3637	J6	O4
3637A	J54	—
3638	J6	O4
3638A	J55	—
3639/40	J6	O4
3640A	J4	—
3641/2/3	J4. V2	O4
3644	J4*. V2	O4
3645	V2	O4
3646	J4. V2	O1
3647	V2	O4
3648	J4. V2	O4
3649	V2	O4
3650	V2	O1
3651	V2	O4
3652	V2	O1
3653-8	V2	O4
3659	G2*. V2	O4
3660/1/2	V2	O4
3663	V2	O1
3664-9	V2	O4
3670	V2	O1
3671	V2	O4
3672	J55. V2	O4
3673	J54*. J55. V2	O4
3674	J55*. V2	O4
3675	J54*. V2	O4
3676	J54. V2	O1
3677	J55. V2	O4
3678	J55. V2	O1
3679/80	J54. V2	O4
3681	J54*. V2	O4
3682	G2*. V2	O4
3683	V2	O4
3684/5/6	J57. V2	O4
3687	J57. V2	O1
3688	J54.*. J55. V2	O4
3689	J54. J55. V2	O1
3690	J54*. J55. V2	O4
3691	J54. V2	O4
3692	J54*. J55. V2	O4
3693	J54. V2	O4
3694/5	G2*. V2	O4
3696	G2. A2	O4
3697/8/9	A2	O4
3700-10	—	O4
3711/2	—	O1
3713/4	—	O4
3715	E1*	O4
3716	J4*. J3	O4
3717	J3	O4
3718/9	J4	O4
3720	—	O4
3721	J4*. J3	O4
3722/3	—	O4
3724	J4*. J3	O4
3725	J4	O1
3726/7	J4	O4
3728	—	O4
3729	J4	O4
3730	J4*. J3	O4
3731	J4. J3	O4
3732/3	—	O4
3734	J4	O4
3735-9	—	O4
3740	—	O1
3741/2/3	—	O4
3744	J4*	O4
3745	J4	O4
3746	J4	O4. O1†
3747	—	O4
3748	J4*. J3	O4
3749	—	O4
3750	J4*	O4
3751	—	O4
3752	—	O1
3753	E1*	O4
3754	—	O4
3755	E1*	O1
3756/7	—	O4
3758	E1*	O4
3759	—	O4
3760	E1*	O1
3761-4	—	O4
3765	G2*	O4
3766	G1	O4
3767	G1*	O4
3768	—	O1
3769/70	G1*	O4
3771/2	—	O4
3773	—	O1
3774/5/6	—	O4
3777	—	O1
3778	—	O4
3779	J55	O4
3780	J54	O1
3781	J54	O4
3782/3	J55	O4
3784	J54	O1
3785	J54*. J55	O4
3786	J54	O1
3787	J55	O4
3788	J54*	O4
3789	J54*. J55	O1
3790	J55	O4
3791	—	O4
3792	J4. J3	O1
3793	J4*. J3	O4
3794	—	O4
3795/6	—	O1
3797	J4	O4
3798	—	O4
3799	J4*. J3	O4
3800	—	O4
3801	J54	O4
3802	J55	O4
3803	J55	O1
3804	J54. J55	O4
3805	J54	O4
3806	J55	O1
3807	J54*. J55	O4
3808	J54	O1
3809	J55	O4
3810	J55	—
3811	—	
3812	E1*	O4
3813	K3	O4
3814	E1. K3	—
3815	K3	—
3816	K3	O4
3817	K3	O1
3818	E1*. K3	O4
3819	K3	O4
3820	K3	—
3821/2/3	K3	O4
3824	G1*. K3	O4
3825/6	K3	—
3827/8	G1*. K3	O4
3829	K3	O4
3830	G1*. K3	—
3831	J4. K3	—
3832	J4*. K3	O4
3833	J4. O2	O4
3834	J4. O2	
3835/6	O2	O4
3837	J4*. J3. O2	O4
3838	J4. O2	O4. O1†
3939	J4. O2	O4
3840	J4*. O2	O4
3841/2	O2	O4
3843	J4. O2	O4
3844	J4. O2	—
3845/6	J4. O2	O4
3847	O2	O4
3848/9	J4. O2	O4
3850	J4. J3. O2	O4
3851	J55. O2	O4
3852/3	J54. O2	O4
3854	J55. O2	O1
3855	J54. J55. O2	O4
3856	J54. O2	O4. O1†
3857	J54. O2	O4
3858	J54	O4
3859	J54. J55	O4
3860	J54	O4
3861	E1*	O4
3862	—	O4
3863	—	O1
3864	E1*	O4
3865	—	O1
3866	—	
3867/8	E1*	O1
3869	—	O1
3870	—	O4
3871	—	—
3872	—	O1
3873	—	O4
3874	—	O1
3875	—	—
3876/7/8	—	O4
3879	—	O1
3880/1	—	O4
3882-5	E1*	O4
3886	—	O1
3887	E1*	O1

No.	Pre-1946	Post-1946
3888/9	—	O4
3890	—	O1
3891	—	O4
3892	—	—
3893	E1*	O4
3894/5	—	O4
3896	—	—
3897	E1*	O4
3898/9	—	O4
3900	—	O4
3901	J54*. J55	O1
3902	J54	O4
3903	J54	—
3904-7	J54	O4
3908	J54*. J55	O4
3909	J54	—
3910	J54*. J55	—
3911	J54. J55	O4
3912	J54*. J55	O4
3913	J55	O4
3914	J54	O4
3915	J55	O4
3916	J55	—
3917	J55	O4
3918	J55	—
3919	J54. J55	—
3920	J54	O4
3921-4	J53*. J52	O2
3925	J53. J52	O2
3926	J53*. J52	O2
3927	J53. J52	O2
3928	J53	O2
3929	J53*. J52	O2
3930	J53. J52	O2
3931	—	O2
3932	G1*	O2
3933-8	—	O2
3939/40	G1*	O2
3941/2	—	O2
3943	G1*	O2
3944-8	—	O2
3949/50	C2	O2
3951-60	—	O2
3961	J53. J52	O2
3962	J53*. J52	O2
3963-9	J53. J52	O2
3970	J52	O2
3971	J53. J52	O2
3972/3/4	J53*. J52	O2
3975	J53. J52	O2
3976	J53*. J52	O2
3977	J52	O2
3978	J53*. J52	O2
3979	J53. J52	O2
3980	J53*. J52	O2
3981	—	O2
3982-7	C2	O2
3988/9/90	C2	—
3991	—	—
3992-5	E1*	—
3996/7	—	—
3998/9	E1*	—
4000	K3	—
4000A	E1*	—
4001-9	K3	—
4009A	C12	—
4010	C12	—
4011/2	J4. J3	—
4013-20	C12	—
4021	J7	—
4022	—	—
4023/4	J7	—
4025/6	—	—
4027-30	J7	—
4031/2/3	J4. J3	—
4034	J4	—
4035	J4. J3	—
4036/7	J4*. J3	—
4038	—	—
4039	J4*. J3	—
4040/1	J4	—
4042	—	—

No.	Pre-1946	Post-1946
4043/4	J4	—
4045	J3	—
4046	J53. J52	—
4047-54	J53*. J52	—
4055	J53. J52	—
4056/7	J53*. J52	—
4058	J53. J52	—
4059	J53*. J52	—
4060	J52	—
4061-4	E1*	—
4065/6	—	—
4067/8/9	E1*	—
4070	E1	—
4071-6	D3	—
4077	D4*. D3	—
4078	D3	—
4079	D4. D3	—
4080	D3	—
4081	J4*. J3	—
4082	J3	—
4083/4/5	J4	—
4086	J4*. J3	—
4087/8	J4. J3	—
4089	—	—
4090	J4	—
4091	J3	—
4092/3	J4*. J3	—
4094	J3	—
4095	J4*. J3	—
4096	J3	—
4097	J4*. J3	—
4098	J4. J3	—
4099	J3	—
4100	J3	—
4101/2	J4*. J3	—
4103/4	J3	—
4105	J3	J3
4106/7	J4	J3
4108/9	J3	J4
4110	J4*. J3	J4
4111	J4*. J3	J3
4112	J4*. J3	J4
4113/4/5	J3	J3
4116/7/8	J4*. J3	J3
4119	J3	J3
4120	J3	J4
4121	J4*. J3	J4
4122/3/4	J3	J3
4125	J4*. J3	J3
4126	J3	J3
4127/8	J3	J3
4129	J4*. J3	J3
4130	J3	J3
4131	J4*. J3	J3
4132/3/4	J3	J3
4135	J4*. J3	J3
4136/7	J3	J3
4138	J4. J3	J3
4139	J3	J3
4140	J4*. J3	J3
4141/2	J3	J3
4143/4	J4*. J3	J3
4145	J4	J3
4146/7	J3	J3
4148	—	J3
4149	J4*. J3	J3
4150	J4. J3	J3
4151/2	J3	J3
4153	J4. J3	J3
4154/5	J4*. J3	J3
4156	J3	J3
4157	J3	J4
4158	J4*. J3	J3
4159	J3	J4
4160	J4*. J3	J4
4161	J3	J3
4162	J3	J4
4163	J3	J3
4164	J3	J4
4165	J3	—
4166	J4*. J3	—
4167	J3	J4

No.	Pre-1946	Post-1946
4168/9	J3	—
4170	J3	J6
4171/2	J4*. J3	J6
4173	J3	J6
4174-9	J3	J6
4180	D2	J6
4181-99	—	J6
4200	—	J6
4201-10	J52	J6
4211	J53. J52	J6
4212	J53*. J52	J6
4213/4/5	J53. J52	J6
4216-79	J52	J6
4280-90	J52	J11
4291-9	—	J11
4300	C1*	J11
4301-4	D3	J11
4305	D3*. D2	J11
4306-12	D3	J11
4313	D4*. D3	J11
4314-9	D3	J11
4320	D3. D2	J11
4321-40	D2	J11
4341-55	D3	J11
4356	D4. D3	J11
4357	D3	J11
4358	D4. D3	J11
4359	D3	J11
4360	D4. D3	J11
4361-99	D2	J11
4400-53	C1	J11
4454-9	C1	—
4460/1	C1	J35
4462-9	A4	J35
4470	A1	J35
4471	A1. A3	J35
4472	A1 (A10)	J35
4473/4	A1. A3	J35
4475/6	A1 (A10)	J35
4477-80	A1. A3	J35
4481	A1 (A10)	J35
4482-99	A4	J35
4500	A4	J35
4501-7	C12	J35
4508	C12	—
4509-35	C12	J35
4536-50	C12	J37
4551-99	N1	J37
4600-5	N1	J37
4606-15	N2	J37
4616-29	—	J37
4630	K1. K2	J37
4631	K2	J37
4632/3/4	K1. K2	J37
4635	K2	J37
4636-9	K1. K2	J37
4640-74	K2	J19
4675-99	K2	J20
4700-4	K2	J39
4705-20	—	J39
4721-70	N2	J39
4771-99	V2	J39
4800	J54. J55. V2	J39
4801/2/3	Y1. V2	J39
4804-99	V2	J39
4900-3	A4	J39
4904-88	—	J39
4989	—	—
4990	J55	—
4991/2/3	Y1	—
4994-9	—	—
5000	—	J1
5001	O4	J1
5002	C13	J1
5003	A5	J1
5004	B8	J1
5005	O4	J1
5006/7	A5	J1
5008	O4	J1
5009	C13	J1
5010-4	O5. O4	J1
5015	O5. O4	J2

No.	Pre-1946	Post-1946	No.	Pre-1946	Post-1946	No.	Pre-1946	Post-1946
5016	... J11	J2	5172	... J10	J10	5501-11 ... D11		J17
5017	... O5. O4	J2	5173	... N5	J10	5512/3/4 ... N4		J17
5018	... C13	J2	5174/5/6 .. J10		J10	5515-37 ... N5		J17
5019	... O5. O4	J2	5177	... J11	J10	5538	... J63	J17
5020	... C13	J2	5178/9 ... C13		J10	5539-48 ... N5		J17
5021	... N5	J2	5180-7 ... B5		J10	5549	... J8	J17
5022	... O5. O4	J2	5188	... C13	J10	5550	... J8*	—
5023	... A5	J2	5189	... N5	J10	5551-8 ... J8		J17
5024	... A5	—	5190/1 ... C13		J10	5559	... J8*	J17
5025	... N5	J21	5192	... C4	J10	5560	... J8	J17
5026	... O4	J21	5193	... C13	J10	5561-7 ... D7		J17
5027/8/9 .. C13		J21	5194	... C4	J10	5568-73 ... J13		J17
5030	... A5	J21	5195/6 ... B1 (B18)		J10	5574-89 ... F1		J17
5031/2/3 .. B7		J21	5197/8 ... J11		J10	5590-9 ... F1		—
5034	... B7	—	5199	... C13	J10	5600	... F1	J24
5035-8 ... B7		J21	5200	... N5	J10	5601-12 ... N4		J24
5039	... Q4	J21	5201-9 ... J11		J10	5613	... N4	—
5040-3 ... N6		J21	5210/1 ... J11		J36	5614/5 ... N4		J24
5044	... Q4. Q1	J21	5212/3 ... Q4		J36	5616	... N4	—
5045/6 ... A5		J21	5214-50 ... J11		J36	5617-29 ... N4		J24
5047	... C13	J21	5251	... N5	J36	5630	... N4	—
5048	... Q4. Q1	—	5252-7 ... J11		J36	5631-4 ... N4		J24
5049	... Q4	J21	5258/9 ... C5		J36	5635	... N4	—
5050	... C13	—	5260/1 ... C4		J36	5636	... N4	J24
5051	... N5	J21	5262	... C4	—	5637/8 ... N4		—
5052/3 ... B6		J21	5263-7 ... C4		J36	5639-42 ... J10		J24
5054	... N5	—	5268/9/70 . D6		J36	5643	... J10	—
5055	... C13	—	5271	... O4	J36	5644	... J10	J24
5056/7 ... Q4		J21	5272-6 ... L1 (L3)		J36	5645-51 ... J9		J25
5058	... Q4. Q1	J21	5277	... J63	J36	5652	... J9	—
5059	... Q4	J21	5278	... J61	J36	5653-69 ... J9		J25
5060/1 ... J63		J21	5279/80 ... B8		J36	5670-81 ... J10		J25
5062/3/4 ... Q4		J21	5281-99 ... J11		J36	5682	... D7	—
5065	... Q4	—	5300-9 ... J11		J36	5683-93 ... D7		J25
5066	... N6	J21	5310	... C13	J36	5694-9 ... D5		J25
5067	... Q4	J21	5311-20 ... J11		J36	5700-8 ... D7		J25
5068	... Q4. Q1	J21	5321	... J63	J36	5709	... D7	—
5069	... O4	J21	5322-30 ... J11		J36	5710	... D7	J25
5070	... Q4. Q1	J21	5331-5 ... O4		J36	5711	... D7	—
5071	... Q4	J21	5336-45 ... L1 (L3)		J36	5712-8 ... N4		J25
5072/3 ... B7		J21	5346	... O4	J36	5719	... N4	—
5074-7 ... J10		J21	5347/8/9 .. O4		—	5720-5 ... N4		J25
5078	... B7	J21	5350-5 ... O4		J15	5726/7/8 .. F1		J25
5079-84 ... J10		J21	5356	... Q4	J15	5729	... F1	—
5085	... Q4	—	5357	... C13	J15	5730-7 ... F1		J26
5086	... Q4	J21	5358	... C4	J15	5738-43 ... J9		J26
5087	... Q4. Q1	J21	5359	... C13	J15	5744-75 ... N5		J26
5088	... A5	J21	5360-3 ... C4		J15	5776-9 ... F2		J26
5089	... J63	J21	5364/5 ... C5		J15	5780-5 ... F2		J27
5090	... J10	J21	5366-70 ... L1 (L3)		J15	5786-99 ... J10		J27
5091/2 ... Q4		J21	5371-4 ... A5		J15	5800-51 ... J10		J27
5093	... O4	J21	5375-84 ... O4		J15	5852-81 ... D6		J27
5094-9 ... J10		J21	5385	... O4. O1	J15	5882-93 ... J62		J27
5100/1 ... J10		J21	5386-93 ... O4		J15	5894	... N5	J27
5102	... O4	J21	5394	... O4. O1	J15	5895-9 ... N5		—
5103	... J10	J21	5395-9 ... O4		J15	5900-34 ... N5		J38
5104-13 ... D9		J21	5400	... O4	J15	5935-46 ... N5		—
5114/5 ... C13		J21	5401	... Q4	J15	5947-55 ... J11		—
5116-23 ... J10		J21	5402-7 ... O4		J15	5956/7/8 .. Q4		—
5124/5 ... J10		—	5408	... O4. O1	J15	5959	... Q4. Q1	—
5126	... J10	J10	5409/10 ... N5		J15	5960	... Q4	—
5127	... N5	J10	5411	... A5	J15	5961	... Q4. Q1	—
5128	... A5	J10	5412/3 ... O4		J15	5962-5 ... Q4		—
5129	... A5	—	5414/5 ... O5. O4		J15	5966	... O4	—
5130/1/2 .. J10		J10	5416	... B6	J15	5967/8 ... X4*		—
5133	... O4	J10	5417-22 ... O5. O4		J15	5969	... X4	—
5134	... J11*. J10	J10	5423-8 ... B2 (B19)		J15	5970	... X4*	—
5135/6/7 .. Q4		J10	5429-38 ... D10		J15	5971	... X4*. J12	—
5138	... Q4. Q1	J10	5439-46 ... B8		J15	5972	... X4	—
5139/40 ... Q4		J10	5447-52 ... A5		J15	5973-99 ... J11		—
5141	... J10	J10	5453-7 ... C13		J15	6000	... J11	Elec.(EM1)
5142-6 ... Q4		J10	5458-78 ... B7		J15	6001-12 ... J11		—
5147	... Q4. Q1	J10	5479	... J12*. B7	J15	6013-42 ... D9		—
5148-53 ... Q4		J10	5480-3 ... B7		J5	6043-51 ... J11		—
5154	... A5	J10	5484	... J12*. B7	J5	6052/3/4 ... Q4		—
5155	... O4	J10	5485	... J12*	J5	6055-66 ... C13		—
5156	... A5	J10	5486-9 ... J12		J5	6067-72 ... B5		—
5157	... J63	J10	5490/1/2 .. J12*		J5	6073-6 ... Q4		—
5158	... A5	J10	5493-7 ... J12		J5	6077	... Q4. Q1	—
5159-64 ... Q4		J10	5498	... J12*	J5	6078-82 ... J11		—
5165-70 ... A5		J10	5499	... J12	J5	6083-94 ... C4		—
5171	... C13	J10	5500	... J12	J17	6095-9 ... B4		—

No.	Class Pre-1946	Post-1946
6100-4	B4	—
6105-14	B9	—
6115-9	J11	—
6120-31	C14*	—
6132-8	Q4	—
6139	Q4. Q1	—
6140-4	Q4	—
6145-53	M1	—
6154-7	N6. M2	—
6158-63	N6. L2	—
6164-9	B3	—
6170-3	S1	—
6174-8	Q4	—
6179	Q4. Q1	—
6180/1/2	Q4	—
6183-94	O4	—
6195	O4. O1	—
6196-9	O4	—
6200-12	O4	—
6213	O4. O1	—
6214/5	O4	—
6216	O4. O1	—
6217/8/9	O4	—
6220	O4. O1	—
6221-30	O4	—
6231	O4 O1	—
6232-42	O4	—
6243/4/5	O4. O1	—
6246-62	O4	—
6263	O4. O1	—
6264-82	O4	—
6283	O4. O1	—
6284-7	O4	—
6288	O4. O1	—
6289-99	O4	—
6300-23	O4	—
6324	O4. O1	—
6325/6/7	O4	—
6328	O4. O1	—
6329-33	O4	—
6334	O4. O1	—
6335-40	O4	—
6341	O4. O1	—
6342-9	O4	—
6350	O4. O1	—
6351-5	O4	—
6356	O4. O1	—
6357/8	O4	—
6359	O4. O1	—
6360-70	O4	—
6371	O4. O1	—
6372/3	O4	—
6374	O4. O1	—
6375/6/7	O4	—
6378-99	D11	—
6400/1	D11	—
6402-7	G3	—
6408-11	J60	—
6412/3/4	N6	—
6415	D8. H2	—
6416	E2*. H2	—
6417-22	J12. H2	—
6423-9	J12	—
6430/1	Y2	—
6432/3/4	J12	—
6435	J12*	—
6436/7	J12	—
6438	J12*	—
6439-43	J12	—
6444	J12*	—
6445	J12	—
6446/7	J12*	—
6448/9/50	J12	—
6451	J59	—
6452	J59*	—
6453	J59	—
6454	J59*	—
6455/6	E8*	—
6457/8/9	J12	—
6460	D12	—
6461/2	J59*	—
6463	D12*	—

No.	Class Pre-1946	Post-1946
6464	D12	—
6465	D12*	—
6466/7	D12	—
6468	D12*	—
6469	J61	—
6470	J59	—
6471/2	J59*	—
6473	J59	—
6474	J59*	—
6475/6	J59	—
6477	J8*	—
6478	J59	—
6479	J59*	—
6480	J59*	ES1 (Elec.)
6481	J59	ES1 (Elec.)
6482	J59	—
6483-9	J58	—
6490/1	J58	EF1 (Elec.)
6492	J58*	EF1 (Elec.)
6493/4	J58	EF1 (Elec.)
6495/6/7	O4	EF1 (Elec.)
6498	O4	EB1 (Elec.)
6499	O4	EF1 (Elec.)
6500-4	O4	—
6505	O4. O1	—
6506	O4	—
6507	O4. O1	—
6508-12	O4	—
6513	O4. O1	—
6514	O4	—
6515	O4. O1	—
6516/7/8	O4	—
6519	O4. O1	—
6520-5	O4	—
6526	O4. O1	—
6527-32	O4	—
6533	O4. O1	—
6534	O4	—
6535	O4. O1	—
6536-44	O4	—
6545	O4. O1	—
6546-54	O4	—
6555	O4. O1	—
6556-65	O4	—
6566	O4. O1	—
6567-74	O4	—
6575	O4. O1	—
6576/7	O4	—
6578	O4. O1	—
6579-94	O4	—
6595	O4. O1	—
6596-9	O4	—
6600	O4	—
6601	O4. O1	—
6602-23	O4	—
6624/5/6	O4. O1	—
6627/8/9	O4	—
6630	O4. O1	—
6631-5	O4	—
6636	O4. O1	—
6637-41	O4	—
6642	O4. O1	—
6643-99	—	—
6700	—	—
6701	EM1 (Elec.)	—
6702-99	—	—
6800	—	—
6801	D39*	—
6802/3	D39	—
6804	D42	—
6805/6	D46	—
6807	D42	—
6808	J90	—
6809/10	D42	—
6811	J90	—
6812/3/4	D43	—
6815/6	J90	—
6817/8	D42	—
6819-24	D41	—
6825-9	D40	—
6830	Z5	—
6831	D40	—

No.	Class Pre-1946	Post-1946
6832	Z5	—
6833-6	D40	—
6837/8	J91	—
6839	J90	—
6840	D45	—
6841	J91	—
6842	J90	—
6843/4	Z5 (Z4)	—
6844A	D47*	—
6845	D40	—
6845A	D47*	—
6846/7/8	D40	—
6848A	D47*	—
6849	D40	—
6849A	D47*	—
6850	D40	—
6850A	D47*	—
6851	D45	—
6852	D40	—
6852A	D47*	—
6853	D45	—
6854	D40	—
6854A	D47*	—
6855/6	D47*	—
6857	D45*	—
6858/9	D45	—
6860	D45*	—
6861	D45	—
6862	D45*	—
6863/4	D44*	—
6865	D44	—
6866	D44*	—
6867	D44	—
6868	D44*	—
6869/70/1	D48	—
6872/3/4	D42	—
6875/6/7	D38	—
6878-83	D41	—
6884-92	G10	—
6893-9	D41	—
6900-12	D41	—
6913/4/5	D40	—
6916-98	—	—
6999	—	EE1 (Elec.)
7000	—	—
7001-10	F6	—
7011-20	J67	—
7021-36	J68	—
7037/8/9	J15*. J68	—
07038/9	J15	—
7040-6	J68	—
7047	J68. J67. J68	—
7048/9/50	J68	—
7051-60	J69	—
7061-70	F6	—
7071-80	F4	—
7081	J69	—
7082	J69. J67	—
7083/4/5	J69	—
7086	J69. J67. J69	—
7087-90	J69	—
7091	F5	—
7092	F4	—
7093	F4	F7
7094	F5	F7
7095	F5	F1
7096	F5	—
7097	F4	F1
7098	F4	—
7099	F4	F1
7100	F5	F1
7101	F4	F1
7102	F4	—
7103	F5	—
7104	F5	F2
7105/6/7	F4	F2
7108/9/10	F5	F2
7111	F4	F2
7112/3	—	F2
7114-8	—	F3
7119-22	J15	F3
7123	—	F3

No.	Pre-1946 Class	Post-1946 Class
7124	J15	F3
7125/6	J70	F3
07125/6	Y6	—
7127/8/9	J70	F3
07129	Y6	—
7130/1	J70	F3
7132/3/4	Y6	F3
7135-9	J70	F3
7140	F4	F3
7141-5	F5	F3
7146	F4	F3
7147	F5	F3
7148/9	F4	F3
7150	J65	F3
7151-9	J65	F4
7160	J69	F4
7161	J67	F4
7162/3	J69. J67	F4
7164	J67	F4
7165-8	J69	F4
7169	J67	F4
7170	F5	F4
7171-8	F4	F4
7179	F5	F4
7180-7	F4	F4
7188	F5	F5
7189	F4	F5
7190	J69. J67	F5
7191	J69	F5
7192/3	J69. J67. J69	F5
7194-8	J69	F5
7199	J67	F5
7200-8	J67	F5
7209	Y5	F5
7210	Y4	F5
7211-7	F4	F5
7218/9	F4	F6 (F5†)
7220-5	F4	F6
7226/7/8	Y4	F6
07228	Y5	—
7229	Y4	F6
7230/1	Y5	F6
7232-9	F4	F6
7240-4	F4	G5
7245-54	J65	G5
7255-64	J67	G5
7265-74	J69	G5
7275-99	J66	G5
7300-4	J66	G5
7305	J69	G5
7306	—	G5
7307-26	J66	G5
7327	J67	G5
7328	J69	G5
7329/30	J67	G5
7331/2	J67. J69	G5
7333/4	J67	G5
7335	J69	G5
7336	J67	G5
7337/8	J69	G5
7339	J69. J67. J69	G5
7340-9	J69	G5
7350/1	J69	C12
7352	J69. J67	C12
7353	J69	C12
7354	J69. J67	C12
7355-8	J69	C12
7359	J69. J67	C12
7360	J69. J67. J69	C12
7361/2	J69	C12
7363	J69. J67	C12
7364/5	J69	C12
7366	J69. J67. J69	C12
7367-70	J69	C12
7371	J69. J67	C12
7372-6	J69	C12
7377	J69. J67. J69	C12
7378-81	J69	C12
7382	J69. J67. J69	C12
7383	J69	C12
7384	J69. J67. J69	C12
7385-95	J69	C12
7396	J69. J67	C12
7397/8/9	J67	C12
7400-6	J67	C13
7407-25	E4	C13
7426	E4. B12	C13
7427-36	E4	C13
7437	E4. B12	C13
7438/9	E4	C13
7440-8	E4	C14
7449	E4. B12	C14
7450/1	E4	C14
7452-66	E4	C15
7467	E4. B12	C15
7468/9	E4	C15
7470	E4. B12	C15
7471	E4	C15
7472	E4. B12	C15
7473/4/5	E4	C15
7476	E4. B12	C15
7477/8	E4	C15
7479	E4. B12	C15
7480/1	E4	C15
7482	E4. B12	C16
7483-7	E4	C16
7488	E4. B12	C16
7489/90	E4	C16
7491	E4. B12	C16
7492-9	E4	C16
7500/1/2	E4	C16
7503/4	E4	—
7505	E4	G10
7506	E4	—
7507-10	J15	—
7511/2	J15	H2
7513	—	—
7514-35	J15	—
7536/7	J15*	—
7538-71	J15	—
7572-88	F4	—
7589/90	F5	—
7591	F4	—
7592	J15	—
7593-8	J15. F7	—
7599	J15	—
7600	J15	V1. V3†
7601/2/3	—	V1
7604	J14*	V1. V3†
7605-8	—	V1. V3†
7609	J15	V1. V3†
7610	J15	V1
7611-8	J15	V1. V3†
7619	—	V1. V3†
7620/1	J15	V1. V3†
7622	J15	V1
7623	J15	V1. V3†
7624	—	V1. V3†
7625	J15	V1. V3†
7626	—	V1. V3†
7627/8	J15	V1. V3†
7629/30/1	J15	V1
7632	—	V1. V3†
7633	J15	V1. V3†
7634	J15	V3
7635/6	J15	V1. V3†
7637	—	V1
7638	J15	V1. V3†
7639	J15	V1
7640	J15	V1. V3†
7641	J15	V1
7642-8	J15	V1. V3†
7649	J15	V1
7650	F4	V1. V3†
7651/2	O6	V1. V3†
7653	F4*. O6	V1. V3†
7654	F4. O6	V1. V3†
7655	F4. O6	V1
7656	D16. O6	V1. V3†
7657	F4. O6	V1. V3†
7658	O6	V1. V3†
7659	F4*. O6	V1
7660	F4*. O6	V1. V3†
7661	O6	V1. V3†
7662	F4. O6	V1. V3†
7663	F4*. O6	V1. V3†
7664	O6	V1
7665	F4. D16. O6	V1
7666	F4. O6	V1. V3†
7667	O6	V1. V3†
7668	F4. O6	V1. V3†
7669	F4. O6	V3
7670	F4. O6	V1. V3†
7671	O6	V1
7672	O6	V3
7673	O6	V1
7674	F4*. O6	V1. V3†
7675	F4. O6	V3
7676	F4	V1. V3†
7677	F4*	V1. V3†
7678	F4	V1. V3†
7679	F4*	V1. V3†
7680	J15	V1
7681	J15	V1. V3†
7682-6	J15	V3
7687	—	V3
7688	J15*	V3
7689/90/1	J15	V3
7692	J15. D16	—
7693/4	J15	—
7695	D16	—
7696-9	J15	—
7700	D13	—
7701/2/3	—	L1†
7704/5/6	D13	L1†
7707/8	D13. D16	L1†
7709	—	L1†
7710	D13	L1†
7711	—	L1†
7712	D13. D16	L1†
7713	D13	L1†
7714/5/6	—	L1†
7717/8/9	D13	L1†
7720-6	—	L1†
7727	D16	L1†
7728	D13. D16	L1†
7729	D13	L1†
7730	D13*	L1†
7731-5	D13	L1†
7736	—	L1†
7737/8/9	D13	L1†
7740	D16	L1†
7741/2	D13	L1†
7743	—	L1†
7744/5	D13	L1†
7746/7	—	L1†
7748	D13	L1†
7749/50	—	L1†
7751	D13	L1†
7752-5	—	L1†
7756	D13	L1†
7757-63	—	L1†
7764	D15	L1†
7765/6/7	D13	L1†
7768/9	—	L1†
7770	D16	L1†
7771	—	L1†
7772	D13. Y1	L1†
7773/4	Y1	L1†
7775	D13. Y10	L1†
7776	Y10	L1†
7777	D13	L1†
7778	—	L1†
7779	D13	L1†
7780-8	F5	L1†
7789/90	F6	L1†
7791	F4*. E4	L1†
7792	F4	L1†
7793	F4*	L1†
7794	F4*. E4	L1†
7795	F4	L1†
7796	F4*	L1†
7797	F4. E4	L1†
7798/9	F4	L1†
7800	F4	L1†
7801	J15	—

No.	Pre-1946	Post-1946
7802	J15. E4	—
7803	J15	—
7804	—	—
7805	J15. E4	—
7806/7	J15	—
7808	—	—
7809/10	J15	—
7811	—	—
7812-21	J15	—
7822	—	—
7823-31	J15	—
7832	J15*	—
7833-57	J15	—
7858	J15*	—
7859-81	J15	—
7882	—	—
7883	J15	—
7884/5	—	—
7886-99	J15	—
7900-34	J15	—
7935	—	—
7936-45	J15	—
7946-50	—	—
7951	J14*	—
7952-8	—	—
7959	J14*	—
7960/1/2	—	—
7963/4	J14*	—
7965-9	—	—
7970	J14*	—
7971/2	—	—
7973	J14*	—
7974/5	—	—
7976/7	J14*	—
7978	J14*. N7	—
7979	N7	—
7980/1	J14*. N7	—
7982	N7	—
7983/4/5	J14*. N7	—
7986	N7	—
7987	J14*. N7	—
7988-92	N7	—
7993	J14*. N7	—
7994-7	N7	—
7998	J14*. N7	—
07998	J14*	—
7999	N7	—
8000-3	N7. J45 (DES1)	DES1 (Diesel)
8004/5	N7	—
8006-11	N7	J94
8012/3	D13	J94
8014	—	J94
8015/6	D13	J94
8017	—	J94
8018	D13*	J94
8019	—	J94
8020/1	D13	J94
8022	—	J94
8023	D13	J94
8024	—	J94
8025-33	D13	J94
8034	—	J94
8035/6/7	D13	J94
8038	—	J94
8039	D13	J94
8040-9	F3	J94
8050-9	—	J94
8060-80	F3	J94
8081	F3	Y5
8082/3	F3	Y6
8084/5	F3	—
8086	F3	Y7
8087	F3	—
8088/9	F3	Y7
8090/1	F3	Y8
8092-9	F3	Y9
8100-24	G4	Y9
8125-9	G4	Y4
8130-9	G4	Y1
8140-9	J19	Y1
8150/1/2	J16. J17	Y1
8153	J17	Y1

No.	Pre-1946	Post-1946
8154/5	J16*. J17	Y3
8156	J17	Y3
8157	J16*. J17	Y3
8158/9/60	J16. J17	Y3
8161/2	J16*. J17	Y3
8163	J16. J17	Y3
8164	J16*. J17	Y3
8165	J16. J17	Y3
8166	J16*. J17	Y3
8167/8	J16. J17	Y3
8169	J17	Y3
8170	J17	—
8171/2	J16. J17	Y3
8173/4	J17	Y3
8175/6	J16. J17	Y3
8177/8	J16*. J17	Y3
8179-85	J16. J17	Y3
8186/7	J16. J17	Y10
8188	J16*. J17	Y11 (Petrol)
8189	J17	Y11 (Petrol)
8190/1	J16. J17	Z4
8192	J16*. J17	Z5
8193	J17	Z5
8194	J17	—
8195/6	J16. J17	—
8197/8	J17	—
8199	J16*. J17	—
8200	J16. J17	J62
8201/2	J17	J62
8203	J16. J17	J62
8204/5/6	J16. J17	J63
8207	J17	J63
8208/9	J16. J17	J63
8210	J17	J63
8211-5	J17	J65
8216-26	J17	J70
8227/8/9	J17	—
8230-9	J17	J71
8240-9	J18. J19	J71
8250-4	J19	J71
8255-9	—	J71
8260-9	J19	J71
8270-94	J20	J71
8295-9	—	J71
8300	F7	J71
8301-10	F7. B1	J71
8311	F7	J71
8312/3	F9	J71
8314	N18	J71
8315	—	J71
8316	J64	J71
8317	J64	J55
8318/9	—	J55
8320-54	—	J88
8355-64	—	J73
8365	—	J75
8366-9	—	J60
8370-88	—	J66
8389	—	—
8390-3	—	J77
8394	—	—
8395-9	—	J77
8400/1/2	Y1	J77
8403	Y10	—
8404	Y10	J77
8405-10	—	J77
8411	—	—
8412-7	—	J77
8418	—	—
8419-29	—	J77
8430/1	Petrol (Y11)	J77
8432-8	—	J77
8439	—	—
8440/1	—	J77
8442-81	—	J83
8482	—	J93
8483	—	—
8484/5	—	J93
8486/7	—	—
8488/9	—	J93
8490	—	J67. J69†
8491	—	J69

No.	Pre-1946	Post-1946
8492/3	—	J67
8494/5	—	J69
8496	—	J67
8497	—	J69
8498	—	J67. J69†
8499	—	J69
8500-5	B12	J69
8506	—	—
8507/8	B12	J69
8509	B12	J67
8510	B12	J67. J69†
8511	B12	J67
8512/3	B12	J67. J69†
8514/5/6	B12	J67
8517	B12	J67. J69†. J67†
8518	B12	J67
8519	B12	J67. J69†
8520	B12	J67. J69
8521	B12	J67
8522	B12	J67. J69†
8523	B12	J67
8524-8	B12	J69
8529	B12	J67. J69†
8530	B12	J69
8531	B12	J67
8532-5	B12	J69
8536	B12	J67
8537/8	B12	J69
8539	B12	—
8540	B12	J67
8541-6	B12	J69
8547	B12	J67
8548-63	B12	J69
8564	B12	—
8565-71	B12	J69
8572	B12	J67
8573-9	B12	J69
8580	B12	—
8581	—	J69
8582	—	—
8583/4	—	J67
8585	—	J67. J69
8586	—	J67
8587	—	J67. J69
8588	—	J67. J69†
8589/90	—	J67
8591	—	J67. J69†
8592-5	—	J67
8596	—	J69
8597	—	J67
8598/9	—	J69
8600-3	—	J69
8604	—	—
8605	—	J69
8606	—	J67
8607	—	J69
8608	—	J67
8609	—	J67. J69†
8610/1	—	J67
8612/3	—	J69
8614/5	—	—
8616	—	J67
8617/8/9	—	J69
8620	—	—
8621	—	J69
8622	—	—
8623	—	J69
8624	—	—
8625/6	—	J69
8627	—	—
8628	—	J67
8629-33	—	J69
8634	—	—
8635/6	—	J69
8637	—	—
8638-66	—	J68
8667/8/9	—	J92
8670-99	—	J72
8700-54	—	J72
8755/6	—	—
8757-79	—	J52
8780-9	D16	J52

No.	Class Pre-1946	Class Post-1946
8790-9	D15. D16	J52
8800-61	D15. D16	J52
8862	D14*. D15. D16	J52
8863	D15. D16	J52
8864	D14*. D15. D16	J52
8865	D14. D15. D16	J52
8866	D14*. D15. D16	J52
8867	D14*. D15	J52
8868	D14. D15. D16	J52
8869	D15. D16	J52
8870/1/2	D14*. D15. D16	J52
8873	D14. D15. D16	J52
8874	D15. D16	J52
8875/6	D14. D15. D16	J52
8877	D14. D15	J52
8878/9	D14. D15. D16	J52
8880	D15. D16	J52
8881	D14. D15	J52
8882-5	D15. D16	J52
8886	D14*. D15. D16	J52
8887/8	D15. D16	J52
8889	D15	J52
8890/1	D15	J50
8892/3	D14. D15	J50
8894	D15	J50
8895	D14. D15	J50
8896/7/8	D15	J50
8899	D15. D16	J50
8900	D14*. D15. D16	J50
8901-91	—	J50
8992-9	—	—
9000	L1	L1
9001-6	C15	L1. J72†
9007	N15	L1. J72†
9008	J37	L1. J72†
9009/10/1	Y9	L1. J72†
9012	C15	L1. J72†
9013	J37	L1†. J72†
9014	Y9	L1†. J72†
9015	C15	L1†. J72†
9016	C15	J72†
9017	Y9	J72†
9018	J34*	J72†
9019/20	N15	J72†
9021	J33	J72†
9022/3	N15	J72†
9024	J33	J72†
9025/6	C15	J72†
9027/8	J34*	J72†
9029	N15	—
9030	J34*	—
9031	N15	—
9032	Y9	—
9033	J37	—
9034/5	D34	—
9036/7	D31	—
9038	J35	—
9039	C15	—
9040	Y9	—
9041	C15	—
9042	Y9	—
9043	C15	—
9044	J37	—
9045	J36	—
9046	J37	—
9047	N15	—
9048	C15	—
9049	N15	—
9050	Y9	L3
9051	C15	L3
9052	N15	L3
9053	C15	L3
9054/5	N15	L3
9056-9	J35	L3
9060/1	N15	L3
9062	J37	L3
9063	Y9	L3
9064	C15	L3
9065	N15	L3
9066	J88	L3
9067	N15	L3
9068	J36	L3

No.	Class Pre-1946	Class Post-1946
9069	N15	L3
9070/1	N15	L2
9072/3	J37	—
9074/5	N15	—
9076/7	N15	M2
9078/9	N15	—
9080/1	J33	—
9082	J33	M1
9083	J33	—
9084	J37	—
9085	J33*	—
9086	J35	—
9087	J88	—
9088	J37	—
9089	J37	N12
9090-5	G7	N10
9096/7	N15	N10
9098	J37	N10
9099	N15	N10
9100	D34	N10
9101	J37	N10
9102	C15	N10
9103/4/5	J37	N10
9106/7/8	N15	N10
9109	J37	N10
9110/1	J37	N13
9112	J33	N13
9113	J37	N13
9114	J88	N13
9115	J35	N13
9116-9	J88	N13
9120	J35	N14
9121	J88	N14
9122	C15	N14
9123	J37	N14
9124	J35	N14
9125	J34*. N15	N14
9126/7	J35	N15
9128	J37	N15
9129	J35	N15
9130	J88	N15
9131	C15	N15
9132	J88	N15
9133/4/5	C15	N15
9136	J37	N15
9137	J33	N15
9138	J34	N15
9139	J37	N15
9140	J33*	N15
9141	C15	N15
9142	N15	N15
9143	J37	N15
9144	Y9	N15
9145	J36	N15
9146	Y9	N15
9147	N15	N15
9148	J33	N15
9149	D34	N15
9150	J33	N15
9151	J37	N15
9152	J88	N15
9153	D34	N15
9154	N15	N15
9155	C15	N15
9156	J33	N15
9157/8	J37	N15
9159/60	J33	N15
9161/2	J37	N15
9163	J34	N15
9164	C15	N15
9165/6	N15	N15
9167	J37	N15
9168/9	J33	N15
9170	J33*	N15
9171	J37	N15
9172/3	J36	N15
9174	N15	N15
9175	J37	N15
9176/7	J36	N15
9178	J33	N15
9179-83	J36	N15
9184	J34*	N15

No.	Class Pre-1946	Class Post-1946
9185-99	J35	N15
9200-8	J35	N15
9209/10	N15	N15
9211-8	D31	N15
9219	N15	N15
9220	J35	N15
9221	D34	N15
9222	J37	N15
9223/4	N15	N15
9225	N15	N4
9226	J35	N4
9227	N15	N4
9228	J35	N4
9229/30	N15	N4
9231/2	D50	N4
9233-8	J88	N4
9239	G9	N4
9240	N15	N4
9241/2	D34	N4
9243/4/5	D29	N4
9246	N15	N4
9247	J36	N4
9248	J36	—
9249	J33	—
9250	J36	N5
9251/2	N15	N5
9253/4	J35	N5
9255	J37	N5
9256	D34	N5
9257	N15	N5
9258	D34	N5
9259	N15	N5
9260/1	J37	N5
9262	D31	N5
9263	J37	N5
9264	N15	N5
9265	C15	N5
9266	D34	N5
9267	C15	N5
9268	—	N5
9269	J33	N5
9270	D34	N5
9271	J88	N5
9272/3/4	J37	N5
9275	—	N5
9276	N15	N5
9277	J88	N5
9278	D34	N5
9279	J88	N5
9280	J36	N5
9281	D34	N5
9282	N15	N5
9283/4/5	—	N5
9286	J34*	N5
9287	D34	N5
9288/9/90	J88	N5
9291	D34	N5
9292	J37	N5
9293	D31	N5
9294	—	N5
9295/6/7	J37	N5
9298	D34	N5
9299	J37	N5
9300-6	J37	N5
9307	D34	N5
9308	Y9	N5
9309	C15	N5
9310	Y9	N5
9311	J34*	N5
9312	D31	N5
9313/4/5	J37	N5
9316	—	N5
9317	D26*	N5
9318	D26	N5
9319	—	N5
9320	D26*	N5
9321	—	N5
9322	D26	N5
9323	D26*	N5
9324-7	D26	N5
9328	—	N5
9329/30	J35	N5

No.	Pre-1946	Post-1946
9331/2/3	D33	N5
9334	G9	N5
9335/6/7	J35	N5
9338/9/40	D29	N5
9341-4	—	N5
9345	J34	N5
9346	—	N5
9347/8	J35	N5
9349-56	G9	N5
9357/8	J36	N5
9359-62	D29	N5
9363	D30	N5
9364-70	J35	N5
9371-81	J35	N8
9382-5	D33	N8
9386/7	N15	N8
9388	N15	—
9389-93	N15	N8
9394/5	—	N8
9396-9	N15	N8
9400	D30	N8
9401	J37	N8
9402/3	J37	—
9404	D31	—
9405-8	D34	—
9409	D30	—
9410-6	D30	N9
9417	D30	—
9418-28	D30	N9
9429	J37	N9
9430-7	J37	N1
9438-52	C16	N1
9453	N15	N1
9454-73	J37	N1
9474/5	G9	N1
9476-80	J37	N1
9481/2	J34*	N1
9483	—	N1
9484	J33	N1
9485	J37	N1
9486-9	J37	—
9490	D34	N2
9491	J37	N2
9492-6	D34	N2
9497/8/9	D30	N2
9500/1	D30	N2
9502-5	D34	N2
9506/7/8	J37	N2
9509/10	C11	N2
9511-6	C16	N2
9517/8	J37	N2
9519-28	J34*. N15	N2
9529	J34*. Y1	N2
9530-3	J34*	N2
9534	J34	N2
9535	J34*	N2
9536	J34	N2
9537	J34*	N2
9538	J34	N2
9539-45	J34*	N2
9546/7	Y9	N2
9548/9	J34*	N2
9550	J34	N2
9551/2	J34*	N2
9553	J34	N2
9554-65	J34*	N2
9566	J33*	N2
9567/8	J33	N2
9569	J33*	N2
9570/1/2	J33	N2
9573	J33*	N2
9574-9	D31	N2
9580/1/2	J33	N2
9583/4	J33*	N2
9585	J33	N2
9586-91	G7	N2
9592	D25	N2
9593/4	D25*	N2
9595/6	D25	N2
9597	D25*	—
9598/9	D25	—
9600/1	D25	N7

No.	Pre-1946	Post-1946
9602	D25*	N7
9603	D25	N7
9604-9	J36	N7
9610	Y9	N7
9611-32	J36	N7
9633-42	D31	N7
9643-92	J36	N7
9693/4	—	N7
9695	D36	N7
9696-9	—	N7
9700-4	—	N7
9705-28	J36	N7
9729-33	D31	N7
9734-40	D31	—
9741-64	J36	—
9765-9	D31	—
9770	D31	A7
9771-89	J36	A7
9790-4	J36	A6
9795-9	J83	A6
9800-34	J83	A5
9835	Y9	A5
9836-42	J88	A5
9843-7	J88	—
9848/9	J35	—
9850-7	J35	A8
9858-63	N14	A8
9864-7	D33	A8
9868-81	C11	A8
9882-93	D32	A8
9894	D33	A8
9895-9	D29	—
9900	D29	S1
9901-5	C10*. C11	S1
9906	C10*. C11	—
9907/8/9	N15	—
9910-22	N15	T1
9923/4	N15	—
9925/6	N15	Q1
9927/8	—	Q1
9929	Y9	Q1
9930/1	—	Q1
9932	Y9	Q1
9933-7	—	Q1
9938-41	—	—
9942	Y9	—
9943-88	—	—
9989/90	E7	—
9991-8	—	—
9999	—	U1
10000	W1	W1
10001-6	—	—
10007	J82	—
10008/9/10	—	—
10011	Y10*	—
10012-22	—	—
10023	J82	—
10024-69	—	—
10070	J31*	—
10071-81	—	—
10082	J31*	—
10083/4	Y9	—
10085/6	—	—
10087-98	Y9	—
10099	—	—
10100/1/2	Y9	—
10103	Y9*	—
10104-13	—	—
10114	J31*	—
10115-21	—	—
10122	J31	—
10123-31	—	—
10132/3/4	J31*	—
10135/6	—	—
10137/8	J31*	—
10139	—	—
10140-4	J31*	—
10145	—	—
10146	J31	—
10147/8/9	J31*	—
10150-6	—	—
10162	J31	—

No.	Pre-1946	Post-1946
10163	—	—
10164	J31*	—
10165	—	—
10166	J31	—
10167	—	—
10168	J85*	—
10169-72	—	—
10173	J86*	—
10174-7	—	—
10178	J31*	—
10179	—	—
10180	J31	—
10181/2	—	—
10183	J31*	—
10184-7	—	—
10188	J31	—
10189/90	J31*	—
10191-4	—	—
10195	J31*	—
10196-9	—	—
10200	J31*	—
10201-5	—	—
10206	J31	—
10207	—	—
10208	J31*	—
10209-13	—	—
10214	J31*	—
10215	—	—
10216	J81*	—
10217-20	—	—
10221	J31*	—
10222	—	—
10223/4	J31*	—
10225/6	—	—
10227	J31	—
10228-38	—	—
10239	E7*	—
10240-4	—	—
10245	E7*	—
10246/7	E7	—
10248	—	—
10249	E7	—
10250-5	—	—
10256	E7*	—
10257	J84*	—
10258	—	—
10259	J84*	—
10260-9	—	—
10270	J84*	—
10271-88	—	—
10289	J82	—
10290	—	—
10291	J82*	—
10292/3	—	—
10294	J82*	—
10295	—	—
10296	J31*	—
10297/8	J32*	—
10299	J82*	—
10300	J32*	—
10301/2/3	—	—
10304/5	J32*	—
10306	J82*	—
10307/8/9	—	—
10310/1/2	J32*	—
10313	—	—
10314/5	J32*	—
10316/7/8	—	—
10319	J32*	—
10320	G8*	—
10321	D27*	—
10322	D28*	—
10323/4	D27*	—
10325/6/7	G8*	—
10328	J82*	—
10329	J32*	—
10330	J82	—
10331/2/3	J82*	—
10334	G8*	—
10335/6	J82*	—
10337	J32*	—
10338	G8*	—

No.	Pre-1946	Post-1946
10339	J32*	—
10340	—	—
10341	J32*	—
10342	—	—
10343-6	J32*	—
10347	—	—
10348-57	J82*	—
10358	J82	—
10359	J82*	—
10360	—	—
10361	D28	—
10362/3	—	—
10364-9	J34*	—
10370	J34	—
10371-6	—	—
10377	J34*	—
10378/9	—	—
10380/1	J34*	—
10382	—	—
10383	J34*	—
10384/5	—	—
10386	J34*	—
10387	D28	—

No.	Pre-1946	Post-1946
10388	D28*	—
10389	—	—
10390/1	D50	—
10392	D50*	—
10393-7	J34*	—
10398/9	—	—
10400	J34*	—
10401/2	D51*	—
10403	—	—
10404/5	D51*	—
10406	D51	—
10407	J34*	—
10408	—	—
10409	J34	—
10410	J34*	—
10411	D51	—
10412-23	J34*	—
10424	D51*	—
10425-9	D51	—
10430/1/2	J34*	—
10433	—	—
10434	D35*	—
10435-8	—	—

No.	Pre-1946	Post-1946
10439	D35*	—
10440/1	—	—
10442	D35*	—
10443-7	—	—
10448/9	D35*	—
10450/1	—	—
10452/3	D35*	—
10454/5	D51*	—
10456	D51	—
10457	D51*	—
10458/9	D51	—
10460	D51*	—
10461/2	D51	—
10463	D51*	—
10464/5	D51	—
10466	D51*	—
10467	D51	—
10468	D51*	—
10469	D51	—
10470	D51*	—
10471	D51	—
10472-81	J34*	—

Appendix A

H. & B.R. locomotives numbered between 3013 and 3161 in the N.E.R. series took L.N.E.R. numbers 2405-2542 during 1924/25, as follows:—

N.E.R. No.	L.N.E.R. No.	Class
3013	2405	N13
3014	2406	J28
3015	2407	N13
3016/7	2408/9	J28
3018	2410	N13
3019-22	2411-4	J28
3023	2415	N13
3024/5/6	2416/7/8	J28
3027	2419	N13
3028-32	2420-4	J28
3033/5/8/41/2	2425-9	D24
3049-66	2430-47	J23
3067/8/9	2448/9/50	J80
3070-96	2451-77	J23
3097/8/9	2478/9/80	N11
3100/1	2481/2	N11
3102-10	2483-91	N12
3111-6	2492-7	J75
3117/8	2498/9	Q10
3119-31	2500-12	Q10
3132-41	2513-22	J23
3142-51	2523-32	J75
3152-6	2533-7	N13
3157-61	2538-42	J28

Appendix B

Engines in the G.C.R. Duplicate List still in stock on 15th January 1924 were allotted L.N.E.R. numbers 6402-94 as follows:—

G.C.R. No.	L.N.E.R. No.	Class
3B	6457	J12
5B	6487	J58
6B	6427	J12
7B	6426	J12
8B	6483	J58
22B	6494	J58
30B	6459	J12*
34B	6458	J12
35B	6425	J12
37B	6424	J12
41B	6489	J58
45B	6429	J12
46B	6428	J12
52B	6485	J58
53B	6484	J58
62B	6431	Y2
63B	6430	Y2
72B	6493	J58
73B	6491	J58
78B	6492	J58*
88B	6486	J58
128B	6460	D12
156B	6490	J58
158B	6488	J58

G.C.R. No.	L.N.E.R. No.	Class	G.C.R. No.	L.N.E.R. No.	Class
272B	6482	J59	477B	6436	J12
275B	6481	J59	478B	6435	J12*
276B	6480	J59*	480B	6434	J12
279B	6479	J59*	481B	6433	J12
280B	6478	J59	482B	6432	J12
309B	6477	J8*	483B	6459	J12
336B	6476	J59	484B	6419	J12
339B	6475	J59	501B	6421	J12
340B	6474	J59*	502B	6420	J12
342B	6473	J59	503B	6419	J12*
367B	6472	J59*	504B	6418	J12
371B	6471	J59*	505B	6417	J12
374B	6470	J59	506B	6416	E2*
407B	6469	J61	510B	6415	D8
413B	6462	J59*	1145B	6414	N6
415B	6461	J59*	1146B	6413	N6
417B	6454	J59*	1147B	6412	N6
418B	6453	J59	1148B	6406	G3
420B	6452	J59*	1149B	6405	G3
421B	6451	J59	1150B	6404	G3
425B	6468	D12*	1151B	6403	G3
428B	6467	D12	1152B	6402	G3
430B	6466	D12	1153B	6411	J60
439B	6465	D12*	1154B	6410	J60
442B	6464	D12	1155B	6409	J60
443B	6463	D12*	1156B	6408	J60
449B	6456	E8*	1169B	6407	G3
450B	6455	E8*			
459B	6450	J12			
460B	6449	J12			
461B	6448	J12			
462B	6447	J12*			
463B	6446	J12*			
464B	6445	J12			
465B	6444	J12*			
466B	6443	J12			
469B	6442	J12			
470B	6423	J12			
471B	6422	J12			
472B	6441	J12			
473B	6440	J12			
474B	6439	J12			
475B	6438	J12*			
476B	6437	J12			

*Engine withdrawn before being renumbered.

NOTE — Nos. 6459 and 6419 were at first allotted to class J12 Nos. 30B and 503B but these two engines were withdrawn before the renumbering scheme commenced and the numbers 6459 and 6419 were re-allotted to J12 Nos. 483B and 484B.

Appendix C

The following locomotives were not allotted a number in the L.N.E.R. series:—

Company	No.	Class
G.N.R.	"Doncaster Works"	(Crane 0-4-4T)
G.C.R.	10B	"7" (0-6-0T)
,,	11B	"7" (0-6-0T)
,,	31B	J12
,,	32B	J12
,,	36B	J12
,,	38B	J12

Company	No.	Class
G.C.R.	66B	J58
,,	154B	J58
,,	169B	"12A" (2-4-0)
,,	273B	J58
,,	274B	J58
,,	277B	J58
,,	338B	J58
,,	368B	J58
,,	370B	J58
,,	372B	J58
,,	400B	(0-8-0T)
,,	414B	J58
,,	423B	D12
,,	434B	D12
,,	440B	D12
,,	441B	D12
,,	446B	D12
,,	458B	J12
,,	467B	J12
,,	468B	J12
,,	507B	E2
,,	508B	D8
,,	509B	E2
,,	511B	D8
G.E.R.	B§	Z4 (J92)
,,	C§	Z4 (J92)
,,	D§	Z4 (J92)
E.W.Y.U.R.	3	J84
,,	6	N19
C.V.H.R.	1	(0-4-2T)
,,	4	F9
M.S.L.R.	3	J64

§ Running numbers (8667/8/9) were given to these engines in the 1946 general renumbering.

Appendix D

M. & G.N. stock taken over in 1936. Former numbers prefixed by "0".

L.N.E.R. No.	Class
01	D52
02	D53
03/4	D52*
05	D52
06	D53
07	D52
09	C17
011/2/3	D52
014	D52*
015/6	J93
016A	(0-6-0T)*
017/8	D52*
020	C17
023	"A Rebuild" (4-4-0)*
025	"A Rebuild" (4-4-0)
026	"A Rebuild" (4-4-0)*
027	"A Rebuild" (4-4-0)
028	"A Rebuild" (4-4-0)*
036	D53*
037	D52*
038	D52
039	D54
041	C17
042/3	D52
044	D53
045	D54*
046	D54
047	D52
048	D52*
049/50	D53
051-6	D54
057	D54*
058-61	J40
062	J41
063/4/5	J40
066/7	J40*
068/9	J41
070	J40
071	J41
072	J40*
073	J40
074/5	D52*
076	D52
077	D53
078/9	D52
080	D52*
081	J3
082	J3*. J4
083	J3
084/5	J3*. J4

L.N.E.R. No.	Class
086	J3
087	J3*. J4
088	J3
089-92	J3*. J4
093-9	J93

* Engine withdrawn (or rebuilt) without receiving cypher.

Appendix E

L.N.E.R. type locomotives numbered by B.R. other than into the 60,000 series.

L.N.E.R. No.	B.R. No.	Class
3000-3100	90000-90100	O7
3101-99	90422-90520	O7
6000	26000	Electric EM1
—	26001-57	,, ,,
—	27000-6	Electric EM2
6480/1	26500/1	Electric ES1
6490-7	26502-9	Electric EF1
6498	26510	Electric EB1
6499	26511	Electric EF1
6999	26600	Electric EE1
8000-3	15000-3	Diesel DES1
(8004)	15004	Diesel DES2
L4	15097	Petrol Y11
8188/9	15098/9	,, ,,
10000	60700	W1

Index of Locomotive Class Articles

Wheel Type	Class	Book Part
4-6-2	A1-A4	2A
4-6-2T	A5-A8	7
4-6-2	A10	2A
4-6-0	B1-B19	2B
4-4-2	C1-C11	3A
4-4-2T	C12-C17	7
4-4-0	D1-D12	3B
,,	D13-D24	3C
,,	N.E.R. "38"	,,
,,	D, D25-D54	4
,,	M.G.N. "A Rebuild"	,,
2-4-0	E1-E7	,,
,,	G.C.R. "12A"	,,
,,	N.E.R. "901" & "1440"	,,
2-4-0T	E8	7
2-4-2T	F1-F9	,,
0-4-4T	G1-G10	7
,,	G.N.R. Crane	10A
4-4-4T	H1, H2	7
0-6-0	J1-J37	5
,,	N.E.R. "398" & "1001"	,,
,,	J38-J41	6A
0-6-0T	J45 (Diesel)	10A
,,	J50-J70	8A
,,	G.C.R. "7"	,,
,,	J71-J91	8B
,,	N.E.R. "44"	,,
,,	G.N.R. 3470A	10A
,,	M.G.N. 16A	,,
,,	J92	,,
,,	J93, J94	8B
2-6-0	K1-K5	6A
2-6-4T	L1-L3	9A
0-6-4T	M1, M2	,,
0-6-2T	N1-N19	,,
2-8-0	O1-O7	6B
2-8-2	P1, P2	,,
0-8-0	Q1-Q10	6C
0-8-0T	Q1	9B
,,	G.C.R. 400B	,,
0-8-2T	R1	,,
0-8-4T	S1	,,
4-8-0T	T1	,,
2-8-0+0-8-2	U1	,,
2-6-2T	V1	,,
2-6-2	V2	6C
2-6-2T	V3	9B
2-6-2	V4	6C
4-6-4	W1	,,
2-2-4T	X1-X3	9B
4-2-2	X4	6C
0-4-0T	Y1-Y10	9B
0-4-0	Y10	6C
0-4-0T	Y11 (Petrol)	10A
,,	G.N.R. Tram loco	,,
0-6-0T	Z4	,,
0-4-2T	Z4, Z5	9B
,,	C.V.H.R. 1	,,
0-6-0T	DES1, DES2 (Diesel)	10A
Electric locos		10B

ACKNOWLEDGEMENTS

This part is mainly the work of Messrs. M. G. Boddy, E. V. Fry, W. Hennigan, K. Hoole and W. B. Yeadon, with particular assistance from Messrs. E. Neve, P. Proud and D. F. Tee. The line drawings were kindly prepared by Messrs. J. M. Edgson, L. V. Wood and the late B. W. Calvert. Many other people willingly helped with information and advice, also the loan of photographs from their collections. The Society is grateful to them all.

Acknowledgment of illustrations:—

E. Woods (Fig. 1), W. Potter (Figs. 2, 131), E. R. Wethersett (Fig. 3), K. A. C. R. Nunn (Figs. 4, 24), E. V. Fry (Figs. 5, 13/6/9, 126), H. C. Casserley (Figs. 7, 47, 54, 118), A. W. Croughton (Figs. 9, 61, 77), A. R. Goult (Figs. 10/1, 32/6, 51/5, 93), W. S. Sellar (Figs. 12, 123), N. E. Stead (Fig. 15), L.N.E.R. (Figs. 17, 57, 79, 99, 130/49), R. J. Buckley (Figs. 18, 22, 85, 96), P. H. Groom (Figs. 20/1, 40, 90/5), G.N.R. (Fig. 23), J. P. Mullet (Fig. 31), H. N. James (Figs. 33/7, 41), L. W. Perkins (Fig. 34), C. Major (Figs. 35, 52), N. Fields (Figs. 38/9, 43, 91/2/7), Dr. I. C. Allen (Fig. 42), P. Ransome Wallis (Figs. 45/9), W. L. Good (Fig. 56), W. B. Greenfield (Fig. 59), L. G. Charlton (Fig. 60), R. B. Hadden (Fig. 64), J. G. Gregory (Fig. 65), P. J. Hughes (Fig. 67), W. D. Edwards (Figs. 69, 74), C. H. S. Owen (Fig. 70), D. Barham (Figs. 71/2), D. A. Dant (Figs. 73/5), Topical Press Agency (Figs. 80-3), B. O. Hilton (Figs. 84, 127), L. Hanson (Fig. 89), A. B. Crompton (Fig. 94), M. Smith (Fig. 98), W. A. Brown (Fig. 103/48), J. L. Stevenson (Figs. 120/34/42), A. Dow and K. Pirt (Fig. 124), B. V. Franey (Fig. 125), P. Proud (Fig. 132), E. Neve (Figs. 135/6), W. H. Whitworth (Figs. 140/1/5), W. A. Camwell (Fig. 143).

Figs. 4 and 24 are reproduced by courtesy of The Locomotive Club of Great Britain from the Ken Nunn collection, Fig. 14 of the *Railway Magazine,* Figs. 17, 23, 57/9 of the National Railway Museum (Crown copyright), Figs. 29 and 48 of Ian Allan Ltd., Figs. 44/6, 128/9/33/7/8/9/47 of Photomatic Ltd., and Fig. 77 of Lens of Sutton.